Competition Law and Economics

KDI/EWC SERIES ON ECONOMIC POLICY

The Korea Development Institute (KDI) was established in March 1971 and it is Korea's oldest and best-known research institute in the fields of economic and social sciences. Its mission is to contribute to Korea's economic prosperity by drafting socioeconomic development plans and providing timely policy recommendations based on rigorous analysis. Over the decades KDI has effectively responded to rapidly changing economic conditions at home and abroad by conducting forward-looking research as well as putting forth significant efforts in formulating long-term national visions.

The East-West Center promotes better relations and understanding among the people and nations of the United States, Asia and the Pacific through cooperative study, research and dialogue. It serves as a resource for information and analysis on critical issues of common concern, bringing people together to exchange views, build expertise and develop policy options. The Center is an independent, public, nonprofit organization with funding from the U.S. government, and additional support provided by private agencies, individuals, foundations, corporations, and governments in the region.

The KDI/EWC series on Economic Policy aims to provide a forum for scholarly discussion, research and policy recommendations on all areas and aspects of contemporary economics and economics policy. Each constituent volume in this series will prove invaluable reading to a wide audience of academics, policy makers and interested parties such as NGOs and consultants.
Titles in the series include:

Global Economic Crisis
Impacts, Transmission and Recovery
Edited by Maurice Obstfeld, Dongchul Cho and Andrew Mason

Social Policies in an Age of Austerity
A Comparative Analysis of the US and Korea
Edited by John Karl Scholz, Hyungpyo Moon and Sang-Hyop Lee

Macroprudential Regulation of International Finance
Managing Capital Flows and Exchange Rates
Edited by Dongsoo Kang and Andrew Mason

Economic Stagnation in Japan
Exploring the Causes and Remedies of Japanization
Edited by Dongchul Cho, Takatoshi Ito and Andrew Mason

Competition Law and Economics
Developments, Policies and Enforcement Trends in the US and Korea
Edited by Jay Pil Choi, Wonhyuk Lim and Sang-Hyop Lee

Competition Law and Economics

Developments, Policies and Enforcement
Trends in the US and Korea

Edited by

Jay Pil Choi

*Professor, Department of Economics, Michigan State
University, USA and Department of Economics, Yonsei
University, Republic of Korea*

Wonhyuk Lim

Professor, KDI School of Public Policy, Republic of Korea

Sang-Hyop Lee

*Senior Fellow, East-West Center, Professor, Department of
Economics, University of Hawaii at Manoa, USA*

KDI/EWC SERIES ON ECONOMIC POLICY

A JOINT PUBLICATION OF THE KOREA DEVELOPMENT INSTITUTE,
THE EAST-WEST CENTER, AND EDWARD ELGAR PUBLISHING LTD

Cheltenham, UK • Northampton, MA, USA

Published by
Edward Elgar Publishing Limited
The Lypiatts
15 Lansdown Road
Cheltenham
Glos GL50 2JA
UK

Edward Elgar Publishing, Inc.
William Pratt House
9 Dewey Court
Northampton
Massachusetts 01060
USA

A catalogue record for this book
is available from the British Library

Library of Congress Control Number: 2019956770

This book is available electronically in the **Elgar**online
Economics subject collection
DOI 10.4337/9781839103414

ISBN 978 1 83910 340 7 (cased)
ISBN 978 1 83910 341 4 (eBook)

Typeset by Servis Filmsetting Ltd, Stockport, Cheshire
Printed and bound in Great Britain by TJ International Ltd, Padstow

Contents

PART V   VERTICAL RESTRAINTS

Contributors

Se Hoon Bang is an assistant professor in the Department of Economics at Ewha Womans University.

Woohyun Chang is a fellow in the Performance Management Team at the Korea Institute of Public Finance.

Jay Pil Choi is a university distinguished professor in the Department of Economics at Michigan State University and a professor in the School of Economics, Yonsei University.

Joseph Farrell is a professor in the Department of Economics at the University of California, Berkeley.

Yangsoo Jin is an assistant professor and Chair of the Department of Economics at Sungshin Women's University.

William E. Kovacic is the Global Competition Professor of Law and Policy, Professor of Law, and Director of the Competition Law Center, The George Washington University Law School.

Sang-Hyop Lee is a senior fellow in the East-West Center and a professor in the Department of Economics of the University of Hawai'i at Mānoa.

Suil Lee is a professor in the KDI School of Public Policy and Management at the Korea Development Institute.

Wonhyuk Lim is a professor in the KDI School of Public Policy and Management at the Korea Development Institute.

Robert C. Marshall is a distinguished professor of economics at Penn State University.

Leslie M. Marx is the Robert A. Bandeen Professor of Economics in The Fuqua School of Business at Duke University.

Claudio Mezzetti is the Colin Clark Professor of Economics at the University of Queensland.

Ralph A. Winter is the Canada Research Chair in Business Economics and Policy and Professor of Strategy, Business Economics and Finance

Strategy in the Sauder School of Business, University of British Columbia.

Yong Hyeon Yang is the Director and Vice President of the Department of Markets and Institutions at the Korea Development Institute.

Preface

Jeong Pyo Choi

In the early stages of export-oriented industrialization, the Korean government shared the investment risks of private-sector firms, encouraged firms to invest for international competitiveness and regulated dominant firms to prevent abuses. The Monopoly Regulation and Fair Trade Act was promulgated in 1981, but the ensuing liberalization was asymmetric. Restrictions and investment controls were relaxed, and conglomerates expanded aggressively through debt financing. The combination of weakening control and continuing government guarantees helped to set the stage for economic crisis in 1997. After many large business groups failed, firms reassessed investment risks and increasingly focused on building core competence.

The 1981 Act was supplemented through amendments and other changes in line with the increasing competition-advocacy role of the Fair Trade Commission. The 1999 Omnibus Cartel Repeal Act removed legal exemptions for some 20 cartels. The same year, the legal standard for anticompetitive practices was changed from substantial restraint to unreasonable restraint of competition, making it no longer possible to defend a restrictive agreement on the grounds that it has an insignificant actual effect.

During the subsequent two decades, there has been a shift in emphasis from industrial policy to competition policy, with increasing reliance on market mechanisms. Many industries are still highly concentrated, however, and market concentration began increasing again. The Fair Trade Commission is committed to its competition-advocacy role, but institutional legacies tend to affect progress on core competition issues and efforts to make markets work better for consumers.

In the context of these issues, the Korea Development Institute and the East-West Center organized a study titled "Competition Law and Economics: Beyond Monopoly Regulation." An international team of market experts compared market structures, with particular reference to the impacts of foreign competition on market concentration and ways to improve market structure. They also examined core competition issues, including international experience with abuses of dominance, mergers and collusion, and vertical restraints. Their findings, presented in this book in both global and Korean contexts, will be helpful for better understanding the problems and designing future policies.

On publishing this volume, I would like to thank Dr. Jay Pil Choi, Professor of Economics at Michigan State University, Dr. Wonhyuk Lim, Professor in the KDI School of Public Policy and Management, and Dr. Sang-Hyop Lee, Senior Fellow in the East-West Center and Professor of Economics at the University of Hawai'i at Mānoa, for organizing and editing the chapters for publication. I also wish to thank the chapter writers and reviewers who contributed to improving the quality of this volume.

Jeong Pyo Choi
President
Korea Development Institute

Abbreviations and acronyms

BE	Bureau of Economics (US Federal Trade Commission)
CC	Competition Commission (United Kingdom)
CV	conjectural variation
DOJ	Department of Justice (United States)
DRAM	dynamic random-access memory
EC	European Commission (European Union)
EU	European Union
FTC	Federal Trade Commission (United States)
GDP	gross domestic product
GMM	generalized method of moments
HMG	*Horizontal Merger Guidelines* (United States)
ICN	International Competition Network
IPR	illustrative price rise
KDI	Korea Development Institute
KFTC	Korea Fair Trade Commission (Republic of Korea)
KSIC	Korea Standard Industry Classification (Republic of Korea)
MOFCOM	Anti-Monopoly Bureau of the Ministry of Commerce (China)
MRFTA	Monopoly Regulation and Fair Trade Act (Republic of Korea)
OEM	original equipment manufacturers
PNB	*Philadelphia National Bank* (US Supreme Court decision)
R&D	research and development
RPM	resale price maintenance (Republic of Korea)
SCIST	Standing Committee on Industry, Science and Technology (Canadian Parliament)
SOE	state-owned enterprise
SPC	specific purchase contract (Republic of Korea)
SSNIP	small but significant and nontransitory increase in price
TFEU	Treaty on the Functioning of the European Union (European Union)
UK	United Kingdom
UPP	upward pricing pressure
US	United States

1. Introduction and overview

Jay Pil Choi, Wonhyuk Lim and Sang-Hyop Lee

In the early stages of export-oriented industrialization, the Korean government shared the investment risks of private-sector firms. Implicit government protection encouraged firms to undertake aggressive investment under the logic of optimum-efficiency scales for international competitiveness. The government was reluctant to seek fundamental solutions to the problems of monopolization and collusion and instead opted to regulate the behavior of dominant firms to prevent "abuses."

This approach continued under the 1981 Monopoly Regulation and Fair Trade Act (MRFTA), but the ensuing liberalization was asymmetric. As market-entry restrictions and investment controls were relaxed, institutional reforms and credible market signals were not introduced to replace weakening government control. The conglomerates, confident that they were too big to fail, expanded aggressively through debt financing. The explosive combination of weakening government control and continuing expectations of government guarantees set the stage for Korea's economic crisis of 1997.

In the aftermath of the crisis, 16 large business groups failed. Firms reassessed investment risks and increasingly focused on building core competence. The problems inherent in the MRFTA were addressed through amendments and other changes in line with the increasing competition-advocacy role of the Fair Trade Commission. The 1999 Omnibus Cartel Repeal Act removed legal exemptions for 20 cartels under 18 statutes. In addition, the legal standard for anticompetitive practices was changed from substantial restraint to unreasonable restraint of competition, making it no longer possible to defend a restrictive agreement on the grounds that it has an insignificant actual effect.

During the past decade and a half there has been a marked shift in emphasis from industrial policy to competition policy, with increasing reliance on market mechanisms rather than "the rule of government officials." Yet many challenges remain. Many industries are still highly concentrated and, in a reversal of the recent trend, overall market concentration has increased since the mid-2000s. The Fair Trade Commission is still committed to its competition-advocacy role, but institutional legacies tend to impede progress on core competition issues. The commission should conduct rigorous market studies and adopt appropriate remedies to make markets work better for consumers. Policy on contentious issues should be based on sound economic theory and empirical analysis.

The book examines these issues. The chapters are authored by experts from Canada, Korea and the United States and provide international comparisons of market structures with particular reference to the impacts of foreign competition on market concentration. The book also examines core competition issues, including international experiences with abuses of dominance, mergers and collusion, and vertical restraints.

In Chapter 2, Jay Pil Choi discusses several issues that arise with "decentralized" enforcement of antitrust across jurisdictions due to the proliferation of independent antitrust authorities.

The author begins with recent developments in competition law and enforcement. Recent years have witnessed a dramatic increase in the number of countries introducing antitrust laws and creating antitrust agencies to enforce them (126 competition agencies from 111 jurisdictions, as of 26 April 2013). At the same time, the increasingly global nature of business transactions has resulted in a growing number of firms operating in multiple jurisdictions. In addition, antitrust authorities often take action against foreign firms if the firms affect competition in their jurisdictions. These developments, taken together, inevitably invite potential conflicts among competition authorities if their rules and procedures are not harmonized.

Choi provides an overview of potential pitfalls of antitrust proliferation with a focus on enforcement externalities. On the one hand, decentralized enforcement may lead to the "strictest regime wins" problem and the risk of over-regulation in the case of unilateral conduct by a dominant firm as the conduct needs to be cleared by each antitrust agency. On the other hand, the author adds that, if we consider enforcement costs, the enforcement externalities can also lead to a collective-decision dilemma and the concomitant free-rider problem in antitrust enforcement, which may lead to under-regulation.

From the perspective of business entities, independent and uncoordinated antitrust enforcement can be a considerable burden for multinational firms operating in many different countries if the antitrust rules differ and/or procedural rules of enforcement vary across countries. To make it worse, there may be countries that pursue additional or different objectives with antitrust policies, which would certainly create inconsistencies in the policy implementation. A nightmare scenario may be the case where different agencies require conflicting rules that cannot be satisfied simultaneously. Finally, the lack of uniform antitrust enforcement across jurisdictions raises the possibility of "forum shopping" in the presence of antitrust enforcement externalities. With multiple antitrust authorities in different jurisdictions, competitors of the merging parties or an allegedly dominant firm have incentives to bring the case to the antitrust authority with the most sympathetic ear, which ensures that the strictest antitrust rule is enforced in the global economy.

With this backdrop, the author moves on to consider specific enforcement areas in more detail. The areas in which enforcement externalities pose a serious problem and are discussed include mergers and acquisition, single-firm conduct by dominant firms and international cartels.

To address the potential downside associated with the proliferation of antitrust agencies and decentralized antitrust enforcement, Choi considers potential pathways to achieve policy harmonization across jurisdictions. In the pursuit of policy convergence through various channels such as the International Competition Network (ICN) and bilateral agreements between countries, the author proposes that the best way to achieve any commonality and harmonization is through movement towards effects-based antitrust enforcement guided by sophisticated economic reasoning rather than a formalistic approach. In practice, differences—cultural, political, legal and economic conditions—across countries can be a challenge in achieving harmonization of global antitrust enforcements. In this respect, effects-based antitrust enforcement with sound economic models and empirical foundations can mitigate the problem. The effects-based approach with the use of sound economic analysis can be applied across national boundaries with a common methodology. It enables antitrust agencies to find common ground and be insulated from political considerations and subjective beliefs, thereby promoting predictability and uniformity in antitrust enforcement.

In Chapter 3, William E. Kovacic examines different types of market studies—ranging from narrow analyses of single industries or parts of single industries to very broad work on competitive behavior or regulatory effects across sectors—and how they can be used to inform and design government policy.

The author points out that market studies serve three important functions for a competition agency. The first is to expand the base of knowledge on which an agency depends in order to understand commercial phenomena, to identify market failures and to devise forms of intervention that improve economic performance. The second is to facilitate the preparation of reports about competitive conditions within and across commercial sectors. The third is to enable the competition agency to engage in competition advocacy and to prepare recommendations for regulatory reform.

Good market studies require three principal inputs: (1) skilled human capital and (2) resources to collect and analyse information are self-explanatory; (3) political capital is less straightforward because market studies can arouse strong political opposition to the competition agency's recommendations. A competition agency must anticipate such opposition and may have to select cautiously among controversial issues that it can reasonably address at any given time. The more effective the study is in redressing substantial monopoly power, the greater the political hazards it can pose to the agency.

To confront these challenges, an agency must assemble a skilled research team, anticipate demands on resources (notably from legislative and executive branches of government), anticipate political risks (notably from the private sector and other interested parties) and devise strategies for effective implementation. For smaller, poorly funded, agencies, cooperation to pool research efforts can overcome resource limitations.

The author concludes that high-quality market analysis is a necessary ingredient for good policymaking, and the resources, manpower and time needed to produce good studies should not be underestimated. The author's examples of healthcare and the US Federal Trade Commission show how great the number and complexity of competition issues can be, even within a single industry, in any attempt to provide satisfactory answers to questions about interconnected markets within an industry.

In Chapter 4, Suil Lee identifies the importance of the foreign sector in investigating the degree of competition in the domestic market of Korea. For this purpose, Lee examines the import penetration and domestic market-concentration ratios by linking mining and manufacturing statistics and trade statistics. He then carries out empirical analyses on the relationship between the profitability of the domestic industry and the degree of import penetration.

The main results of the chapter can be summarized as follows. First, related to the import penetration, there has been a very big cross-industry difference in the level and variability of import penetration in the 2000s in Korea. There are also a number of industries in which the level of import penetration is very high or showing very severe volatility. This demonstrates the need for a new concentration-ratio index that reflects the actual degree of competition in the foreign sector. When the foreign sector was considered in the computation of the concentration ratio, Lee finds a number of industries where the decrease in the value of the index is very large or the annual volatility of the index changes significantly. These findings suggest that the impacts of the foreign sector need to be integrated into the process of assessing the competitiveness of domestic markets for open economies like Korea.

In addition, the empirical analysis on potential and actual competitive pressure from the foreign sector shows that potential competitive pressure, which is defined as a response of the import-penetration ratio to changes in an industry's profitability, operates with a one-year time lag in Korea. When it comes to actual competitive pressure, which is the negative impact of increasing import penetration on industry profitability, however, there was no empirical evidence on the existence of such pressure in Korea. Combining these findings on the potential and actual competitive pressures, Lee argues that it is possible to make an interpretation that imports increase in response to an increase in the profitability of the domestic industry but that importers who increase imports may try to enjoy a higher profit rate stringing along with domestic firms rather than fiercely competing with the domestic firms. This interpretation provides a policy implication that calls for the removal of entry barriers facing independent importers not affiliated with domestic producers.

In Chapter 5, Yong Hyeon Yang proposes a procedure to apply a "structured rule of reason" analysis for tying arrangements, which can be relied on by both the Korea Fair Trade Commission (KFTC) and the defendant in the investigation procedure.

Recently, a *per se* approach has been replaced by the rule of reason approach in many countries. In Korea, the Supreme Court ruled in 2007 that the KFTC has to prove anticompetitive effects of abusive behaviors of dominant firms. In Korea, abusive behaviors can be challenged under both Article 3-2 and Article 23 of the MRFTA. The only difference is that Article 23 can be applied to a larger set of firms as it concerns unfair trade practices, whereas an application of Article 3-2 requires market dominance because it prohibits abuse of dominance.

The author claims that behaviors of dominant firms should be condemned under the article on abuse of dominance (that is, Article 3-2) if the behaviors may harm competition only when engaged in by dominant firms. Tying arrangements are viewed as such an example.

The author further argues that the assessment of tying arrangements should be guided by a "structured rule of reason" approach that considers all the possible effects, negative or positive, in turn. The commission first has to prove anticompetitive effects, if any, of the behaviors using available data. He proposes the following four-step procedure.

First, identify tying and tied products. This involves market definition and, if necessary, a separate product test. Second, show the existence of market power or, more clearly, of market dominance. Third, find a theory of harm. This requires a decision on whether the tying arrangements have exploitative or exclusionary effects or both. Fourth and lastly, provide empirical evidence of the harm.

In response, the defendant firm should be given a chance to make counterarguments, which may consist of two distinct assertions. One is to disprove the arguments of the commission. The other defense is to claim that their behaviors enhance efficiency thereby canceling out the harm. The author concludes with a discussion of some practical issues in implementing the proposed rule.

In Chapter 6, Joseph Farrell, who has played a key role in the revision of the 2010 US *Horizontal Merger Guidelines* (HMG) as the director of the Bureau of Economics at the US Federal Trade Commission, comments on the role of merger guidelines and economic issues associated with recent revisions.

Farrell first explains the multiple purposes and multiple audiences that merger guidelines serve and provides a brief discussion of the intellectual and substantive history of merger guidelines. He then discusses some of the modern economic principles behind the 2010 revisions to the HMG in particular. He dispels the common misconception that the current guidelines abandon market definition and the use of market shares and concentration measures. Instead, he argues that the guidelines strike a sensible balance by respecting the traditional analysis based on market definition and concentration while, at the same time, incorporating modern economic analysis.

In his discussion of the unilateral effects of a merger, the author points out the sensitivity of merger-simulation analysis to functional forms for demand and cost, which can potentially limit the usefulness of merger simulation as a price predictor. Instead, he proposes two alternative approaches: measures of upward pricing pressure (UPP) and the illustrative price rise (IPR). UPP is essentially an idea to capture the changes in pricing incentives by the merging entities. It can be measured by the extent to which a unit sale by one of the merging firms cannibalizes sales by the merger partner and its profits, which were not taken into account before the merger. IPR simply assumes a "for instance" demand function and can be viewed as a simple illustration of how the UPP measure can be translated into price terms, rather than as a prediction of price.

Farrell also discusses how the 2010 guidelines incorporate coordinated effects with a broadened view of ordinary oligopoly conduct. Reactions by one oligopolist to another's competitive initiatives can reflect ordinary responses to a changed competitive environment, rather than an enforcement-oriented and perhaps prenegotiated discipline device in response to departures from an (implicit or explicit) agreement. This kind of Markov response is sometimes viewed as a coordinated effect and sometimes as a unilateral effect, but the chapter argues that such classifications are not important. In any case, this type of "parallel accommodating conduct" deserves discussion in the guidelines because otherwise there is a risk that merger analysis could improperly bifurcate into a static version of unilateral effects on the one hand and identifiable consciously coordinated (even if not necessarily illegally collusive) activity on the other hand. That would risk being misleading because a focus on the latter tends to encourage the analyst to look for conduct consisting of, or at least tantamount to, goal-oriented discussions or feelers along the lines of negotiation/deterrence, and to look for outcomes close to joint monopoly, while there is no reason to expect either in general.

The author concludes by lamenting the fact that the antitrust agencies' current practices do not fully exploit the learning opportunities from realized mergers. He thus advocates more systematic post-merger retrospective studies that would offer valuable lessons. Finally, he points out that guidelines are living documents that need to be subject to constant updating as we learn more about the effects of mergers with the accumulation of experience and new knowledge.

In Chapter 7, Robert C. Marshall, Leslie M. Marx and Claudio Mezzetti consider firms' strategies related to settlement negotiation and leniency applications once they are being prosecuted for collusion. When a firm is investigated for participation in a cartel, there is some flexibility for cartels to negotiate settlement with the government. Considering record-breaking fines and prison sentences for cartel firms and their employees in recent years, this *ex post* negotiation flexibility can have important implications for antitrust policy and deterrence of cartel formation, as settlement negotiations offer opportunities to reduce the penalties ultimately imposed on the colluding firms.

The authors consider two types of *ex post* negotiation. First, cartel members being prosecuted can negotiate settlement terms that favor them in terms of limiting future penalties from civil litigation. When there is a criminal finding of collusion, it often triggers follow-on civil litigation by consumers who were harmed. Cartel members can limit penalties from civil litigation in exchange for concessions to the competition authority, which may include the amount of criminal fines, the number of individuals receiving prison terms or the total length of prison terms. Second, leniency programs such as Amnesty Plus allow a multi-product firm being prosecuted for collusion in a market to qualify for reduced fines by applying for leniency in a separate product market in which it is also engaged in collusion.

The authors suggest that limited criminal pleas—for example in terms of plea length, customers affected or geography—can handicap the ability of civil litigants to pursue damages and hence reduce deterrence. Amnesty Plus can also have negative effects on detection and deterrence because it reduces the preemption effect. The reason is that a firm has less incentive to apply for leniency as it can obtain a similar fine reduction through Amnesty Plus in the event that any other member of the cartel applies for leniency.

The authors' analysis suggests that antitrust enforcement authorities should recognize potential negative effects of settlement negotiations as deterrence relies on civil as well as criminal penalties in addition to the potential for strategic abuse of leniency programs, especially the possibilities that arise when collusion in one product affects incentives for leniency applications in another product. Moreover, they recommend that enforcement agencies continue to adjust and enhance the tools available to them, including potentially such changes as encouraging whistleblowers for collusive conduct or expanding the opportunities and benefits for individual leniency applicants.

In Chapter 8, Ralph Winter reviews the economic foundations of competition policy towards vertical restraints with an emphasis on resale price maintenance (RPM). The author advocates competition policy guided by the basic economic principles and argues for the potential of still-greater movement in competition law on vertical restraints towards strong economic foundations. To this end, he first reviews the economic theory of the incentives for vertical restraints and discusses, against the background of this review, policy implications.

More specifically, he lays out two main economic principles for competition policy towards vertical restraints. First, agreements among firms in vertical relationships should be considered *prima facie* legal in the absence of any *horizontal* effects. A policy intervention on vertical agreements, regardless of their effect on intrabrand competition, would be justified only when they reduce interbrand competition by inducing collusive pricing or facilitate the exclusion of entry into upstream manufacturing by another brand or downstream retailing sector by discounters. Second, a manufacturer benefits from downstream competition. This implies that the manufacturer would impose vertical restraint only if it results in some other private benefits such as promotion of sales efforts. The manufacturer's incentives to trade off competition for sales effort in its decision to use vertical restraint may not be perfectly aligned with social incentives. However, this possibility alone cannot be a justification for intervention.

Winter points out that competition law in most jurisdictions fails to accord with the basic principles above. In particular, he lists six fallacies that plague current policy discussions and debunks them. First, a sensible policy would be to allow vertical restraints only when they are efficient. Second, in competition policy towards vertical restraints, the burden of proof should be on the side of the firm to demonstrate a legitimate business justification for the practice. Third, the likelihood of an anticompetitive use of a vertical restraint by a firm is always increasing with any increase in the market share or dominance of the firm. Fourth, a problem with RPM is the suppression of intrabrand competition, leading to higher prices. This effect can justify legal restrictions against the practice. Fifth, empirical evidence shows that the RPM practice generally increases price and reduces quantity and, therefore, reduces welfare. The evidence thus favors prohibition of the practice. The sixth and final fallacy comes from the laissez-faire side of the debate. It argues for *per se* legality of the practice and no need for a rule of reason approach because we already have laws against cartels.

In Chapter 9, Se Hoon Bang and Yangsoo Jin provide an analysis of the competitive effect of RPM in a market environment where multiple producers can offer RPM simultaneously and distributors have incentives to free-ride on each other's presale services.

The authors construct a simple theoretical model in which distributors provide product information via presale services. The information is useful to consumers because it helps consumers determine whether a product is the right match with his or her preference. This information may also be useful as a consumer can take advantage of it to evaluate the degree of match with another product. That is, the information is, to some extent, transferable across products, and therefore creates incentives for distributors to free-ride on competing distributors' presale services.

The transferability of the information across different vendors' products, of course, can vary depending upon the nature of products and market conditions. The effects of producers' RPM on the market outcome, in turn, will depend on the extent to which this type of information is transferable. If the information is non-transferable, for example, there is no free-rider problem in the provision of presale services by distributors. RPM thus is irrelevant to the provision of presale services. However, if the information is transferable, RPM can rectify the free-rider problem and restore incentives to provide presale services. In this case, the competitive effects of RPM depend on the degree of information transferability. For instance, if the information is not easily transferable across products, the main effects of presale information would be to increase product differentiation and hence soften producers' price competition. This may make consumers worse off in the end although they are served presale services that allow them to choose a right-match product.

By considering the interplay among multiple producers and multiple distributors, Band and Jin's analysis enhances our understanding of RPM's competitive effects and complements policy guidelines of competition authorities. In particular, the European Commission's "Guidelines on Vertical Restraints" emphasizes RPM's anticompetitiveness for a market situation with multiple producers, whereas it stresses procompetitiveness for a situation with distributors' free-rider problem. The analysis in this chapter shows that these two market conditions, if they exist at the same time, interact to determine RPM's competitive effects, being either procompetitive or anticompetitive. This implies that competition authorities should look into the market conditions more carefully when they assess individual RPM cases. The authors also suggest a few points that deserve to be considered in the assessment of RPM cases in practice.

In Chapter 10, Woohyun Chang reviews potential anticompetitive effects of so-called Specific Purchase Contracts widely used by Korean department stores as a mechanism to coordinate retail prices.

A specific purchase contract (SPC) is a legal form of agreement between a producer and a retailer in which the producer does not sell directly to the retailer, but merely rents the retail space and pays a sales fee proportional to the sales volume to the retailer (department store). As a result, the producer retains the property rights of the product until it is sold and can set the final consumer price, whereas the retailer effectively sets a part of the producer's costs. In Korea, it is observed that the price of a specific product is the same in all department stores nationwide, regardless of the location and the retail chain to which the store belongs. This price uniformity is enabled by the producer's ability to set the price through SPCs. The SPC price-coordination mechanism can be similar to other retail price coordination such as RPM in that it can facilitate collusion among firms. Chang develops a simple model with one producer and two retailers to analyse potential anticompetitive effects of SPCs. His analysis suggests that SPCs' anticompetitive effects can be more pernicious than other collusive mechanisms. The reason can be explained by externalities between retailers in setting their sales fee: each retailer does not take into account the other retailer's lost profit due to a higher retail price that would result from raising its own sales fee. As a result, the equilibrium retail price can be set even higher than the collusion price (which, in turn, is higher than the socially optimal retail price).

Chang's analysis offers the following lessons for researchers and policymakers. First, competition authorities should pay as much or greater attention to potential retail price coordination mechanisms other than RPM cases. Second, it is worth studying traditional business practices in depth as they can be used as disguised tools of anticompetition actions for firms. Finally, the SPC-based price coordination can be a valuable area of research, as this practice is widely used not only by department stores in Korea and Japan but also by rapidly growing department stores in China. It thus would have significant welfare implications to properly understand the potentially harmful effects of these types of contracts and business practices.

PART I

Setting the stage

2. Competition law and economics: international cooperation and convergence in competition policy

Jay Pil Choi

INTRODUCTION

The recent trend toward trade liberalization has greatly increased the movement of goods and services across national boundaries by reducing government-imposed trade barriers. Simply reducing trade barriers such as tariffs and quotas, however, may not be enough to realize the full benefits of trade liberalization without simultaneously implementing additional policies that can complement existing trade policies. In particular, the enhanced competition and vibrant innovation promised by trade liberalization require sound competition policy to assure a level playing field on which businesses across nations can compete "on the merits."

Thus it is a welcome development that more countries are adopting competition laws and plan to implement competition policies. For instance, when the International Competition Network (ICN) was formed in 2001, only 16 competition agencies from 14 developed countries were participating members. The number stood at 126 competition agencies from 111 jurisdictions in April 2013 (see Federal Trade Commission 2013). One of the most noteworthy developments on this front is China's adoption of the Anti-Monopoly Law, which took effect on 1 August 2008 after more than ten years of drafting. Promulgating competition law and setting up a competition agency, however, are not enough. In fact, mushrooming competition agencies in every country may turn out to be counterproductive if competition laws are applied in an inconsistent manner.

As the globalization of the world economy entails a growing interdependence among national economies, a nation's competition policies are no longer confined to domestic firms within the nation's jurisdiction. With the prominence of multinational firms, what counts is not the nationalities of firms but the locus of their economic effects. Antitrust authorities often take action against foreign firms if the firms affect competition in their jurisdictions. As a result, it is a distinct possibility that multinational firms may be subject to contradictory policies in the absence of policy harmonization among countries. This may significantly add to the complexity and costs of doing business and severely hamper the proper functioning of the market economy.

In this chapter, I discuss several issues that arise with "decentralized" enforcement of antitrust across jurisdictions due to the proliferation of independent antitrust authorities. These issues necessitate harmonization and coordination of policies in antitrust enforcement. However, divergence in economic conditions and policy goals in different jurisdictions presents a stumbling block in achieving harmonization in antitrust enforcement. Thankfully, economic analysis has a common methodology that is applicable across national boundaries in the assessment of antitrust enforcement effects. Antitrust law enforcement thus should be effects based and be guided by the economic model of competition.

The section on "Potential Pitfalls of Antitrust Proliferation" discusses these problems with a focus on enforcement externalities. Next, "Discussion of Specific Enforcement Areas" considers areas in which enforcement externalities pose a serious problem. And "What To Do for Policy Harmonization" considers potential pathways to achieve policy harmonization across jurisdictions with brief comments on the use of economics as a facilitating analytical tool in the harmonization of antitrust enforcement.

POTENTIAL PITFALLS OF ANTITRUST PROLIFERATION

The proliferation and potentially independent implementation of antitrust enforcement across more than a hundred different jurisdictions can lead to a variety of problematic issues, especially when the rules and enforcement procedures vary across jurisdictions. Below, I discuss some of the most important issues, which call for harmonization of antitrust rules and cooperation among enforcement agencies.

Enforcement Externalities

With the globalization of the economy and with many multinational firms operating in so many different jurisdictions, the effects of an antitrust enforcement activity in one country are not necessarily confined to the country of enforcement. This often leads to the problem of what Geradin (2009) calls the "strictest regime wins" and the risk of overregulation. To see the nature of the problem, imagine that there are two independent antitrust authorities in two different countries. Consider a unilateral conduct by a dominant firm such as tying or rebates. Let the effects of such a conduct on national welfare be W_1 and W_2, in country 1 and country 2, respectively. Such conduct will be globally efficient if $W_1 + W_2 \geq 0$. However, such conduct will be prohibited and subject to antitrust enforcement in country i, if $W_i < 0$, where $i = 1, 2$. Suppose that a unilateral conduct confined to an individual country is *not* feasible. Then, the unilateral conduct in question will be allowed only when $W_1 \geq 0$ *and* $W_2 \geq 0$,[1] which is a more stringent condition to satisfy than $W_1 + W_2 \geq 0$, and may lead to overregulation of unilateral conducts. The shaded areas in Figure 2.1 represent the overregulated areas. In both areas A and B, the unilateral conduct is globally efficient. However, the antitrust authority in country 1 prohibits such conduct in area A and the antitrust authority in country 2 does the same in area B. The same logic applies to other areas of antitrust enforcement.

If we consider enforcement costs, the enforcement externalities can also lead to a collective decision dilemma and the concomitant free-rider problem in antitrust enforcement. To see this, let us now assume that

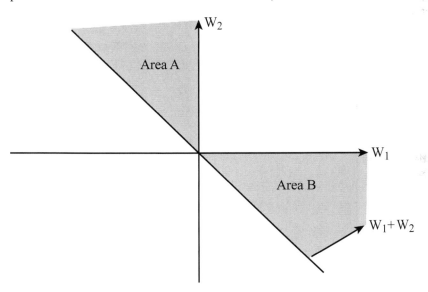

Source: Bank of Korea, Economic Statistics System data (ECOS, available at HYPERLINK "http://ecos.bok.or.kr" http://ecos.bok.or.kr).

Figure 2.1   *Areas of overregulation by two antitrust authorities in two countries*

the welfare effects of the unilateral conduct are the same and harmful for both countries, that is, $W_1 = W_2 = W < 0$. In addition, assume that there are enforcement costs C. Then it is optimal to enforce against this conduct in one country as long as $2W + C < 0$. There can be two types of inefficiencies. If $W + C > 0$ and $2W + C < 0$, no country is willing to enforce against this conduct unilaterally, because the cost of enforcement is not justified although the enforcement is globally efficient. In this case, the only way to enforce against this conduct is to share the enforcement costs between the two countries. If $W + C < 0$, each country is willing to unilaterally enforce against the conduct, but each country may have incentives to free ride on the other country's enforcement efforts unless both countries can coordinate.

Burden of Compliance Costs with Multiple Agencies

Independent and uncoordinated antitrust enforcement can be a considerable burden for multinational firms operating in many different countries if the antitrust rules differ or procedural rules of enforcement vary across countries or both. Merger proposals may need to satisfy the conditions of the agency with the strictest antitrust rules. The same applies to unilateral conduct. A nightmare scenario may be the case where different agencies require conflicting rules that cannot be satisfied simultaneously.

Multiple jurisdictions with independent agencies can also significantly increase the complexity of defense strategies of a firm that is investigated for an alleged antitrust violation. Defense lawyers need to be extra cautious so that a position taken in one country cannot be adversely used against the alleged violator in other countries with different rules and procedures. The need to adopt a cohesive defense strategy in the face of many different antitrust rules may severely limit the ability to defend the alleged violations. Language can be another issue. The in-house general counsels of firms investigated for alleged violations need to formulate coordinated defense strategies in multiple languages without anything being "lost in translation."

Pursuit of Different Objectives across Jurisdictions

There is a broad consensus that the main objective of antitrust enforcement should be the protection of consumers. However, there may be countries that pursue additional or different objectives with antitrust policies, which would certainly create inconsistencies in the policy implementation. For instance, the Anti-Monopoly Law in China states that one of its objectives is to "promote the socialist market economy." Considering the growing importance and influence of the Chinese economy, it may be a concern if the antitrust authority in China actively pursues this objective, though it is still too early to tell. Its merger review also considers among other factors the "effect on the development of the national economy and public interest." It remains to be seen how this consideration will affect actual merger decisions in China.

Even in countries where the stated goal of antitrust authorities is purely the protection of consumers, we cannot rule out the possibility that antitrust authorities misuse their power for other purposes or succumb to "regulatory capture" to which any regulatory agency is susceptible. This possibility is especially worrisome in developing countries where antitrust authorities are not completely independent and are usually political appointees.

First, there is a concern that antitrust decisions can be used as a disguised protectionist policy. This is especially so in antitrust cases pitting domestic firms against foreign multinational firms and where domestic firms have previously been shielded from foreign competition. In such cases, antitrust policy could be enforced in a discriminatory fashion against foreign companies as an instrument of protectionist policy.

Second, politically minded and overzealous enforcement officials may also see high-profile antitrust cases (especially those against foreign multinationals) as stepping stones leading to promotion in their bureaucratic or political career. They can use such opportunities to portray themselves as crusaders who bravely stand against powerful foreign multinationals to protect domestic interests. There could be a race to be the toughest in an attempt to be a relevant player, which can preclude many procompetitive mergers and single-firm conducts.

Forum Shopping

Finally, the lack of uniform antitrust enforcement across jurisdictions raises the possibility of "forum shopping" in the presence of antitrust enforcement externalities. With multiple antitrust authorities in different jurisdictions, competitors of the merging parties or an allegedly dominant firm have incentives to bring the case to the antitrust authority with the most sympathetic ear, which ensures that the strictest antitrust rule is enforced in the global economy.

DISCUSSION OF SPECIFIC ENFORCEMENT AREAS

This section focuses on three important classes of antitrust enforcement in which enforcement externalities become a problem due to the proliferation of antitrust agencies.

Mergers and Acquisitions[2]

If multiple antitrust jurisdictions are in place, enforcement externalities naturally arise in cases of international mergers. The increasingly global nature of business transactions has resulted in a growing number of mergers falling under multiple jurisdictions and corresponding competition authorities. This inevitably invites potential conflicts among competition authorities.

For instance, the EC can block or force changes to company mergers and takeovers, even when they do not involve any European firms, if they are deemed to adversely affect the competitive landscape in the European market.[3] The same applies to United States (US) antitrust authorities such as the Department of Justice (DOJ) and the Federal Trade Commission (FTC). They routinely take actions against foreign firms if the firms' actions harm competition and adversely affect consumers in the US market.[4] The current situation naturally raises concerns about the potential for intergovernmental disagreements about the effects of antitrust actions. This type of potential conflict is best illustrated by the proposed merger between General Electric and Honeywell, which was approved in the US but blocked by the EC (see Choi 2007 for more details).

With the proliferation of antitrust authorities enforcing merger regulations, this type of conflict can only be magnified. As of 2001, the American Bar Association identified 46 international merger notification requirements (see Leary 2001).

China is now an active player in this area. For instance, the Anti-Monopoly Bureau of the Ministry of Commerce (MOFCOM) reviews the filing of "concentration of operators" under the Anti-Monopoly Law and denied the acquisition of Huiyuan by Coca-Cola by claiming that Coca-Cola would have the ability to transmit its dominant position in the soda/soft-beverage market into the juice-beverage market.[5]

The proliferation of decentralized antitrust enforcement agencies implies that any planned mergers between large multinational firms having a presence in multiple countries requires notification and approvals, without a single exception, from each country in which they do business. A veto from any of these countries can torpedo the proposed merger.

The problem with the current regime, without any harmonization of policies, is that any international merger will essentially be determined by the least permissive agency without any considerations of its effect on consumers in other jurisdictions. This decision mechanism is likely to be inefficient and the degree of inefficiency will be exacerbated as more agencies are involved, since the view reflected in the decision would be the one most extreme.

This is true even if all antitrust agencies pursue the same economic goal (either social- or consumer-welfare maximization) without any political considerations and the effects of mergers are uniform across jurisdictions. If we consider the outcome of each investigation as an independent estimate of the effects of the proposed merger, the best estimate in the statistical sense would be the average view unless there is systematic bias in the evaluation process. With the current system, however, the merger enforcement would be driven by the "first-order statistic," that is, by the competition authority with the most pessimistic view about the proposed merger.

Even if there is no uncertainty in the evaluation of the effects of mergers, there could be conflicts if the effects of mergers are *not* uniform across jurisdictions. Suppose that there is a proposed merger that affects two countries, 1 and 2. The welfare impacts of the merger on each country are given by W_1 and W_2. As discussed above, the merger is globally efficient if and only if $W_1 + W_2 \geq 0$. However, the merger will be approved if and only if $W_1 \geq 0$ and $W_2 \geq 0$ under the current system. The latter condition is more stringent than the former condition, which implies that efficient mergers can be blocked since each agent ignores external effects. Once again, the scope of this type of inefficiency certainly increases as more agencies are involved.

Single-firm Conduct

The issue of externalities also arises in the context of single-firm conduct. As in the merger cases, the decision of one agency may have positive or negative impacts on consumers in other jurisdictions. If a country has no antitrust enforcement, other countries' enforcement against unilateral conduct can have positive effects on the country's welfare. However, if the country also has an active enforcement agency and deems a firm's unilateral conduct efficient and welfare enhancing, other countries' enforcements against the same conduct can eliminate efficiency-enhancing business practice by the firm, leading to overregulation.

Recent examples in which the US antitrust agencies and the EC made divergent decisions include the British Airways conditional-rebate case. In the US, the rebate scheme used by British Airways was deemed to be permissible, but the same conduct was condemned as anticompetitive by the EC.[6] Intel was another case in which the conduct was deemed lawful in the US but condemned as anticompetitive in Europe and Korea.

The Microsoft case is another example in which the company was subject to allegations of antitrust violations in multiple jurisdictions and faced different remedies that are not necessarily consistent. In antitrust cases that involve intellectual property rights, additional issues may arise. As an example, consider the case of compulsory licensing as an antitrust remedy to solve an interoperability problem. (See Choi 2010 for more details.)

When an "essential facility" is a physical property, the access can be limited to a particular geographic area. Thus, the issue of different antitrust approaches can be confined to the areas of dissonance without affecting others. In contrast, if the essential facility is intellectual property, limiting the use of the property in other areas or related fields may be difficult. To use the example of the Microsoft case in Europe, it would be impractical to enforce the limitation that the interoperability information shared with third party vendors of Windows server software be limited to the products sold only in Europe. Thus, compulsory licensing enforced in Europe can affect competitive conditions in other areas as well. This also raises the possibility of "forum shopping," as explained above. With multiple antitrust authorities in different jurisdictions, competitors of the essential-facility owner have incentives to bring the case to the antitrust authority with the most sympathetic ear for the competitors. This possibility highlights the need to harmonize competition policies across jurisdictions.

International Cartel

There is a near consensus that the first priority of antitrust enforcement should be to combat price fixing and the economic harms caused by hardcore cartels are universally recognized. Thus there is less conflict in this area among antitrust agencies. In addition, the enforcement in this area usually confers positive benefits on other countries. The main issue in this area is under-enforcement rather than over-enforcement.

When multinational firms operate in several jurisdictions in the presence of arbitrage opportunities across markets, the sustainability of collusion in one local market can be affected by the existence of collusion in other markets. Consider, for example, the vitamin cartel case of *Empagran S.A. v. F. Hoffman-LaRoche*. Empagran S.A. of Ecuador and other foreign companies (that purchase and resell vitamins) filed a suit against F. Hoffman-LaRoche of Switzerland and numerous other foreign companies for an alleged international price-fixing conspiracy.[7] The case concerned a price-fixing conspiracy that allegedly took place overseas even though the case itself was filed in a US federal district court. The foreign plaintiffs, suing under the US Foreign Trade Antitrust Improvement Act, claimed that "the cartel raised prices around the world in order to keep prices in equilibrium with United States prices in order to avoid a system of arbitrage" and therefore that "the foreign plaintiffs were injured as a direct result of the increases in United States prices even though they bought vitamins abroad."

The interdependence of cartel stability across markets leads to potential externalities in antitrust enforcement across jurisdictions with independent antitrust authorities. For instance, cartel detection and desistance in one market can lead to cartel breakdown in other markets, conferring positive externalities. The "domino effect" may induce each antitrust agency to free ride on other agencies' enforcement efforts. This calls for cooperation and coordination among antitrust agencies to eliminate a collective decision problem.

To understand the nature of the free-rider problem when there are enforcement costs, consider the following simple cartel-enforcement game. There are two antitrust agencies that must decide whether or not to spend resources on cartel detection and prosecution. For simplicity, assume that the welfare effect of a hardcore cartel on consumers is the same across jurisdictions. Let us denote the welfare loss due to the cartel in each country by L. The cartel should desist, but the agency's enforcement cost is C. The game can be described by the following matrix (Table 2.1). Each enforcement agency independently decides whether or not to enforce. We assume that the cartel in both countries can be broken up by enforcement in any one of the two countries due to the domino effect. We further assume that $L > C > 0$, which implies that the cartel enforcement is beneficial in each country if there is no other enforcement agency.

There are multiple equilibria in this game, with two asymmetric pure-strategy equilibria and one symmetric mixed-strategy equilibrium. In the two asymmetric pure-strategy equilibria, one agency enforces while the other chooses not to, and the resulting equilibrium is efficient. However, the most natural equilibrium may be the symmetric mixed-strategy equilibrium since both agencies are symmetric in this game. Without any coordination and information sharing, the unique, symmetric equilibrium is that each agency enforces with probability $p = \frac{L-C}{L}$. With the symmetric mixed-strategy equilibrium, however, we have a coordination failure and the price fixing will continue with probability $(1-p)^2$. Another source of inefficiency with independent investigations is the possibility of duplicative

Table 2.1   Payoff matrix of the simultaneous cartel enforcement game

	Enforce	Do not enforce
Enforce	–C, –C	–C, 0
Do not enforce	0, –C	–L, –L

Note: C = agency's enforcement cost; L = welfare loss due to the cartel.

efforts in the event that both agencies decide to enforce, which occurs with probability p^2.

In this stylized situation, it would be beneficial for both parties to consider the designation of a "lead agency" to eliminate duplication and streamline the process. All the reasons listed above support a more integrated approach in the enforcement of international mergers.

In addition, information sharing among antitrust authorities would be a very important tool in the fight against hardcore cartels. Information-sharing arrangements would allow antitrust agencies to coordinate their investigative strategies and provide them with access to subjects, evidence and witnesses located outside each country's borders.[8]

WHAT TO DO FOR POLICY HARMONIZATION

Previous sections point out potential perils from the proliferation of antitrust agencies and emphasize the need for policy harmonization and coordination across jurisdictions. It is important not to impose any additional burden on businesses with unnecessary regulatory uncertainty. Different substantive and procedural regimes make conducting businesses with an international locus of effects complex, time consuming and expensive. Clear and consistent standards across jurisdictions will facilitate global businesses and eliminate any bureaucratic burdens associated with uncertainty. Given this broad consensus on the high desirability of a uniform substantive and procedural antitrust regime, the difficult question is a more practical one of how we can achieve the needed policy harmonization among countries with sovereign rights.

Cabral (2003) suggests that the externality problem can be mitigated if antitrust enforcement policy is considered as a repeated game. In international-merger cases, for instance, each agency compromises and approves efficient mergers even though its own country's welfare will decrease under the belief that the partner country will reciprocate the favor in the future. However, the efficacy of this framework is highly suspect since it depends on the assumption that the policymakers are infinitely lived long-run players and are sufficiently patient.

One obvious solution would be the creation of a supranational, global antitrust agency. The Competition Directorate of the EC can be considered a supranational agency at the regional level. The question is whether we can create a truly global supranational agency. In fact, there have been several attempts to create such an organization over the years. However, such attempts have, so far, failed.[9]

Paradoxically, one of the main reasons for the past failures was the objection of the US government. The US Congress was not ready to concede any antitrust jurisdiction to an international agency and found the language of the agreements either too weak or not satisfactory to their purpose compared with the prevailing US standards (see Wood 1992 and 2005).

As learned from past experiences, there are several reasons to believe that the creation of a supranational agency is impractical, at least for now. First, there is simply too much divergence in economic conditions and policy goals at present between the developed and the developing countries. For instance, in the US, antitrust is understood to be the body of law purely targeted at business practices that harm economic welfare in the marketplace. However, in many other countries, especially in developing countries, competition law is linked to broader national economic goals; antitrust policy is expected to deliver other social objectives such as ensuring "fair" business practices, promoting small- to medium-size businesses and maintaining price stability. Until these countries' economic conditions improve to allow the role of antitrust to be limited to competition matters, or there is a convergence in philosophical viewpoints, it may be difficult to reconcile the purpose of antitrust law at the international level.

Second, differences in procedural rules and enforcement mechanisms make an immediate and meaningful consensus among all countries difficult. Even between the US and the European Union (EU), two jurisdictions that have arguably the most sophisticated and advanced antitrust regimes, we can find substantial differences. For instance, the US allows private parties to bring antitrust suits and also has two federal antitrust agencies, whereas the Competition Directorate of the EC has near-monopoly power and is largely responsible for antitrust enforcement. The US allows treble damages and criminal conviction for hardcore cartels, but antitrust agencies have to go to court to block mergers and hence are "exposed to the crucible of cross-examination before an independent fact-finder" (Majoras 2001). In contrast, the directorate general for competition of the EC is said to act as investigator, prosecutor, judge and jury. To appeal for a judicial review, firms must petition the Court of First Instance in Luxembourg. The review process, however, is slow and the court has been considered as an ally of the commission. The list of differences goes on, even though these two are believed to be in the vanguard of antitrust enforcement. Finding a solution acceptable to all countries with so many procedural variations would be a daunting task and perhaps politically infeasible at this point.

This implies that the only plausible option is to adopt a more piecemeal and gradual convergence path. (See also Wood 2002, who proposes a "soft" harmonization approach.) In this respect, there are already many encouraging signs and new developments along this line. One notable example is the formation of the ICN. The ICN was founded in 2001 by the US DOJ, the FTC and 13 other jurisdictions. By April 2013 it had grown to include 126 competition agencies from 111 jurisdictions (OECD 2014). It is a member-driven virtual network working as a platform to achieve global antitrust convergence with the understanding that consistency in enforcement policy and elimination of unnecessary or duplicative procedural burdens stands to benefit consumers and businesses around the globe. The ICN's goals are to "encourage the dissemination of antitrust experience and best practices, promote the advocacy role of antitrust agencies and seek to facilitate international cooperation" (International Competition Network undated).

To achieve these goals, the network runs several working groups in the areas of advocacy, agency effectiveness, cartel, merger and unilateral conduct. To disseminate best practices, they also hold regular workshops and annual conferences for officials of antitrust agencies.

In the area of merger enforcement, the network promotes the adoption of best practices in the design and operation of merger-review regimes in order to (1) enhance the effectiveness of each jurisdiction's merger-review mechanisms, (2) facilitate procedural and substantive convergence, and (3) reduce the public and private time and cost of multijurisdictional merger reviews. In particular, ICN members have adopted eight "Guiding Principles for Merger Notification and Review Procedures" around which a merger regime should be built and have issued a set of "Recommended Practices for Merger Notification and Review Procedures" that have been identified as very important in facilitating convergence toward best practices in merger review. Even though these "principles" and "recommended practices" are nonbinding, many governments and agencies have already made changes to their laws, practices and procedures to conform to the ICN practices or are in the process of developing or amending their laws, practices and procedures to conform (see Delrahim 2004).

In the area of unilateral conduct, the ICN Working Group aims to "facilitate greater understanding of the issues involved in analyzing unilateral conduct, and to promote greater convergence and sound enforcement of laws governing unilateral conduct." To this end, the group is developing guidelines on the analysis of conduct. Similarly, in the area of cartels, it is constantly improving the *Anti-Cartel Enforcement Manual* and the *Anti-Cartel Templates* to address hardcore cartels directed at price fixing, bid rigging, market sharing and market allocations. The multilateral approach of the ICN can also be complemented by bilateral agreements between countries sharing similar competition goals and procedures to deepen their level of coordination and to formulate consistent substantive and procedural rules.[10]

In the pursuit of policy convergence through various channels such as the ICN and bilateral agreements between countries, the best way to achieve any commonality and harmonization seems to be movements toward effects-based antitrust enforcement guided by sophisticated economic reasoning rather than a formalistic approach. In this respect, as most officials of newly created antitrust agencies tend to have backgrounds in the field of law and lean toward a more formalistic approach, training programs in economics provided through the ICN to educate such officials would be highly desirable. Differences in cultural, political, legal and economic conditions across countries challenge achieving harmonization of global antitrust enforcements. Effects-based antitrust enforcement with sound economic models and empirical foundations can mitigate the problem. The effects-based approach with the use of sound economic analysis can be applied across national boundaries with a common methodology. It enables antitrust agencies to find common ground and be insulated from political considerations and subjective beliefs, thereby promoting predictability and uniformity in antitrust enforcement.

One caveat in the use of economic analysis as a centerpiece of antitrust enforcement is that it should be based on widely accepted economic theory disciplined by empirical support. One of the lessons learned in the past few decades with the development of the so-called "new empirical industrial organization" is that each industry is distinct with its own idiosyncratic characteristics (Bresnahan 1989). Proper industry analysis thus requires intimate knowledge of market specifics and institutional details. Along with this recognition, there has been a plethora of game-theoretic oligopoly models explaining various business conducts and their competitive effects with all sorts of "possibility theorems" (Fisher 1989). This leads to the "proliferation of economic models" problem. The best practice should be to rely on the best available theory that fits with industry specifics, preferably one that has been empirically validated. The use of novel theories not yet empirically tested should be avoided when possible.

Perhaps the best example of economic analysis in antitrust enforcement is the evolution of merger enforcement in the US. The evolution of the *Horizontal Merger Guidelines* (HMG) (US Department of Justice and Federal Trade Commission 2010) exemplifies how new knowledge in industrial organization has been successfully integrated in antitrust enforcement over time. For instance, the revised 2010 HMG make it clear that the measurement of market shares and market concentration is not an end in itself, but is useful to the extent it illuminates the mergers' likely competitive effects. This statement reflects the long-held consensus view among economists that concentration measures are not a reliable instrument to assess competitive effects of mergers, and simplistic and mechanical enforcements based on market shares and concentration measures without proper attention to the likely competitive effects are not desirable. (See Shapiro 2010 for more details.) The 2010 HMG continue the trend of downplaying the role of market concentration and put more emphasis on competitive effects based on the concepts of the "diversion ratio" and "upward pricing pressure."

Finally, I cannot overemphasize the roles the US and EU play in the harmonization efforts of global antitrust. Naturally, antitrust agencies all over the world—especially the ones in developing countries—seek guidance from the US agencies and the EC. Just as quarreling parents cannot set an example for their children and may not have any moral authority to control fighting siblings, when the US and EC make conflicting decisions, antitrust agencies in other countries feel free to choose whichever side is more convenient for them. They may, in addition, even be emboldened to make decisions that are far from the best practices. Thus close cooperation between the US and the EC to show a unified front is particularly important.

CONCLUDING REMARKS

Recent years have witnessed a dramatic increase in the number of countries introducing antitrust laws and creating antitrust agencies to enforce them. At the same time, the increasingly global nature of business transactions has resulted in a growing number of firms operating in multiple jurisdictions. These developments, taken together, inevitably invite potential conflicts among competition authorities if their rules and procedures are not harmonized. This chapter discusses the potential downside of these new developments. The discussion reveals potential problems that can arise when multiple antitrust agencies independently pursue their own goals and it calls for harmonization and international coordination in antitrust enforcement. The ICN and numerous bilateral agreements between antitrust agencies are, albeit *ad hoc* and piecemeal, important developments toward convergence in antitrust policy. One convergence path that is most agreed seems to be effects-based antitrust enforcement guided by economic principles.

NOTES

1. The European Commission (EC), for instance, has jurisdiction only over actions that distort trade in the Common Market; arguably, if it were to approve a merger with

WUS + WEU > 0 and WEU < 0, it would be in violation of its mandate. By the same token, US antitrust authorities seek to maximize US welfare, not world welfare. One such example is the Webb–Pomerene Act of 1918, which is US federal legislation that exempts certain exporters' associations from certain antitrust regulations.

2. The discussion in this section draws heavily from Choi (2007).
3. The EC's Merger Control Regulation adopted in 1989 (Council Regulation EEC No 4064/89 of 21 December 1989 on the control of concentrations between undertakings) requires that all companies, regardless of where they are based, notify the Commission about planned mergers if their combined worldwide annual sales exceed 5 billion euros and at least 250 million euros worth of their business is done among the 15 EU nations. The regulation has been substantially amended. For the new EC Merger Regulation of 20 January 2004, see https://eur-lex.europa.eu/legal-content/EN/TXT/PDF/?uri=CELE X:32004R0139&from=en (accessed on 18 December 2019).
4. One such example is the block of a merger between Ciba-Geigy and Sandoz, two Swiss pharmaceutical firms, by the US FTC in 1997.
5. For the case of the proposed acquisition of Anheuser-Busch by InBev, MOFCOM approved the merger with some restrictive conditions under China's Anti-Monopoly Law, such as the pledge not to increase either Anheuser-Busch's or InBev's current shareholding percentage in other Chinese beer-manufacturing companies or to seek any shareholding percentage in other Chinese beer-manufacturing companies.
6. *Virgin Atlantic Airways Ltd. v British Airways PLC*, 257 F.3d 256 (2d Cir. 2001) and Case T-219/099 *British Airways PLC v Commission* (2003) ECR II-5917.
7. *SA v F. Hoffman-LaRoche, Ltd.*, 315F.3d 338, 431 (DC Cir. 2003).
8. See Hammond (2003). However, there may be a need to put some limits to information sharing with other antitrust authorities when the information is obtained during leniency-program applications. See Choi and Gerlach (2012a, b) for more details on information sharing in the context of leniency programs.
9. See Geradin (2009) for a synopsis of past attempts to create multilateral antitrust rules.
10. Over the last two decades, the US DOJ Antitrust Division has entered into bilateral antitrust cooperation agreements with Brazil, Canada, the EU, Germany, Israel, Japan and Mexico.

REFERENCES

Bresnahan, Timothy F. (1989), "Empirical studies of industries with market power," in Richard Schmalensee and Robert D. Willig (eds), *Handbook of Industrial Organization*, vol. 2, Amsterdam: North Holland, pp. 1011–57.

Cabral, Luis M.B. (2003), "International merger policy coordination," *Japan and the World Economy*, **15**(1), 21–30.

Choi, Jay Pil (2007), "The economics and politics of international merger enforcement: a case study of the GE/Honeywell merger," in Viveck Ghosal and John Stennek (eds), *The Political Economy of Antitrust*, Amsterdam: North-Holland, pp. 241–58.

Choi, Jay Pil (2010), "Compulsory licensing as an antitrust remedy," *The WIPO Journal*, **2**(1), 74–82.

Choi, Jay Pil and Heiko Gerlach (2012a), "Global cartels, leniency programs and international antitrust cooperation," *International Journal of Industrial Organization*, **30**(6), 528–40.

Choi, Jay Pil and Heiko Gerlach (2012b), "International antitrust enforcement and multi-market contact," *International Economic Review*, **53**(2), 635–58.

Delrahim, Makan (2004), *Antitrust Enforcement Priorities and Efforts towards*

International Cooperation at the US Department of Justice. Washington, DC: US Department of Justice, available at www.usdoj.gov/atr/public/speeches/208479. htm (accessed on 28 November 2019).

Federal Trade Commission (2013), *International Competition Network Advances Convergence through Initiatives on Enforcement Cooperation and Investigative Process*. News release, 26 April. Washington, DC: Federal Trade Commission, available at www.ftc.gov/opa/2013/04/icn1.shtm (accessed on 28 November 2019).

Fisher, Franklin M. (1989), "Games economists play: a noncooperative view," *RAND Journal of Economics*, **20**(1), 113–24.

Geradin, Damien (2009), "The perils of antitrust proliferation: the globalization of antitrust and the risk of overregulation of competitive behavior," *Chicago Journal of International Law*, **10**(1), 189–212.

Hammond, Scott D. (2003), "Beating cartels at their own game: sharing information in the fight against cartels," paper presented at the Inaugural Symposium on Competition Policy, Tokyo, Japan, 20 November, available at www.justice.gov/atr/public/speeches/201614.pdf (accessed on 28 November 2019).

International Competition Network (undated), Memorandum on the establishment and operation of the International Competition Network, available at www.internationalcompetitionnetwork.org/wp-content/uploads/2019/07/ICNMemo_on_Establishment.pdf (accessed on 18 December 2019).

Leary, Thomas B. (2001), "A comment on merger enforcement in the United States and in the European Union," paper presented at the Transatlantic Business Dialogue Principals Meeting, Washington, DC, 11 October 2001, available at www.ftc.gov/speeches/leary/tabd010111.htm (accessed on 28 November 2019).

Majoras, Deborah Platt (2001), "GE-Honeywell: the US decision," remarks before the Antitrust Law Section, State Bar of Georgia, Washington, DC: US Department of Justice, available at www.justice.gov/atr/public/speeches/9893.htm (accessed on 28 November 2019).

OECD (2014), "Challenges of international co-operation in competition law enforcement," available at www.oecd.org/daf/competition/Challenges-Competition-Internat-Coop-2014.pdf (accessed on 28 November 2019).

Shapiro, Carl (2010), "The 2010 horizontal merger guidelines: from hedgehog to fox in forty years," *Antitrust Law Journal*, **77**(1), 701–59.

US Department of Justice and Federal Trade Commission (2010), *Horizontal Merger Guidelines*, Washington: US Department of Justice and Federal Trade Commission.

Wood, Diane P. (1992), "The impossible dream: real international antitrust," *The University of Chicago Legal Forum*, 1992, 277–314.

Wood, Diane P. (2002), "International harmonization of antitrust law: the tortoise or the hare," *Chicago Journal of International Law*, 2002, 391–407.

Wood, Diane P. (2005), "Antitrust at the global level," *The University of Chicago Law Review*, 2005, 309–24.

PART II

Market structure

3. Market structure and market studies
William E. Kovacic

INTRODUCTION

Academics, practitioners and public officials often equate "competition law" with the enforcement of prohibitions against specific forms of business behavior. When asked to describe their main function, competition agency officials frequently answer, "Law enforcement." This orientation explains why the prosecution of cases provides the chief benchmark by which we assess the quality of a system of competition law.[1]

The past two decades have featured growing recognition that the historical concept of competition law is inadequate and that competition agencies should invest resources in pursuits beyond the prosecution of cases.[2] At least two considerations caused this change in perspective. The first is awareness that a system of competition law can achieve important competition-policy goals through the application of policy instruments other than law enforcement.[3] Among other means, the preparation of reports and other forms of advocacy can discourage legislatures and other government bodies from adopting policies that suppress business rivalry.[4] Unless it is supplemented by effective advocacy, robust law enforcement against private anticompetitive conduct simply may encourage business decision makers to seek and obtain government intervention that accomplishes the same ends.[5]

A second stimulus to rethink the traditional case-centric view of competition law is the realization that competition agencies must invest in accumulating knowledge to diagnose business phenomena correctly and to intervene wisely. Knowledge about markets and business practices is a vital input to making competition policy. Routine investments in the public-policy equivalent of research and development (R&D) are essential to agency proficiency. Particularly for dynamic, innovation-intensive sectors, regular upgrades in a competition agency's base of knowledge are indispensable elements of good public policy.[6]

Market studies—research that analyses trends within and across industries—are valuable forms of competition-policy R&D. As described below, the market-studies framework in some jurisdictions enables the competition agency to impose remedies to correct the market failures identified in a market inquiry. With or without remedial powers, a market-studies regime can be a useful element of the diversified portfolio of policy tools that enable a competition agency to serve as an effective advocate for competition and to assemble a strong base of knowledge for law enforcement and other forms of policy making. Over 120 jurisdictions today have systems of competition law and an increasing number are employing market studies as one way to achieve competition-policy goals.[7]

This chapter considers the role that market studies can play to increase understanding of market structures and practices, to identify the causes of poor performance and to effectuate improvements. It analyses the rationale for performing market studies, examines the institutional prerequisites for conducting market studies and suggests an approach to using this technique for policy making. The chapter begins by describing the menu of inquiries often grouped under the umbrella of "market studies." It then discusses the role of market studies as valuable forms of competition R&D and as useful foundations for effective competition-agency programs. The next part describes the institutional prerequisites for conducting market studies. The final section discusses pitfalls in using market studies as policy-making tools and offers a strategy for overcoming these pitfalls. The chapter uses the experience of the US Federal Trade Commission (FTC) to illustrate many of its points.

MARKET STUDIES: FORMS AND FUNCTIONS

Market studies are research projects that analyse specific industries or examine commercial phenomena across industries. They can vary according to their substantive scope, the nature of the legal mandate that authorizes the agency to conduct studies, the means by which the agency may acquire information to examine industry conditions and the remedial force of the agency's findings or recommendations.

Scope

The most common and a narrower form of market study consists of a detailed examination of conditions or practices within a single industry. In some instances, the agency reports broadly upon trends related to the industry's structure, important behavioral features and the sector's impact on economic performance.[8] In other cases the market study focuses upon a more narrowly defined topic concerning the sector.[9]

At the same time, a market study can be an occasion for a more comprehensive examination of private behavior and public policies that affect competition within a sector. This inquiry can provide the basis for microeconomic policy-reform proposals to improve sector performance. A competition agency that uses market studies in this manner plays a role similar to the public agencies that some governments have created to spearhead microeconomic regulatory reforms. An example is Australia's Productivity Commission, which conducts studies and issues recommendations for regulatory reform.[10]

Other market studies examine commercial phenomena or structural features across sectors. For example, an agency might examine the effect of mergers upon aggregate concentration[11] or use a market study to collect data on profitability and other performance indicators across industries.[12] Other multisector inquiries might examine the significance of specific policies—for example, the functioning of laws and policies governing the issuance of intellectual property rights—for economic performance.[13]

Legal Mandate

For many competition agencies, the authority to conduct market studies and publish reports is expressly provided in the statute creating the jurisdiction's competition-law system. In other systems, the power to perform market studies has risen by implication. In the latter instance, competition agencies have inferred the power to report on industry conditions as an adjunct to their law-enforcement responsibilities.

Experience in competition-law implementation indicates that express statutory authority is not the only possible foundation for an agency's market studies.[14] Nonetheless, an express delegation of power is the most secure and confident basis for a competition agency to implement a market-studies regime. As discussed below, the performance of a market study can have powerful political consequences—especially when the agency uses compulsory methods to acquire data or when the agency's findings and recommendations indicate severe deficiencies in a sector and suggest major policy reforms. Without express statutory authorization, an agency is more vulnerable to political backlash when the targets of the agency's inquiry claim that the agency has acted outside the scope of its legislatively granted powers. An express statutory mandate provides somewhat stronger armor to shield the agency from political attack when affected commercial interests challenge its performance of market studies.

Information-gathering Powers

Less intrusive market-study regimes require the competition agency to base its inquiry on information in the public domain or to use data that companies provide voluntarily. In this circumstance, an agency can draw upon publicly available data and employ various forms of voluntary consultations to collect information from industry participants. Despite the limitations of voluntary data collection, it is possible to prepare informative reports from public sources and voluntary industry cooperation.

More powerful market-study mechanisms allow the competition agency to use compulsory process to collect information. The power to use compulsory process typically is spelled out in the competition law.[15] The market-study mandate of the US FTC is illustrative. The FTC's market-study mandate is spelled out in the FTC Act and the statute, in Section 6, authorizes the FTC to collect information with compulsory process and to issue reports—a power previously exercised by the agency's predecessor, the Bureau of Corporations.[16]

Compulsory process gives the agency direct access to internal company records and, in some cases, allows the agency to require firms to prepare data sets not previously assembled in the ordinary course of business. As compulsory process entails greater administrative burdens for respondents and gives the competition agency access to sensitive business records, it provokes greater resistance. Firms can be expected to contest—at least in the early phase of a competitive regime—compulsory demands for information in court and, in some cases, to lobby elected officials to force the competition agency to back down.[17]

Remedial Consequences

The lighter-handed form of market study allows the agency to influence policy only by persuasion. The agency reports the findings of its inquiry and, in many instances, makes recommendations. In this scheme, the agency has no power to impose its suggestions and reforms of industry structure or conduct will require further intervention by other government bodies—for example, in the form of new legislation or adjustments in regulatory policy within another government ministry.

The power to make recommendations, even without authority to impose them, can give the competition agency substantial influence in policy making. There are numerous instances in which the publication of a report based on a market study created from publicly available sources or voluntary access to information has inspired legislative reforms or induced a government body (such as a sectoral-regulation body) to alter policy in the manner suggested by the competition agency.[18]

A more substantial variant of market study goes beyond persuasion as a mechanism for reform and gives the competition agency power to implement remedial measures to correct deficiencies identified in the agency's inquiry. What arguably is the world's most powerful market-study regime resides in the United Kingdom (UK).[19] The Enterprise Act of 2002 gives the Competition Commission (CC), pursuant to a reference made by the Office of Fair Trading, power to conduct a market study and to take action necessary to remedy, mitigate or prevent the effects of the obstacles to competition identified in the market study.[20] The application of the remedial power is subject to judicial review. Among other measures, the CC's exercise of this power has resulted in a basic restructuring of the ownership of the airports that serve London.

In some respects, the remedial scheme embodied in the UK market investigations regime enables the competition authority to accomplish through industry study and analysis remedial measures—notably, major structure relief—that ordinarily are the province of litigation involving the abuse-of-dominance provisions of a competition law. As applied in the UK, the market study permits direct examination of anticompetitive structural conditions (and the sources of these conditions) and dispenses with the search for exclusionary purposes or practices that ordinarily dominates a substantial amount of antitrust litigation involving single-firm behavior. A market-study regime can, by doing so, avoid the sometimes artificial and tortured efforts to find wrongful behavior that is an essential predicate to the prosecution of abuse-of-dominance cases in the European Union or monopolization cases in the United States.

In the UK, the market-studies mechanism also permits the dissolution of concentrated market positions that owe their existence to public policies that have created or maintained positions of dominance. In developed and developing economies alike, the market-study instrument may be the best means for the competition authority to cure structural competition impediments rooted in collateral public policies. Because of the substantial commercial interests implicated in the application of the UK market-studies remedial scheme, the use of so significant a mandate will press the agency to proceed prudently lest improvident forms of intervention create harmful adverse political responses. The success of the market-studies regime in the UK is a testament to the care exercised by agency leadership in the Office of Fair Trading and the CC in identifying suitable candidates for study and in deciding where the imposition of cures would improve economic performance.

The publication of a market study with mere suggestions for reform can also have powerful political consequences. A negative portrayal of an industry's behavior, coupled with recommendations for dramatic policy intervention, can galvanize formidable political opposition as the targets of the competition agency's criticism mobilize elected officials to restrain the agency.[21] Political backlash can take the form of threats to reduce the agency's budget or to withdraw elements of its statutory authority—including the power to conduct market studies. Thus, even when a jurisdiction's market-studies system does not authorize the competition agency to impose remedies directly, the exercise of this power still requires awareness of possible political implications and demands skill in selecting subjects for study and in carrying out the inquiry.

MARKET STUDIES: POLICY-MAKING CONTRIBUTIONS

Market studies serve three important functions for a competition agency.

The first is to enhance the base of knowledge on which an agency depends to understand commercial phenomena, to identify market failures and to devise forms of intervention that improve economic performance. Agencies can build knowledge in various ways—through academic research, information gathering and report writing, and conferences and workshops bringing together elements from business, government, consumer representatives and the bar to discuss issues related to competition policy and law.

The second significant purpose of market studies is to facilitate the preparation of reports about competitive conditions within and across commercial sectors. Such reports provide an opportunity to recommend legislative measures or adjustments in regulatory policy to remove obstacles to competition more effectively than traditional enforcement of prohibitions on anticompetitive conduct. Compared to the litigation of a traditional antitrust case, a market study can provide a more flexible tool to examine the root causes of a sector's poor economic performance and focus upon considerations (for example, the role of social policies or government-imposed barriers to entry) that might not be relevant to a conventional antitrust case.

The third function, closely related to the second, is to enable the competition agency to engage in competition advocacy and to prepare recommendations for regulatory reform. In a number of countries, the competition agency may be the best suited of all government agencies to promote the abandonment of regulatory controls that unnecessarily impede entry into the market and forestall expansion by private firms.

This section first defines the notion of policy R&D and then discusses the several goals served by engaging in policy R&D. It also examines how the agency sets a research agenda, including the way in which policy R&D topics have been chosen in the past, how they are currently chosen and how the process might be improved in the future. Finally, it presents a set of specific suggestions for policy R&D provided in the course of external consultations.

Policy R&D

Activities that constitute "policy R&D" can take many different forms within a competition agency. To academic economists, "research" sometimes means pursuing the answer to an author-initiated research question using state-of-the-art techniques in the hope of publishing the work in a scientific journal. For a competition agency, the range of relevant policy R&D is broader and includes the convening of workshops and conferences that enable the agency to learn from outsiders about important developments in commerce.

Some competition-policy R&D work is highly analytical in nature. Some research compiles academic and policy literature; and some is more largely descriptive of various informed opinions on policy-relevant questions or the functioning of particular markets. Some research topics are related to specific enforcement programs—for example, to determine the effects of particular mergers on prices. Other topics may focus on policies of other government agencies that have had implications for competition policy and consumer welfare.[22] In the course of law enforcement, a competition agency becomes aware of how other government policies affect competition and may be the primary causes of competitive marketplace failures. These obstacles might be deemed to be the first-order problems and law enforcement may provide a decidedly imperfect way to address them. A market study focusing directly on first-order problems may stand a better chance of correcting fundamental structural obstacles to competition.

Contributions of Market Studies

Market studies can serve to improve agency decision making in law enforcement, rule making and competition advocacy. Some market inquiries seek specifically to improve analysis in the litigation of cases in particular sectors. The use of empirical research work to support a complaint in the case of a consummated hospital merger is one example. Empirical studies complement conceptual work by FTC economists to support the agency's merger-enforcement efforts in merger cases.[23] The FTC also used market studies as one form of policy R&D to complement its recent enforcement efforts to stop anticompetitive conduct designed to delay entry of generic drugs.[24] This combined research and enforcement agenda also informed substantive changes to the US Hatch-Waxman Act. This type of policy R&D helps ensure that FTC actions keep abreast of relevant scholarly learning. For example, research into advertising in the 1970s, 1980s and 1990s played a key part in informing the FTC's advertising enforcement.[25] This research also influenced courts and state policy makers in their approach to the regulation of advertising. By performing high-quality market studies, a competition agency also helps establish a "brand" for thoughtful, informative analysis.

Market studies allow an agency to gain a better understanding of industries that feature prominently in the agency's law-enforcement agenda. For example, the FTC's gasoline and diesel price-monitoring project allows the agency to track changes over time in price-cost margins and to identify anomalies in prices in various cities or regions.[26] Although checking for such anomalies is now a routine measure, this effort initially was a policy R&D prototype. Policy R&D has also been in evidence at the FTC in the healthcare area for over 30 years. Modern examples include the 2003–04 hearings that led to the report, *Improving Health Care: A Dose of Competition*,[27] as well as a workshop on the economics of the pharmaceutical industry.[28]

Other market studies are principally horizon-scanning exercises that gather information about industries an agency expects to be important in its future enforcement and policy efforts. A market study can enable an agency to gather relevant industry and marketplace information to anticipate and address emerging competition issues. For example, the FTC's 1999 pharmaceutical report[29] describing the industry and its idiosyncrasies was a precursor to much of the agency's work in the area of pharmaceutical-patent settlements, which have become a major component of the FTC's competition-law enforcement program. FTC market studies likewise provided insights into aspects of industries with which the agency will be dealing for the foreseeable future. These efforts include examination of the antitrust and consumer-protection implications of broadband Internet access[30] and investigation of the effects of government restrictions on entry into online retailing.[31] Still other FTC projects have included research into new methods of healthcare delivery, examining progress on electronic medical records and the advent of limited-service medical clinics.[32] The FTC is only one of a number of competition agencies that have found market studies and related research to be valuable horizon-scanning tools.[33]

Market studies also help agency personnel gain insight into the effects of practices spanning many industries and product markets. For example, teams of FTC researchers have undertaken a research project to examine

dynamic oligopoly models.[34] Such models lie at the intersection of both
theoretical and empirical economic research on markets and understanding such issues may help the agency untangle knotty problems in the
dynamics of gasoline and refined-products pricing (for example, the
analysis of asymmetric price variations in gasoline markets). A conference
on behavioral economics in 2007 is another example of policy R&D serv-
ing to illuminate important phenomena affecting behavior in numerous
industries.[35] The FTC conference assembled some of the top researchers in
the field to present their work and it gave researchers a clearer view of FTC
programs that build upon, at least implicitly, the principles of behavioral
economics.

A further contribution of market studies is to assist a competition
agency in determining the policy outcomes of its programs. Among other
projects, the FTC has undertaken a noteworthy series of retrospective
studies of past decisions involving mergers,[36] resale-price-maintenance
cases and non-price vertical restraints.[37] Also in the competition realm, an
FTC study in the late 1990s of divestiture remedies in merger cases stands
out as a useful effort to determine whether the agency's intervention passed
at least a minimal standard for efficacy.[38]

Fundamental Structural Reforms

For most competition agencies, the traditional approach to dealing with
impediments to competition is the exercise of law-enforcement authority.
Common strategies include the prosecution of abuse-of-dominance cases
to address improper exclusion by single firms and the prohibition of
mergers that would tend to create positions of dominance or reinforce
oligopoly market structures. The principal means employed to dissolve
existing positions of persistent, substantial monopoly power has been the
abuse-of-dominance lawsuit.[39]

Especially in transition economies, the abuse-of-dominance case may
be an imperfect means to deal with entrenched positions of dominance
and the efforts of incumbent monopolists to sustain control of markets.
The process of conducting law-enforcement investigations or prosecuting
apparent infringements sometimes reveals that substantial, persistent
dominance is not the result simply (or principally) of private exclusionary conduct. Instead, longstanding positions of dominance are likely to
result from significant government involvement. In some instances, the
government chose to reserve all activity in a sector to a single state-owned
enterprise (SOE). In others, the government gave a single private firm an
exclusive franchise to operate within a sector and protected the exclusivity
by forbidding entry. These types of protections are often supplemented by

subsidies, import restrictions and other benefits reinforcing dominance.[40] In still other cases, the true foundations of dominance consist of rights-granting mechanisms for intellectual property that apply insufficiently rigorous tests to determine eligibility for copyrights, patents or trademarks.

The typical focus of an abuse-of-dominance case is private exclusionary behavior. As such, abuse-of-dominance litigation may not fully address other sources of substantial market power—such as the array of public policies sketched above. The most important source of substantial, persistent dominance may be various forms of state intervention. Single-minded pursuit of improper private exclusionary acts will overlook or sidestep this formative influence. An accurate accounting for the causes and consequences of dominance would need to focus more directly on these public-policy contributions to the establishment and maintenance of monopoly power.

The market study can provide a valuable policy tool to address these more complex markets where public and private action accounts for observed dominance. The lower-powered form of market study, where the competition agency identifies deficiencies and proposes solutions, is one way to bring attention to possibilities for reform. Such a study has a greater capacity to illuminate the more important sources of substantial market power and to suggest solutions that deal more directly with these formative influences.

More high-powered market-study regimes, which authorize the competition agency to impose remedies directly, supply still more potent tools to correct market failures at their source. In these studies, the competition agency not only diagnoses market and public-policy failures but also implements solutions.

INSTITUTIONAL PREREQUISITES

Good market studies require three principal inputs: skilled human capital, resources to collect and analyse information, and the shrewd expenditure of what might be called "political capital."

Human capital is necessary as good market studies typically result from a collaboration of skilled analysts with backgrounds in industrial-organization economics and competition law and experience in doing empirical research.

In terms of resources, data collection and analysis require agencies to spend funds on accumulating information (for example, by purchasing data sets) and creating an information technology infrastructure to collect and process information.

Political capital is essential too. Market studies can arouse strong political opposition as the targets of critical analysis respond to a competition agency's findings and recommendations. As they initiate studies, competition agencies must seek to anticipate how affected parties will try to mobilize political institutions to suppress the agency. An agency can take on controversial and difficult issues in its market studies, but it cannot afford to permit its portfolio of work become too top-heavy with matters involving severe political risk. The selection of topics and projects requires attention to how many fights an agency can take on at one time.

The struggle to satisfy these institutional prerequisites will be greatest in relatively new competition systems located in less affluent jurisdictions. Such jurisdictions may find it useful to pool resources and/or perform studies from a regional center to access the human capital and financial resources needed to perform effective market studies.

Among other approaches, regional centers might conduct studies addressing commercial phenomena relevant to two or more countries in the region. An alternative answer for generating effective market studies would be for such jurisdictions to form partnerships with local universities and/or academic-research centers. With this approach competition agencies would rely heavily on universities and/or academic-research centers to develop the analytical capacity and data-collection skills needed to generate effective research.

CHALLENGES, HAZARDS AND SOLUTIONS

In reciting the advantages of market studies as means to identify the causes of market dominance and to propose (or impose) solutions, this chapter has suggested problems associated with their implementation. This section of the chapter spells out some of the challenges and hazards associated with the establishment of a market-study mechanism and its use to dismantle positions of entrenched monopoly power.

Challenges and Hazards

Loss of control over the competition policy agenda
Legislators and other elected officials may take a keen interest in how the competition agency's market-study authority is applied. Lawmakers may demand that the agency use its authority to conduct studies of salient issues of the moment. In doing so, they may decline to provide resources needed to carry out the requested inquiry. The agency may find itself besieged with demands that it perform studies whose accomplishment

will require the diversion of resources from other pursuits. Over time, the agency may lose its capacity to shape a coherent policy strategy.

The FTC's experience illustrates this potential difficulty. The US FTC's broad jurisdiction over industry implies a very broad array of possible research areas. In its early years, most market studies undertaken by the FTC were based on requests from the president or from congress. Even after the commission began to initiate numerous studies on its own, many investigative reports continued to be undertaken based on congressional requests. As congress controlled the agency's budget, these requests had to be taken seriously. In some cases, congress embedded the obligation to perform studies directly into the statute that provided the FTC's budget for the coming year. In many instances, extending to the present, congressional demands have created mismatches between the agency's market-study obligations and the resources to carry them out.

Exercise of political interference
Lawmakers may regard market studies as a way of punishing political rivals or rewarding businesses that provide electoral support. In particular, a legislature may use its budgetary powers to force competition agencies to place disfavored interests under scrutiny. Market studies are not the only focal point of attempted political interference. Legislators can pressure a competition agency to bring cases against business interests controlled by political opponents. At the same time, legislators who are more reluctant to appear to intervene in law enforcement may be less hesitant to call for investigations and related proceedings that do not result in the prosecution of cases or inevitably lead to the imposition of remedies.

Possibilities for political backlash
Market studies can have important adverse political effects for a competition agency. They can draw unfavorable attention to an industry sector or to a range of sectors that use a practice under scrutiny. If the competition agency has authority to impose remedies to correct problems identified in a market study, the application of a market-study mechanism presents a still-greater threat to adversely affected companies. Industries confronting unfavorable publicity or severe remedies (for example, mandatory divestitures of assets or the compulsory licensing of intellectual property) can be expected to mobilize political resources to chasten the competition agency by reducing its budget or reducing its powers.

Need for effective priority-setting and strategy
To use a diversified portfolio of policy-making tools effectively, the competition agency must devise a disciplined approach to selecting priorities and

devising a strategy to achieve its goals. The agency requires a conscious process for defining its economic policy objectives, selecting the best mix of policy tools to attain its goals, matching policy commitments to resources and assessing the risks (political and analytical) associated with each new initiative. Among other tasks, the agency must anticipate how adversely affected economic interests may seek to enlist elected officials to oppose the agency and it must consider how it will deflect pressure to cut its budget or withdraw its authority.

Solutions

Coordination of the research agenda

An important step in devising an effective market-study program is for the competition agency to create an internal mechanism to identify potential topics, evaluate their possible contribution to realizing the agency's priorities and oversee the completion of chosen projects. This function can be assigned to a specific research office or it can be performed by a working group or standing committee. The duty of the office is to assess the likely contributions of a study, to analyse its risks and to place each new project within the existing portfolio of law-enforcement and non-law-enforcement measures. With this perspective, the coordination team can make recommendations to top agency leadership about how to proceed.

Guided by an umbrella coordination office or working group, the formulation of specific proposals and the performance of market-study projects ordinarily is carried out within the agency's operating units. In the recent past, the research-production process within the FTC has been handled largely independently by each economic or legal organization. The choices of topics and the approach to the research problem are generally decided within each group. For example, within the Bureau of Economics (BE), research projects are sometimes initiated by economists who have been given small grants of time to undertake undirected research. This research is monitored twice each year, but the review is intentionally light-handed. As the projects within the BE get larger and more formal, more review is undertaken. For example, if an economist wanted the FTC to purchase relatively low-cost data for a project, the research would be reviewed by an *ad hoc* research committee prior to initiation of the project. Parties outside the BE, however, usually would not be consulted. As projects increase in scope, the BE director and the FTC chairman's office would eventually become involved. If data were to be obtained via a compulsory process of some sort, the relevant legal bureau and the general counsel's office would also become involved with that aspect of the project.

Similarly, other agency units—such as the Office of Policy Planning, the Bureau of Competition's Policy and Coordination Office, and the General Counsel's Policy Studies Group—generate, monitor and produce their own research products. Even if the policy R&D projects are assigned to the organization rather than internally generated, the plans for the project are typically reviewed only within each organization (apart, of course, from informing the chairman and any organization leadership). The organizations typically do not turn to others for review of their proposals or methods. Certain large projects might involve staff from other organizations—particularly economists if data manipulation or analysis is involved in the study—but there would not typically be much cross-organization review of the study proposal or study methods.[41]

Project implementation protocols

There are several steps in the research process for market studies, including defining the broad topic areas of interest for research; generating interesting, policy-relevant and achievable ideas within a topic area; and producing and monitoring the research. As noted above, in the recent past these tasks have largely been handled within each FTC bureau or office. In principle, these tasks could be accomplished either in such a decentralized manner or through a more systematic, centralized process involving the simultaneous collection of research ideas from multiple sources, coordination of topic choices and then monitoring of output.

The selection of an optimal market-study process likely depends on the type of work and output envisioned, as well as the effects on researcher incentives. Staff members who do research and have good research ideas typically are the most motivated to aggressively pursue those ideas. Therefore, it is useful to allow staff members with interesting and feasible research ideas to pursue such ideas. A process that solicits ideas that are then taken from the idea generator will likely produce only very general ideas. Such a process might be useful, however, if it is not costly and if general ideas (as opposed to specific research plans) are the desired output.

There are different approaches for organizing market studies. One method is to combine all of an agency's policy groups into a single central operating unit. By this technique, ideas from a wide variety of sources within the agency are vetted early by a policy planning office or working group that also would oversee production of the market study. Such a group would report to top leadership of the agency. The goals of such an approach would be to better control the chosen topics—for example, to select projects that relate more closely with current enforcement or advocacy priorities—and to coordinate resource deployment across several relatively autonomous groups.

Another method is to centralize market studies within the agency's economics unit, which would be independent of the law-enforcement teams but would enlist contributions from the law-enforcement units. One rationale for such a view would be that the attorney-led organizations tend to produce top-down, workshop-intensive studies of a similar type, while the economists group tends to produce more academic products with a bottom-up orientation.

A third approach consists of what might be called a staff/academic collaborative model of research by which research centers outside the competition agency pursue a systematic research agenda based largely on agency-provided data on competition issues. In this model, the competition agency could gain by inducing collaboration from academics and their graduate students through a data-provision scheme in which academics gain access to the agency's internal and external data for research purposes in exchange for their research efforts. Such collaborations might be furthered through visits to the competition agencies from academics during summers and sabbaticals.

A fourth variant would be for competition agencies to pool their resources in common research projects. The inter-agency collaborative approach might be most useful to relatively small or poorly funded agencies that find it extremely difficult to build a strong internal research capacity.

These suggestions present different notions about the best mechanism to produce high-quality market studies. In practice, these visions may not be as different as they initially appear. If one seeks policy ideas to be explored in public consultations such as workshops or hearings, a formalized topic-selection process and report-production scheme may be feasible. Obtaining ideas from a large set of sources might provide a richer choice set. Some level of coordination of large externally driven projects by the competition agency might also be appropriate. At the FTC, such projects are controlled by an assigned group, but higher-level coordination almost always occurs and centralization might make that process proceed more smoothly. Whether such coordination needs to entail centralized control of production is a more difficult issue, as that may unfavorably alter incentives. As discussed above, individual staff members and organizations may not devote substantial resources to developing good projects if those projects are then taken over by other organizations. In addition, a centralized model would not make much sense for smaller, bottom-up, research projects because centralization would add little value and discourage development. Central planning can identify broad areas of interest, but it is very unlikely to produce specific achievable project ideas. Ideas for any interesting projects likely will have to be generated on a less prescribed basis. Furthermore, the impetus for some of the best policy-relevant economic research is often the recognition of a new data source or method of analysis that could be used to shed light on questions surrounding a particular policy. A high degree of centralization may cause such opportunities to go unrecognized.

Based on discussions with managers in various other governmental economic policy shops, research—particularly bottom-up economic or scientific research—seems to be a decentralized activity in many government organizations.[42] For a segment of the research work, researchers tend to generate their own ideas within relevant bounds and pursue the topics with little oversight.

Another segment of policy R&D work is directed or top-down research and the production of those outputs is more heavily monitored. Even in that context, however, the monitoring appears to be handled within a relatively small group, rather than coordinated across groups.

To generate useful policy R&D topics for large projects, without imposing unnecessary costs on smaller, more research-oriented, projects, perhaps a review process that differs by level of resource commitment might be the best schema. This might maintain flexibility and reduce bureaucracy at the low end while improving monitoring at the upper end. Recent FTC chairmen have used a combination of weekly and monthly reports and semi-annual senior management retreats to review the progress of ongoing projects and to promote potential new ideas.

For relatively smaller projects (for example, proposals by economics staff that do not require significant data purchases and that have working papers or private publication in journals as the envisioned output), little review or monitoring is required. For instance, the BE currently handles such undirected research via a time-grant process and periodic monitoring by managers in its Office of Applied Research and Outreach.[43]

Occasionally, FTC staff members propose projects that may require significant time and some data expense but not require compulsory process or expensive data purchases. For such projects, proposal preparation by the author and bureau/office review has been the norm. Managers within the organization have provided oversight of such projects.

Projects that require major data purchases or that grow directly from the agency's agenda, projects requiring compulsory process and congressionally requested projects may warrant more monitoring and control than do the smaller projects discussed previously. Such large project proposals could be made subject to an intra-agency review process, if such a process would add value or allow for better resource-allocation decisions. The cost would be some loss of autonomy and responsibility for the individual group leading the project and perhaps for the individual authors, but that price may be offset by gains in coordination or in improved topic selection.[44]

Several participants proposed studies of regulatory effects, particularly in the telecommunications arena. Two economists described a previous BE staff study of the Federal Communication Commission's "must carry" rules as a model for future efforts to find opportunistically natural experiments to test theories of exclusion.[45] The idea of looking for natural experiments (that sometimes occur in locally regulated industries) was a theme that reappeared several times during the external consultations in various guises.

CONCLUSION

Market studies can supply an important complement to traditional law enforcement as a way for competition agencies to identify and redress private and public impediments to effective competition in highly concentrated market sectors. Where market dominance is the product of extensive public intervention (for example, through state ownership, subsidies or legal restrictions on market entry), the market study can be superior to law enforcement as a diagnostic tool and as a catalyst for effective remedies.

Market studies have their own costs. Good studies do not come on the cheap. An agency must assemble capable teams of analysts, from its own resources or in alliance with external research bodies, to select topics, conduct investigations, interpret evidence and prepare reports. Market studies also can have important political implications. When a study shines light on private or public behavior that is useful only for its capacity to create and protect monopoly rents, the beneficiaries of that monopoly power will seek to enlist political allies to rebuff the competition agency. The more effective the study is in redressing substantial monopoly power, the greater the political hazards it can pose to the agency.

Experience in various competition agencies teaches a great deal about how to confront these challenges—to organize a research program, to anticipate resource demands and political risks, and to devise strategies for effective implementation. For smaller, poorly funded, agencies, regional cooperation to pool research efforts can be a valuable way to overcome resource limitations.

ACKNOWLEDGMENTS

The author is grateful to Jeffrey Traczynski and the participants in the East-West Center meeting of authors for many useful comments and suggestions. The author also serves as a non-executive director of the UK's

Competition and Markets Authority. The views expressed here are the author's alone.

NOTES

1. For example, the most influential ranking of competition agencies focuses principally on law-enforcement activity. See "Rating enforcement—the annual ranking of the world's leading competition authorities," 16 *Global Competition Review* 6 (June 2013).
2. For an early, influential statement of this point, see R. Shyam Khemani and Mark A. Dutz, "The instruments of competition policy and their relevance for economic development," in Claudio R. Frischtak (ed.), *Regulatory Policies and Reform: A Comparative Perspective* (World Bank, 1995), 16.
3. The importance of assigning the competition agency a diversified portfolio of policy instruments is examined in "More than law enforcement: the FTC's many tools—a conversation with Tim Muris and Bob Pitofsky," 72 *Antitrust L.J.* 773 (2005).
4. For example, South Korea's competition policy system confers upon the Korea Fair Trade Commission (KFTC) a broad competition advocacy mandate regarding regulatory programs that affect competition. *Korea Fair Trade Commission, A Journey toward Market Economy: KFTC's 23 Years of Building Transparent and Fair Market* 173–7 (April 2004).
5. The significant complementarities between law enforcement and competition advocacy are analysed in James C. Cooper and William E. Kovacic, "U.S. convergence with international competition norms: antitrust law and public restraints of competition," 90 *Boston U.L. Rev.* 1555, 1558–62 (2010).
6. William E. Kovacic, "Antitrust in high-tech industries: improving the federal antitrust joint venture," 19 *Geo. Mason L. Rev.* 1097, 1100 (2012).
7. The work of some agencies that have led the development of market studies is discussed in William E. Kovacic, *The Federal Trade Commission at 100: Into Our 2nd Century* (Federal Trade Commission, 2009), 106–9.
8. The FTC's study of electric and natural gas utility holding companies in the late 1920s and early 1930s provides an example of an ambitious, far-ranging examination of an entire sector. See "Federal Trade Commission, summary report on holding and operating companies of electric and gas utilities," S. Doc. No. 92, Pt. 73-A, 74th Cong., 2d. Sess. (1935; presenting a history of the FTC study and its findings and recommendations).
9. In the 1940s and early 1950s, the FTC used a market study to identify and document collusive arrangements among many of the world's leading petroleum companies. See "Federal Trade Commission, the international petroleum cartel—staff report to the Federal Trade Commission," submitted to the Subcommittee on Monopoly of the US Senate Select Committee on Small Business (22 August 1952).
10. On the Productivity Commission and its work, see S.G. Corones, *Competition Law in Australia* (3rd ed., Lawbook Company, 2004), 1–11.
11. The 1950 amendments to the US merger control regime were motivated in part by an FTC study that appeared to link substantial increases in aggregate concentration to mergers. "Federal Trade Commission, report on the merger movement: a summary report" (1948).
12. In the 1970s, the FTC undertook a "line of business" market inquiry that collected data across a large number of sectors to prepare reports on profitability and other performance measures. See "Federal Trade Commission, Bureau of Economics, statistical report: annual line of business report 1973" (March 1979).
13. See, for example, "Federal Trade Commission, to promote innovation: the proper balance of competition and patent law and policy" (2003; examining the effect of the patent system on competition).

14. An agency might treat its law-enforcement authority as an implicit mandate to perform research to guide the selection of new cases and evaluate the impact of past enforcement programs. This type of research might closely resemble what commentators often refer to as "market studies."

15. For example, the Federal Trade Commission Act gives the FTC express authority to use compulsory process to require firms to provide information to be used in a market study. 15 U.S.C. §46.

16. See, generally, Marc Winerman, "The origins of the FTC: concentration, cooperation, control, and competition," 71 *Antitrust L.J.* 1 (2003).

17. The FTC's early experience is representative. Firms contested the exercise of the agency's investigative and reporting powers. See Thomas Blaisdell, *The Federal Trade Commission* (Columbia University Press, 1932), 172, 258–62, 271–3 (discussing litigation challenging exercise of the FTC's information-gathering powers).

18. The FTC's report in 2003 based on an inquiry into the patent system and its effect upon competition, "To promote innovation," relied entirely on public sources and voluntary industry participation in public consultations. The FTC study influenced adoption of subsequent legislation and Supreme Court jurisprudence.

19. The UK market-investigations mechanism is described in Richard Whish, *Competition Law* (5th ed., LexisNexis, 2005), 411–26.

20. Sandra Marco Colino, *Competition Law of the EU and the UK* (Oxford University Press, 2008), 336–47.

21. In its first decade, the FTC conducted a market study of the meat-packing industry and published a highly critical study of the sector. The FTC's report created intense legislative opposition and resulted in legislation that excluded the commission from future involvement in the industry. This episode is recounted in E. Pendleton Herring, *Public Administration and the Public Interest* (McGraw-Hill, 1936), 118–20 and Thomas Blaisdell, *The Federal Trade Commission, supra*, 128–31.

22. For example, work on sectors historically subject to comprehensive public utility regulation (for example, communications and transportation), international trade restraints and licensed professions were major objects of FTC research programs in the late 1970s and early 1980s. These programs are described in William E. Kovacic, "The Federal Trade Commission and congressional oversight of antitrust enforcement," 17 *Tulsa L.J.* 587, 648–9, 663–4 (1982).

23. See, for example, Daniel P. O'Brien and Abraham L. Wickelgren, "A critical analysis of critical loss analysis," 71 *Antitrust L.J.* 161 (2003) (cited in *FTC v. Whole Foods Market, Inc.*, 548 F.3d 1028, 1048 [D.C. Cir. 2008; J. Tatel, concurring]).

24. See "More than law enforcement: the FTC's many tools—a conversation with Tim Muris and Bob Pitofsky," *supra*, at 776–8 (comments by Muris noting how the 2002 generic drug study helped generate cases and reform of the Hatch-Waxman Act).

25. For two formative contributions arising from FTC research, see Pauline M. Ippolito and Alan D. Mathios, "Information, advertising and health choices: a study of the cereal market," 23 *RAND J. Econ.* 459 (1990) and Pauline M. Ippolito and Alan Mathios, "The regulation of science-based claims in advertising," 13 *J. Consumer Policy* 413 (1990).

26. This program is described at "Federal Trade Commission, oil and gas industry initiatives: gasoline and diesel price monitoring," available at www.ftc.gov/ftc/oilgas/gas_price.htm.

27. Federal Trade Commission, *Improving Health Care: A Dose of Competition* (2004).

28. See "FTC Bureau of Economics, roundtable on the economics of the pharmaceutical industry" (Oct. 2006), available at www.ftc.gov/be/workshops/pharmaceutical/pharmaceutical.shtm.

29. FTC Bureau of Economics Staff and Roy Levy, "The pharmaceutical industry: a discussion of competitive and antitrust issues in an environment of change" (1999), available at www.ftc.gov/reports/pharmaceutical/drugrep.pdf.

30. FTC Staff, "Broadband connectivity competition policy" (2007), available at www.ftc.gov/bc/tech/cable/broadband.htm.

31. FTC Workshop, "Possible anticompetitive efforts to restrict competition on the internet" (Oct. 2002), available at www.ftc.gov/opp/ecommerce/anticompetitive/index.shtm.
32. The UK competition regime is a preeminent example. For example, the UK Office of Fair Trading in 2008 commissioned a project to define the upcoming issues that will likely affect consumers. See U.K. Office of Fair Trading, "Consultation on emerging trends: a report prepared for the OFT by GfK NOP" (2008), available at www.oft.gov.uk/shared _oft/about_oft/oft1000.pdf.
33. FTC Workshop, "Innovations in health care delivery" (Apr. 2008), available at www.ftc. gov/bc/healthcare/hcd/index.shtm. Other nations are taking an even more direct route toward predicting future competition and consumer issues. For example, the UK Office of Fair Trading commissioned a project to define the upcoming issues that will likely affect consumers. See U.K. Office of Fair Trading, "Consultation on emerging trends: a report prepared for the OFT by GfK NOP" (2008), available at www.oft.gov.uk/shared_oft/ about_oft/oft1000.pdf.
34. See, for example, Michael R. Baye, "Antitrust economics and policy: some suggestions for research agendas" (26 Sept. 2008), keynote address at the Research Symposium on Antitrust Economics and Competition Policy, Northwestern University Searle Center on Law, Regulation, and Economic Growth, 33–42, available at www.ftc.gov/speeches/baye /080926antitrustnw.pdf.
35. See FTC Bureau of Economics, "Conference on behavioral economics and consumer policy" (Apr. 2007), available at www.ftc.gov/be/consumerbehavior/index.shtml.
36. Retrospective work in the merger area has been done since at least the early 1980s. Several recent merger retrospectives have focused on various refined-products markets in the oil industry and on hospital markets.
37. For a discussion of self-assessments undertaken by the FTC and other competition agencies, see William E. Kovacic, "Using ex post evaluations to improve the performance of competition policy authorities," 31 *J. Corp. L.* 505 (2006).
38. Federal Trade Commission Staff, "A study of the commission's divestiture process" (1999), available at www.ftc.gov/os/1999/08/divestiture.pdf.
39. The US experience is reviewed in William E. Kovacic, "Designing remedies for dominant firm misconduct," 31 *Conn. L. Rev.* 1285 (1999) and William E. Kovacic, "Failed Expectations: The troubling past and uncertain future of the Sherman Act as a tool for deconcentration," 74 *Iowa L. Rev.* 1105 (1989).
40. For example, many dominant enterprises in Armenia owe their market positions to the inability or unwillingness of taxation authorities to force the accurate reporting of income and the payment of taxes on such income. The underreporting of income and the avoidance of income tax gives dominant firms a substantial cost advantage. Thus, in the Armenian case, a major source of dominance is a failure of tax policy and enforcement, not the traditional forms of exclusionary conduct (for example, exclusive dealing or predatory pricing) that figure prominently in litigated antitrust cases. See United Nations Conference on Trade and Development, "Voluntary peer review of competition law and policy: Armenia" (2010).
41. Top managers in each organization in the FTC learn about the existence and status of policy R&D projects from the materials produced for semi-annual management retreats and through monthly and weekly reports prepared by the various organizations describing those activities.
42. This observation is based on interviews regarding the research process and policy work at the Competition Directorate of the European Commission, the US Federal Reserve Board, the US Congressional Budget Office, the US Commerce Department's Bureau of Economic Analysis and the Department of Justice Antitrust Division's Economic Analysis Group. Each institution uses economists for major research projects and each produces some policy outputs. However, the FTC appears to undertake more non-economist research and policy work than do the other organizations.
43. Each of the interviews with other government organizations indicated that offering at

least some amount of this type of research time was important to meet the market for research-capable PhD economists, especially for newly minted PhDs.

44.   One approach to idea generation might entail use of a research staff person who occasionally (perhaps annually) collects general policy R&D ideas from across the agency and from informed outsiders and culls that list down for further consideration. Those general ideas that have the most merit could then be forwarded to organizations within the agency for preparation of specific project proposals. The best proposals might then be chosen for action, with the specific shop that generated the chosen idea/proposal being given responsibility for production. The staffer could monitor and report on progress but would not necessarily control the production process.

45.   See, for example, Michael G. Vita, "Must carry regulations for cable television systems: an empirical analysis," 12 *J. Reg. Econ.* 159 (1997). The natural experiment in Vita's paper was the elimination of the Federal Communications Commission "must carry" rules in the late 1980s on First Amendment grounds. This exogenous change in the regulatory regime gave cable systems discretion as to which (if any) local stations they would carry; it allowed clean testing of various hypotheses about the rationale for cable system carriage decisions.

4. An empirical study of the competitive pressure of the foreign sector in Korea

Suil Lee

INTRODUCTION

Analyses of market structures aim at presenting indirect evidence for the degree of competition in certain markets. A market-structure analysis is primarily based on the market-concentration ratio calculated by the total shipments of domestic firms. However, if a high proportion of shipments were exported or a significant amount of items traded in the market were imported by a variety of importers, the effectiveness of the market-concentration ratio would be potentially degraded to a significant extent.

This problem can be prominent, in particular, in Korea. Looking at the trend of the degree of dependence upon trade in Korea, as shown in Figure 4.1, the index stayed near to 50 percent in the early and mid-1990s and has rapidly risen since 1997, recording 96.8 percent in 2011. Figure 4.2 shows the proportion of exports and imports compared to shipments in mining and manufacturing industries in Korea. From this figure, we see that the proportion maintains a high level of around 40 percent in the 2000s. These facts mean that the effectiveness of the market-concentration ratio as an indirect indicator of the degree of competition could be significantly constrained in Korea.

Based on the awareness of these issues in Korea, this chapter analyses the importance of the foreign sector in the extent of competition in the domestic market in Korea by linking mining and manufacturing statistics and trade statistics. The mining and manufacturing statistics provide us mainly with information on shipments by companies and the trade statistics provide export and import information by product items.

It is important to perceive, however, that advantages of including the foreign sector in the analysis may not be obtained without any cost. First, it is very difficult to link the above-mentioned two statistics reliably since the statistical classification systems of the two statistics are very different

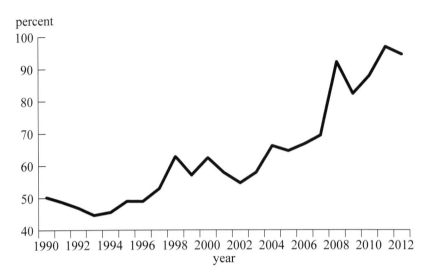

percent

Source: Trade Statistics, Mining and Manufacturing Statistics.

Figure 4.1   Degree of dependence on trade in Korea, 1990–2012

given the difference in their purposes. Thus the conjunction of the two statistics may compromise the reliability of the analyses. In addition, the most detailed industry classification that we can get through the linkage of the two statistics is the Korea Standard Industry Classification (KSIC) three-digit level. However, an industry defined at the three-digit level includes a number of product items. Therefore, the analysis unit of the three-digit level may not be appropriate for the objective to identify the degree of competition in the market.

Competitive pressure from the foreign sector on the domestic market can be conceptually divided into actual competition and potential competition.[1] Actual competition from the foreign sector is related to the question of how, on the one hand, the presence of imported goods traded in the domestic market impacts the competition mode (in terms of production costs, quality, price and so on) and profit margin of domestic firms. On the other hand, potential competition from the foreign sector means that, if there is actual competitive pressure from the foreign sector, such fact in itself could constrain the behavior of domestic firms even before imports occur. The degree of potential competition can be identified in a variety of ways and it can also be analysed by observing how imports react according to the changing conditions in the domestic market. In fact, Choi and Jo

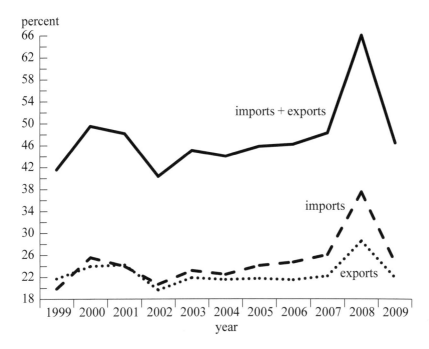

Figure 4.2   Mining and manufacturing exports and imports in Korea,
1999–2009

(2006) defined the potential competitive pressure from the foreign sector as the possibility of trade diversion of imports in response to changes in the domestic price or changes in the import-penetration ratio due to changes in the profitability of the domestic industry.

In previous literature on the relationship among actual competitive pressure from the foreign sector, domestic market structure and the profitability of domestic firms, Bain (1951) found that a higher concentration of domestic market tends to increase profit margin. However, Schwartzman (1959), Jones et al. (1973) and Pagoulatos and Sorensen (1976) reported that such a tendency was not observed in cases of industries with a high degree of openness. Esposito and Esposito (1971), Turner (1980), Levinsohn (1993), Katics and Petersen (1994), Khondker (1996) and Sabido and Mulato (2006) provided empirical evidence that competitive pressure from the foreign sector actually lowers the profitability of the domestic industry. Pugel (1980) showed that such an effect was greater the higher the concentration of the domestic market. In previous studies on the relationship among potential competitive pressure from the foreign sector, domestic market structure and the profit margins of domestic firms, Landes and Posner (1980/81) emphasized the potential competition from the foreign sector and Ghosal (2002) showed that the potential competitive pressures from the foreign sector are high in industries with high concentrations.[2]

There are few preceding studies on the competitive pressure from the foreign sector in Korea. Lee (2002) calculated a domestic-market-concentration ratio for mining and manufacturing industries in Korea and Lee (2007) and Lee et al. (2011) extended the analyses to service industries. Choi and Jo (2006) analysed the potential competitive pressure from the foreign sector in Korea in a similar manner as Ghosal (2002) and have shown the presence of potential competitive pressures from abroad in Korea by analysing the time-series data of seven years from 1996 to 2002. The object of study and the analysis methodology of this chapter are very similar to Choi and Jo (2006). However, as well as a difference in the period of analysis, this chapter also differs from Choi and Jo (2006) in that the analysis on the actual competitive pressure is performed simultaneously with the analysis on the potential competitive pressure in order to fully understand the competitive pressures from the foreign sector.

The remainder of the chapter is organized as follows. In "Import Penetration and Domestic-market Concentration," we calculate import-penetration ratio by industries as an indirect indicator for the actual competitive pressures from the foreign sector. We also construct a market-concentration ratio taking the foreign sector into account and compare it with one based only on the shipments information of domestic firms. In "Empirical Analyses," we conduct econometric analyses on the presence and pattern of competitive pressures from the foreign sector. More specifically, we investigate questions of whether imports may increase in response to an increase in the profitability of the domestic industry and whether these increased imports tend to lower the profitability of the domestic industry. "Summary and Conclusion" finishes the analysis by summarizing the results.

IMPORT PENETRATION AND DOMESTIC-MARKET CONCENTRATION

In this section, the analysis period is set to 11 years, from 1999 to 2009, for consistency with the following section. Yearly market-concentration ratios can be calculated for 54 three-digit industries over the analysis period. Among those, six industries are excluded from the analysis because connecting the mining and manufacturing statistics and trade statistics reliably would be problematic for those industries. Accordingly, the analysis in this section has been conducted using 48 three-digit industries.[3]

During the analysis period, the 48 industries represent 89.3 percent, 62.8 percent and 85.3 percent, respectively, of total shipments, imports and exports in the mining and manufacturing industries. The reason for the relatively small share in the total imports compared to the total shipments and exports is that crude oil, natural gas, mining and related services industries, which accounted for 27.2 percent of total imports of mining and manufacturing industries, are excluded from the analysis. Such industries are far from the analytical purposes of this section of investigating the level of competitive pressures from overseas. Thus, given the purpose of analysis in this section, the 48 industries included in the analysis can be considered to adequately represent the mining and manufacturing industries in Korea.

Import-penetration Ratio

Table 4.1 shows the annual trend of import-penetration ratio in Korea.[4] The first two columns are the mean and standard deviation of import-penetration ratios over the 48 industries weighted by industry shipments for each year. The next two columns are the mean and standard deviation of annual changes in the import-penetration ratio weighted by industry shipments. As can be seen from the table, the average import penetration of the industries included in the analysis, except for the year 2008 when the financial crisis occurred, does not show any particular trend and repeats changes in the range of 14 percent to 16 percent over the analysis period. However, the standard deviations summarized in the second column indicate a very large cross-industry difference with respect to the import-penetration ratio.

Table 4.1   Import-penetration ratio in Korea, 1999–2009

Year	Annual level		Yearly change	
	Mean	Standard deviation	Mean	Standard deviation
1999	0.1445	0.1528	—	—
2000	0.1678	0.1669	0.0245	0.0488
2001	0.1665	0.1490	0.0001	0.0587
2002	0.1438	0.1240	−0.0206	0.0475
2003	0.1593	0.1462	0.0173	0.0307
2004	0.1529	0.1470	−0.0059	0.0429
2005	0.1624	0.1869	0.0106	0.0988
2006	0.1569	0.1597	−0.0045	0.0638
2007	0.1693	0.1638	0.0118	0.0544
2008	0.2251	0.1813	0.0551	0.0445
2009	0.1620	0.1370	−0.0578	0.0638

Competition law and economics

Table 4.2   Cross-industry difference in import-penetration ratio in Korea

	Annual level		Yearly change	
	Mean	Standard deviation	Mean	Standard deviation
Mean	0.245	0.064	0.003	0.064
Standard deviation	0.230	0.078	0.012	0.079
Minimum	0.008	0.002	−0.033	0.003
Maximum	0.922	0.453	0.044	0.450

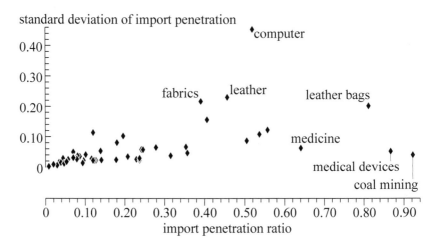

Figure 4.3   Cross-industry differences in import penetration ratio in Korea

The very large cross-industry difference in the import-penetration ratio becomes clearer in Table 4.2 and Figure 4.3. To create Table 4.2, the mean and standard deviation for import-penetration levels and yearly changes over the analysis period were obtained for each industry first, and then the mean, standard deviation, and minimum and maximum values for each item were calculated over industries. The time-series average of import-penetration ratio by industry is 24.5 percent on average, but the standard deviation of the time-series average of import-penetration ratio reaches 0.230, which indicates the presence of a very large cross-industry gap in the time-series average value.

Figure 4.3 shows the mean and standard deviation of import-penetration ratio by industry. As shown in the figure, on the one hand, whereas the time-series average of the import-penetration ratio is less than 10 percent in 15 industries among the 48 industries, there also exist several industries, such as coal mining, medical devices manufacturing, and leather handbags and other leather products manufacturing, for which the average import-penetration ratio is over 80 percent. On the other hand, when it comes to the volatility of the import-penetration ratio, whereas the standard deviation of the import-penetration ratio is less than 0.05 in 28 industries, this number is bigger than 0.2 for computers and office equipment manufacturing, leather manufacturing, fabric manufacturing, and leather handbags and other leather products manufacturing.

If the import-penetration ratio can be interpreted as an effective measure of actual competitive pressure from the foreign sector, the results of the above analysis indicate that there have been very big differences between industries in the levels of actual competitive pressure and the annual changes of such competitive pressure in Korea in the 2000s. In addition, the fact that there are a number of industries for which the level or the volatility of import-penetration ratio is very high suggests that tasks to infer the degree of competition in the domestic market through market concentration calculated based on the shipment of domestic firms can be very constrained.

In order to determine whether significant differences exist in the import penetration depending on market concentration, we divided the sample into high-concentrated industries and low-concentrated industries based on the time-series average value of CR_3 (the sum of top three companies' market shares) and repeated the tasks of Table 4.2 for each sub-sample. Table 4.3 and Table 4.4 summarize the results. As can be seen from the tables, when compared to the low-concentrated industries, the time-series averages of import penetration of high-concentrated industries are considerably lower, on average, whereas the cross-industry gap is larger. Associated with the volatility of import penetration, the cross-industry gap is relatively larger in the case of high-concentrated industries.

Table 4.3   Cross-industry difference in import-penetration ratio in Korea: high concentration

	Annual level		Yearly change	
	Mean	Standard deviation	Mean	Standard deviation
Mean	0.213	0.061	0.004	0.063
Standard deviation	0.242	0.093	0.012	0.099
Minimum	0.008	0.002	−0.033	0.003
Maximum	0.922	0.454	0.030	0.450

Table 4.4   Cross-industry difference in import-penetration ratio in Korea:
low concentration

	Annual level		Yearly change	
	Mean	Standard deviation	Mean	Standard deviation
Mean	0.281	0.067	0.005	0.065
Standard deviation	0.216	0.061	0.013	0.057
Minimum	0.029	0.006	−0.019	0.006
Maximum	0.867	0.230	0.044	0.223

Table 4.5   Market-concentration ratio in Korea, 1999–2009

Year	Annual level		Yearly change	
	Mean	Standard deviation	Mean	Standard deviation
1999	57.48	24.44	—	—
2000	55.73	25.28	−2.25	3.24
2001	53.18	24.68	−2.07	2.50
2002	50.43	23.95	−2.13	2.44
2003	51.74	24.59	1.23	2.98
2004	52.95	24.33	1.36	3.23
2005	51.68	23.64	−1.53	2.85
2006	52.11	22.18	0.51	2.95
2007	54.59	23.53	2.13	4.53
2008	55.74	22.48	0.43	2.83
2009	55.70	22.65	0.41	3.11

Domestic Home Market Concentration Ratio

Table 4.5 shows the annual trend of the market-concentration ratio
(CR_3) based on the shipments of domestic firms in Korea. The table was
constructed in the same way as Table 4.1. According to the table, unlike
the import-penetration ratio, the "average" of the market-concentration
ratio has a clear trend. After recording 57.48 in 1999, it steadily declined
for three years to 50.43 in 2002, began to rise again and recorded 55.70
in 2009. Table 4.6 is made for the market-concentration ratio in the same
way as Table 4.2. Similar to the import-penetration ratio, we can see a
large cross-industry gap in the level and annual change of the market-
concentration ratio, but this cross-industry gap is significantly smaller than
in the case of import penetration.

Table 4.6   Cross-industry difference in market-concentration ratio in Korea

	Annual level		Yearly change	
	Mean	Standard deviation	Mean	Standard deviation
Mean	44.06	5.27	−0.22	3.85
Standard deviation	22.11	3.64	1.16	2.16
Minimum	13.32	1.36	−3.03	1.45
Maximum	95.75	18.03	2.74	12.23

Let us now calculate the domestic market-concentration ratio ($DMCR_3$) to obtain a market-concentration index that reflects the actual degree of competition in the foreign sector. Conceptually, in a specific industry, $DMCR_3$ shall be calculated according to the formula below.

$$DMCR_3 = \sum_{i=1}^{3}(S_i - X_i + M_i)/\sum_{j=1}^{n}(S_j - X_j + M_j) \qquad (4.1)$$

In Equation (4.1), $i=1,2,3$ refers to the top three providers of the industry in question in terms of domestic market share and $j=1,2,...,n$ covers all operators that produce or import products that are traded in the relevant industry. S_i, X_i and M_i refer to firm i's shipments, exports and imports, respectively.

However, firm-specific statistics for exports and imports are not available in Korea. Therefore, the following restrictive assumptions are put in place in order to calculate $DMCR_3$ by currently available statistics: the proportion of total exports compared to total shipments of the top three providers is the same as such proportion of the industry concerned; the import of products that are traded in the industry are done competitively by professional importers. When these assumptions are satisfied, Equation (4.1) can be expressed as the following equation:

$$DMCR_3 = \frac{\sum_{i=1}^{3}\left[S_i = X(\sum_{i=1}^{3}S_i/S)\right]}{S - X + M} = \frac{\sum_{i=1}^{3}S_i - X \cdot CR_3}{S - X + M} \qquad (4.2)$$

In Equation (4.2), S, X and M refer to total shipments, exports and imports, respectively, of the industry in question. Now, using Equation (4.2), we can calculate $DMCR_3$ at KSIC three-digit level by utilizing firm-level shipment data in the mining and manufacturing statistics and industry-level exports and imports data that can be obtained by linking the mining and manufacturing statistics and the trade statistics. Given

Competition law and economics

Table 4.7   Domestic market-concentration ratio in Korea, 1999–2009

Year	Annual level		Yearly change	
	Mean	Standard deviation	Mean	Standard deviation
1999	50.29	25.55	—	—
2000	47.78	25.98	−3.00	3.56
2001	45.27	24.18	−2.21	3.80
2002	43.90	23.14	−0.98	3.53
2003	44.31	24.05	0.28	3.05
2004	45.48	23.95	1.37	4.56
2005	44.02	24.23	−1.76	6.83
2006	44.49	22.15	0.53	4.23
2007	46.14	23.71	1.37	4.46
2008	44.03	22.20	−2.64	3.62
2009	47.72	22.74	3.64	3.68

the definition of import penetration in this section ($IP=M/(S-X+M)$), however, Equation (4.2) can be expressed simply as a function of CR_3 and IP as shown in the following equation:

$$DMCR_3 = \left(\frac{\sum_{i=1}^{3} S_i - X \cdot CR_3}{S}\right)\left(\frac{S}{S-X+M}\right)$$

$$= CR_3\left(\frac{S-X}{S}\right)\left(\frac{S}{S-X+M}\right) = CR_3\left(\frac{S-X}{S-X+M}\right) = CR_3(1-IP) \quad (4.3)$$

Table 4.7 shows the annual trend of domestic market-concentration ratios, which is calculated using $DMCR_3$ data obtained by Equation (4.3). In Korea, $DMCR_3$ of "average" industry has recorded lower levels by about 7 percent, compared to CR_3, reflecting the impact of import penetration. $DMCR_3$ declined continuously until 2002, like CR_3 in Table 4.5, but the rising trend since then is not so pronounced. The latter is due to the fact that, as is clearly illustrated in the case of 2008, the import-penetration ratio of "average" industry has changed in the direction of offsetting the change in CR_3. The results of the work done for $DMCR_3$, in the same way as Table 4.2 and Table 4.6, are summarized in Table 4.8. When compared to Table 4.2 and Table 4.6, the cross-industry gap of $DMCR_3$ observed in Table 4.8 is larger than in the case of CR_3 and smaller than in the case of the import-penetration ratio, which is easily anticipated by Equation (4.3).

Finally, Table 4.9 summarizes changes in the level and volatility of market-concentration ratio, that is, [time-series average of $DMCR_3$ – time-series

Table 4.8   Cross-industry difference in domestic market-concentration ratio in Korea

	Annual level		Yearly change	
	Mean	Standard deviation	Mean	Standard deviation
Mean	34.40	5.52	−0.26	4.59
Standard deviation	22.72	5.49	1.16	4.32
Minimum	4.44	1.35	−3.65	1.37
Maximum	93.82	36.03	3.10	29.26

average of CR_3] and [time-series standard deviation of $DMCR_3$ – time-series standard deviation of CR_3], stemming from reflecting the degree of competitive pressure from the foreign sector. On the one hand, since $DMCR_3$ and CR_3 satisfy the relationship of Equation (4.3) and the import-penetration ratio has a positive value, $DMCR_3$ is always smaller than CR_3. On the other hand, the time-series standard deviation of $DMCR_3$ may be greater or smaller than the time-series standard deviation of CR_3 depending on the direction of time-serial changes in CR_3 and IP. In common with Figure 4.3, which shows a big difference in the level and volatility of cross-industry import penetration, Table 4.9 shows that there is a probable distortion, depending on the industry, if the degree of competition in the domestic market is inferred by market-concentration ratios calculated based only on the shipment data of domestic firms. This is especially true in coal mining, computer and office equipment manufacturing, medical devices manufacturing, the first nonferrous metals industry, and leather handbags and other leather products manufacturing, for which the market-concentration index decreases by more than 20 as the degree of competitive pressure from the foreign sector is reflected in the calculation of market concentrations. The presence of industries for which time-series standard deviation of market-concentration ratios varies significantly according to changes in the method of calculating the market-concentration index also shows the possibility of a distortion when inferring the degree of competition in the domestic market from market-concentration indices calculated by the shipments of domestic firms.

EMPIRICAL ANALYSES

In the previous section, we calculated industry-specific import-penetration ratios and domestic market-concentration ratios as indirect evidence of

Table 4.9   *Change in market-concentration ratio in Korea due to the*
                foreign sector

Change in the time-series standard deviation (% points, absolute value)	Reduction in the time-series average market concentration (% points)			
	0–5	5–10	10–20	≥20
0–5	20 industries	12 industries	leather (10.3) refined petroleum (11.2) basic compounds (16.7) medicine (14.9) glass (16.4) other nonmetallic minerals (13.0) first steel (15.4) other electrical equipment (12.8) other transport equipment (13.9) other products (16.3)	
5–10	—	—	rail transportation equipment (10.1)	coal mining (48.1) leather bags (30.2) first nonferrous metals (31.6) medical devices (32.2)
10–20	—	—	—	—
≥20	—	—	—	computers and office equipment (32.7)

the degree of competitive pressure exercised by the foreign sector. Now we conduct empirical analyses focusing on the following two questions in order to find more direct evidence.

Q1. How does import penetration change responding to changes in the profitability of the domestic industry? Do such changes in the import penetration show a difference depending on the domestic market's market concentration?

Q2. How does the profitability of the domestic industry change responding to changes in import penetration? Do such changes in the profitability show a difference depending on the domestic market's market concentration?

The first question concerns the response of the foreign sector to changing conditions in the domestic market and aims to analyse the competitive pressures that potentially exist in the foreign sector. However, although the corresponding increase in imports responding to an increase in the profitability of the domestic industry is observed, it cannot be fully judged from the results of such an analysis alone whether the foreign sector may exercise the competitive pressure on domestic firms. This is because importers who increase imports in response to the increase in the profitability of the domestic industry may try to enjoy a higher profit rate stringing along with domestic firms rather than fiercely competing with domestic firms. Thus, in order to fully analyse the degree of competitive pressures due to the foreign sector, the analysis on the first question needs to be in parallel with the analysis on the impact of changes in imports on the competition in the domestic market. The second question is designed to analyse the degree of actual competitive pressures from the foreign sector. It is meaningful in itself as well as complementing the analysis on the first question.

It should be noted that the results for the second question do not give a definitive answer on the degree of actual competitive pressure from the foreign sector. In response to an increase in the import penetration, domestic companies can compete with imports by improving the quality of domestic products rather than lowering the prices. It is also possible for them to maintain profitability through cost savings while entering price competition. So, depending on how domestic firms respond to changes in the import penetration, the profitability of the domestic industry may not be lowered even if there is a significant competitive pressure from the foreign sector. However, due to the limitations of available data, it is impossible to include in the analysis the variety of responses to changes in the import penetration that domestic companies can take. Accordingly, in this section, we assume that the quality of domestic products and the cost of production do not change in the short term and that the competition actions that domestic companies can take responding to the competitive pressures from the foreign sector are limited to reductions in price.

Potential Competitive Pressure of the Foreign Sector

To our knowledge, Choi and Jo (2006) is the only study so far to analyse
the potential competitive pressure from the foreign sector in Korea. They
analysed 66 KSIC three-digit industries over the period 1996–2002 and the
following results were obtained:

R1. Potential competition from abroad, defined by the reaction of the
profit rate to changes in import penetration, exists in Korea and occurs
with a lag of one year.

R2. Import penetration tends to decrease as domestic market structure is
more concentrated when other conditions are constant.

In this subsection, in order to answer Q1, we analyse the presence and patterns of the potential competition from the foreign sector and the relationship between the structure of the domestic market and import penetration
in Korea over the period from 1999 to 2009. While doing so, we maintain
the definition and analysis methodology in Choi and Jo (2006) and pay
attention in particular to whether the results obtained from Choi and Jo
(2006) are still valid in the 2000s.

Estimation model
The basic model used to analyse the potential competitive pressure from
the foreign sector is shown in the following equation:

$$IP_{it} = f(PM_{it}, CR_{it}, TR_{it}, GDP_t, EX_t) \tag{4.4}$$

In the above equation, IP_{it}, PM_{it}, CR_{it} and TR_{it} represent import-penetration
ratio, profit margin, market-concentration ratio and barriers to trade of
industry i in year t, respectively. GDP_t and EX_t represent gross domestic
product and foreign exchange rate in year t. Dynamic panel models based
on Equation (4.4) can be set as follows:

$$IP_{it} = \alpha IP_{it-1} + \beta_1 PM_{it} + \beta_2 PM_{it-1} + \gamma_1 CR_{it} + \gamma_2 CR_{it-1} + \delta TR_{it}$$
$$+ \eta_1 GDP_t + \eta_2 GDP_{t-1} + \eta_4 EX_{t-1} + \upsilon_i + \epsilon_{it} \tag{4.5}$$

In Equation (4.5), *GDP* and *EX* are the natural logarithm value of GDP
and the exchange rate. υ_i represents a fixed effect of industry i. ϵ_{it} is an error
term and assumed to be independent of the other variables and have the
same probability distribution. When estimating Equation (4.5), besides

the presence of fixed effects we also have an endogeneity problem due to the variable of profit margin. This is because, rather than exogenously given, the variable of profit margin is likely to be affected by unobserved variables that affect the dependent variable.

Once in order to remove the fixed effects, the following equation can be obtained by taking the difference for each variable in Equation (4.5):

$$\Delta IP_{it} = \alpha IP_{it-1} + \beta_1 \Delta PM_{it} + \beta_2 \Delta PM_{it-1} + \gamma_1 \Delta CR_{it} + \gamma_2 \Delta CR_{it-1} + \delta \Delta TR_{it}$$

$$+ \eta_1 \Delta GDP_t + \eta_2 \Delta GDP_{t-1} + \eta_3 \Delta EX_t + \eta_4 \Delta EX_{t-1} + \mu_{it} \qquad (4.6)$$

In the above equation, $\mu_{it} = \epsilon_{it} - \epsilon_{it-1}$. By taking the difference, as well as eliminating the fixed effects from the estimating equation, we can also address time-series instability embedded in variables *GDP* and *EX*. However, the endogeneity problem of the explanatory variable still exists even if we take the difference. Furthermore, as we take the difference the dependent variable ΔIP_{it} and the error term $\mu_{it} (= \epsilon_{it} - \epsilon_{it-1})$ become correlated with each other.

These problems occurring in estimating Equation (4.5) can be solved by use of the generalized method of moments (GMM) for the dynamic panel model proposed in Arellano and Bond (1991). The econometric issues embedded in Equation (4.5) can then be resolved by using as instrumental variables the lag of the dependent variable and the explanatory variables that are generated by the GMM orthogonality condition shown in Equation (4.7):[5]

$$E(IP_{is} \mu_{it}) = 0, E(PM_{is} \mu_{it}) = 0 \text{ for all } s \leq t - 2 \qquad (4.7)$$

Data

Our data consist of 54 KSIC three-digit industries belonging to mining and manufacturing and its analysis period is 11 years from 1999 to 2009. During the analysis period, the 54 industries included in the analysis represent 92.1 percent and 72.0 percent, respectively, of total shipments and imports in the mining and manufacturing industries. Therefore, the representativeness of the sample may be sufficient.

Industry-specific import-penetration ratio (*IP*) was calculated according to the formula of [imports / (shipments + imports)] using imports data from trade statistics and shipments data from mining and manufacturing statistics. The formula of [imports / (shipments + imports)] rather than [imports / (shipments − exports + imports)] was used since the former is more appropriate for the objective of the analyses in this subsection given that potential competitive pressure from the foreign sector is defined as the possibility of trade diversion in response to changes in domestic prices.

Industry-specific profit margin (PM) was calculated according to the formula of [total revenue / (total revenue − total variable costs)]. For the total revenue, we used annual shipments data from the mining and manufacturing statistics. We calculated the total variable costs by summing salaries, employee benefits and major production costs such as raw materials, fuel and power costs. For market-concentration ratio we used CR_3, the sum of top three companies' market shares. Lastly, for the trade-barriers variable, we employed the tariff rate. The industry-specific tariff rate was calculated by dividing tariff customs by imports.

Table 4.10, Table 4.11 and Table 4.12, respectively, summarize the basic statistics of industry-specific and time-varying import-penetration ratios,

Table 4.10   Import-penetration ratio in Korea

	Annual level		Yearly change	
	Mean	Standard deviation	Mean	Standard deviation
Mean	0.213	0.040	0.004	0.033
Standard deviation	0.200	0.032	0.011	0.019
Minimum	0.008	0.002	−0.023	0.003
Maximum	0.922	0.130	0.036	0.090

Table 4.11   Profit margins in Korea

	Annual level		Yearly change	
	Mean	Standard deviation	Mean	Standard deviation
Mean	0.276	0.048	−0.005	0.053
Standard deviation	0.090	0.062	0.007	0.102
Minimum	0.109	0.015	−0.022	0.012
Maximum	0.606	0.457	0.012	0.738

profit margins and market-concentration ratios. In the previous section, Table 4.2 also provided the basic statistics of the import-penetration ratios, but there the import-penetration ratios were calculated by [imports / (shipments − exports + imports)]. When compared with Table 4.2, Table 4.10 shows that, while the gap between industry in respect to the time-series average of industry-specific import-penetration ratios is observed to

Table 4.12　Market-concentration ratio in Korea

	Annual level		Yearly change	
	Mean	Standard deviation	Mean	Standard deviation
Mean	43.29	5.55	−0.21	3.97
Standard deviation	21.09	3.82	1.26	2.14
Minimum	13.32	1.36	−3.03	1.45
Maximum	95.75	18.03	2.86	12.23

be similar, the time-series volatility of industry-specific import-penetration ratios and the cross-industry gap of such volatility become significantly narrowed by changing the method for calculating the import-penetration ratio. If we compare Table 4.11 with Table 4.10, we see that the cross-industry gap of the time-series average of industry-specific profit margins is much smaller than that of import-penetration ratios. The basic statistics of market-concentration ratio are very similar to Table 4.6 in the previous section, except that there are some changes due to an increase in the number of industries included in the sample.

Estimation results

Table 4.13 summarizes the estimation results obtained by applying the GMM estimation method for a dynamic panel model proposed in Arellano and Bond (1991) to Equation (4.5) with all the 54 industries in the sample. In this subsection we set up a variety of models for estimating Equation (4.5) in order to determine whether the estimation results are robust. Model 1 includes all explanatory variables included in Equation (4.5). Model 2, Model 3 and Model 4 include year dummy variables in the estimation equation instead of variables that are common to all industries, GDP and exchange rates. In order to analyse the pattern of change of the import penetration according to the changes in market structure explicitly, whereas Model 2 does not include any market-concentration variables in the explanatory variables, Model 3 includes the market-concentration ratio in the same year as the dependent variable and Model 4 includes the same year's and the previous year's market-concentration ratios as explanatory variables.

In Table 4.13 AB statistic (Arellano–Bond test for AR (2) in first-difference) tests whether there exists autocorrelation in the error term in Equation (4.6) and indicates that the null hypothesis, that the autocorrelation does not exist, cannot be rejected for all four models. The Hansen statistic is used for testing whether over-identification conditions of instrumental variables provided by GMM are statistically valid. Here the

Table 4.13　Estimation results on potential competitive pressure for 54 Korean industries

	Dependent variable IP_t			
	Model 1	Model 2	Model 3	Model 4
IP_{t-1}	0.6384***	0.6981***	0.6926***	0.6843***
A	(0.0934)	(0.0821)	(0.0845)	(0.0837)
PM_t	0.0115	0.0349	0.0278	0.0305
A	(0.0690)	(0.0833)	(0.0821)	(0.0803)
PM_{t-1}	0.0881**	0.0650***	0.0577**	0.0497**
A	(0.0423)	(0.0231)	(0.0238)	(0.0222)
CR_t	0.0004	—	0.0006	−0.0003
A	(0.0012)	—	(0.0008)	(0.0016)
CR_{t-1}	−0.0014	—	—	0.0014
A	(0.0013)	—	—	(0.0020)
TR_t	−0.1571	−0.1872	−0.1689	−0.1889
A	(0.1435)	(0.1601)	(0.1644)	(0.1773)
GDP_t	0.1475*	—	—	—
A	(0.0869)	—	—	—
GDP_{t-1}	−0.1449*	—	—	—
A	(0.0774)	—	—	—
EX_t	0.0876***	—	—	—
A	(0.0164)	—	—	—
EX_{t-1}	−0.1756***	—	—	—
A	(0.0192)	—	—	—
Year dummies	×	○	○	○
AB test statistic	−1.12	−1.04	−1.08	−0.87
B	<0.261>	<0.299>	<0.286>	<0.310>
Hansen test statistic	48.70	45.48	45.62	43.84
C	[$\chi^2(45)$]	[$\chi^2(42)$]	[$\chi^2(41)$]	[$\chi^2(40)$]
	0.326	0.329	0.286	0.312
Group	54	54	54	54
IV	55	55	55	55
Number of observations	480	480	480	480

Notes:　A = heteroscedasticity and autocorrelation adjusted standard errors.
B = p-value of the test statistic.
C = the probability distribution of the test statistic.
***, ** and * indicate that the estimated coefficient is statistically different from 0 with the significance level of 1%, 5% and 10%, respectively.

null hypothesis is that over-identification conditions are valid. p-values presented in the table mean that we cannot reject the null hypothesis. Group and IV refer to the number of industries and instrumental variables used in estimation. Because the number of instrumental variables is similar to the number of industries, there will be no problem in removing the endogeneity property from explanatory variables vulnerable to endogeneity problems.[6]

Now the estimation results of Equation (4.5) are described as follows. First of all, the previous year's import penetration (IP_{t-1}) coefficient estimate has a positive value and is statistically very significant in all models. This result is interpreted as the presence of a very strong autoregressive nature in the import penetration. The coefficient of the previous year's profit margin (PM_{t-1}) was estimated to have a statistically significant positive value, while the coefficient estimate of the same year's profit margin (PM_t) is not statistically significant. This exactly matches the result (R1) in Choi and Jo (2006) and tells us that, when potential competition from the foreign sector is defined as the reaction of import penetration to changes in the profit margin of domestic companies, such potential competition from the foreign sector has existed in the 2000s and occurred with a lag of one year. However, with regard to the market-concentration variables, the coefficient estimates are not statistically significant in any model. This contradicts the finding (R2) in Choi and Jo (2006). For the time period from 1996 to 2002, they found a tendency that the import-penetration ratio tends to decrease as the domestic market structure is concentrated.

In the previous section, it was reported that the average import penetration between industries with high market concentration and those with low market concentration is statistically different. As a result, we repeated the same estimation process as before, after dividing the sample into two groups depending on the market-concentration ratio, high-concentrated industries and low-concentrated industries, to examine the possibility that the relationship among the import-penetration ratio, profit margin, market-concentration ratio and barriers to trade expressed in Equation (4.5) may be structurally different between the two groups of industries. Table 4.14 summarizes the estimation results for industries for which the time-series averages of market-concentration ratios are less than 50 percent. Table 4.15 reports the estimation results for industries of which the average values exceed 50 percent.[7]

At first, the strong autoregressive nature of the import penetration is retained in the divided samples. The statistical significance of the estimated coefficient of the previous year's profit margin (PM_{t-1}) is maintained only in the high-concentrated industries. Therefore, we may conjecture that the statistical significance of the estimated coefficient of the previous year's

Table 4.14 *Estimation results on potential competitive pressure in Korea:*
            CR₃ ≤ 50 percentile

	Dependent variable IP_t			
	Model 1	Model 2	Model 3	Model 4
IP_{t-1}	0.5858***	0.6529***	0.5597***	0.5496***
A	(0.0996)	(0.0962)	(0.1375)	(0.1263)
PM_t	−0.0551	−0.0532	0.0375	0.0376
A	(0.1180)	(0.1142)	(0.1490)	(0.1557)
PM_{t-1}	−0.1044	0.0080	−0.0354	−0.0272
A	(0.1310)	(0.1241)	(0.1183)	(0.1189)
CR_t	0.0027	—	0.0039***	0.0036*
A	(0.0016)	—	(0.0014)	(0.0020)
CR_{t-1}	−0.0019	—	—	0.0006
A	(0.0017)	—	—	(0.0027)
TR_t	−0.9484	−1.1557*	−0.9398	−0.9183
A	(0.6567)	(0.5733)	(0.6184)	(0.6098)
GDP_t	0.1278	—	—	—
A	(0.1696)	—	—	—
GDP_{t-1}	−0.1718	—	—	—
A	(0.1501)	—	—	—
EX_t	0.0571	—	—	—
A	(0.0345)	—	—	—
EX_{t-1}	−0.1450**	—	—	—
A	(0.0535)	—	—	—
Year dummies	○	×	×	×
AB test statistic	−1.20	−1.00	−1.39	−1.37
B	<0.229>	<0.315>	<0.165>	<0.172>
Hansen test statistic	22.42	22.23	18.97	20.20
C	$[\chi^2(45)]$	$[\chi^2(42)]$	$[\chi^2(41)]$	$[\chi^2(40)]$
	0.998	0.995	0.999	0.996
Group	27	27	27	27
IV	55	55	55	55
Number of observations	240	240	240	240

Notes: A = heteroscedasticity and autocorrelation adjusted standard errors.
B = p-value of the test statistic.
C = the probability distribution of the test statistic.
***, ** and * indicate that the estimated coefficient is statistically different from 0 with the significance level of 1%, 5% and 10%, respectively.

Table 4.15   *Estimation results on potential competitive pressure in Korea:*
             $CR_3 > 50$ *percentile*

	Dependent variable IP_t			
	Model 1	Model 2	Model 3	Model 4
IP_{t-1}	0.6050***	0.6327***	0.6338***	0.6500***
A	(0.1156)	(0.1145)	(0.1169)	(0.1143)
PM_t	−0.0154	−0.0101	−0.0128	−0.0006
A	(0.0430)	(0.0495)	(0.0520)	(0.0528)
PM_{t-1}	0.0774**	0.0673**	0.0641**	0.0569**
A	(0.0381)	(0.0254)	(0.0295)	(0.0208)
CR_t	−0.0005	—	0.0003	−0.0018
A	(0.0013)	—	(0.0008)	(0.0015)
CR_{t-1}	0.0003	—	—	0.0023*
A	(0.0011)	—	—	(0.0013)
TR_t	−0.0093	−0.0206	−0.0163	−0.0748
A	(0.0790)	(0.0756)	(0.0771)	(0.0824)
GDP_t	0.1531	—	—	—
A	(0.0931)	—	—	—
GDP_{t-1}	−0.1309	—	—	—
A	(0.0881)	—	—	—
EX_t	0.0816***	—	—	—
A	(0.0187)	—	—	—
EX_{t-1}	−0.1504***	—	—	—
A	(0.0277)	—	—	—
Year dummies	○	×	×	×
AB test statistic	−1.16	−1.09	−1.07	−0.79
B	<0.248>	<0.274>	<0.283>	<0.431>
Hansen test statistic	23.44	19.59	19.66	20.22
C	$[\chi^2(45)]$	$[\chi^2(42)]$	$[\chi^2(41)]$	$[\chi^2(40)]$
	0.997	0.999	0.998	0.996
Group	27	27	27	27
IV	55	55	55	55
Number of observations	240	240	240	240

Notes: A = heteroscedasticity and autocorrelation adjusted standard errors.
B = p-value of the test statistic.
C = the probability distribution of the test statistic.
***, ** and * indicate that the estimated coefficient is statistically different from 0 with the significance level of 1%, 5% and 10%, respectively.

profit margin (PM_{t-1}) obtained in Table 4.13 was mainly derived from the high-concentrated industries. On the one hand, the analysis result that the potential competitive pressure from the foreign sector is mainly stemming from the high-concentrated industries is consistent with Choi and Jo (2006). On the other hand, unlike when analysing the 54 industries, the estimated coefficients of market-concentration ratio become statistically significant in some models as we separate the samples. At first, when analysing the low-concentrated industries, in Model 3 the estimated coefficient of the same year's market-concentration ratio (CR_t) is positive and highly statistically significant. However, if the previous year's market-concentration ratio (CR_{t-1}) is added as explanatory variable in Model 4, the statistical significance of the estimated coefficient is significantly decreased. In the case of high-concentrated industries, the coefficient of the previous year's market-concentration ratio (CR_{t-1}) was estimated to be positive and statistically significant in Model 4.[8] These empirical results are consistent with theoretical reasoning that higher market concentration is likely to cause higher than normal profit margin and therefore causes greater competitive pressures from the foreign sector represented by the import penetration.

Actual Competitive Pressure of the Foreign Sector

In this subsection, in order to answer the second question (Q2) posed earlier, we investigate whether the increased import penetration corresponding to an increase in the profitability of the domestic industry tends to reduce the profitability of the domestic industry, that is, if there exists import discipline effect in Korea and whether such discipline effect is differential according to the degree of the market concentration of the domestic industry.

Estimation model
To answer the second question (Q2), the following panel model can be considered:

$$PM_{it} = {}_\alpha + \beta IP_{it} + \gamma CR_{it} + \Sigma \delta_j Dyear_j + \omega_i + e_{it} \qquad (4.8)$$

In the above equation, PM_{it}, IP_{it} and CR_{it} represent profit margin, import-penetration ratio and market-concentration ratio of industry i in year t, respectively. $Dyear_j$ is a year dummy and ω_i represents a fixed effect of industry i. e_{it} is an error term and assumed to satisfy $i.i.d.$ conditions. It is unlikely that the autoregressive nature exists in the profit margin. The conjecture that the profit margin will be affected by the previous year's import penetration and market concentration also lacks theoretical basis. Accordingly, unlike Equation (4.5), the lags of the dependent and explanatory variables are not included as explanatory variables in Equation (4.8).

In estimating Equation (4.8), we can assume various possibilities for the endogeneity problem of the explanatory variables. At first, there is a probability that unobserved variables that affect the profit margin may also affect market concentration. In this case, the market concentration variable (*CR*) in Equation (4.8) is vulnerable to the endogeneity problem. We can assume the same possibility for the import penetration. Reflecting the previous result that the import penetration reacts with a lag of one year to changes in the profit margin, however, it is also possible to assume that the import penetration variable (*IP*) is not vulnerable to the endogeneity problem. Accordingly, in this subsection, we carried out a separate estimation task for each possible case considering that a variety of assumptions about the endogeneity problem of the explanatory variables can be realistic. If the market-concentration variable or the import-penetration variable is assumed to be vulnerable to the endogeneity problem, Equation (4.8) will be estimated using the estimation method proposed in Arellano and Bond (1991). For the contrary, if we assume that any explanatory variables are not susceptible to the endogeneity problem, Equation (4.8) is estimated using a conventional fixed-effect model.

Estimation results

Table 4.16 summarizes the results of estimating Equation (4.8) under the assumption that the market-concentration variable and the import-penetration variable are vulnerable to the endogeneity problem. Table 4.17 shows the estimation results when only the market-concentration variable is assumed to be vulnerable to the endogeneity problem. The values of the AB statistics and Hansen statistics indicate that the null hypotheses, that there is no autocorrelation in the error terms and over-identification conditions, are valid cannot be rejected. Note that the number of instrumental variables is consciously limited not to exceed the number of groups in the estimation process in order to control properly the endogeneity problem of the explanatory variables.

Table 4.16 shows that the degree of import penetration did not affect the profitability of domestic industry significantly over the analysis period. This result remains the same regardless of the configuration of the sample. This is in stark contrast to the majority of previous research, which has shown that imports have a discipline effect on the price-cost margin. The coefficient of market-concentration variable was analysed to have a significantly positive sign if 54 industries as a whole were included in the analysis. However, if the sample was divided into high-concentrated industries and

Table 4.16 *Estimation results on actual competitive pressure in Korea: endogenous variables CR, IP*

	Dependent variable PM_t		
	Total sample	$CR_3 \leq 50$ percentile	$CR_3 > 50$ percentile
IP_t	−0.2782	0.1968	−1.9069
A	(0.8545)	(0.2210)	(2.4196)
CR_t	0.0036*	0.0015	−0.0082
A	(0.0020)	(0.0032)	(0.0137)
AB test statistic	−1.00	1.13	−1.23
B	<0.318>	<0.256>	<0.219>
Hansen text statistic	39.82	19.19	18.10
C	[$\chi^2(36)$]	[$\chi^2(14)$]	[$\chi^2(14)$]
	0.304	0.158	0.202
Group	54	27	27
IV	48	26	26
Number of observations	535	267	268

Notes: A = heteroscedasticity and autocorrelation adjusted standard errors.
B = p-value of the test statistic.
C = the probability distribution of the test statistic.
* indicates that the estimated coefficient is statistically different from 0 with the significance level of 10%. Estimation results for the year dummies are not shown for brevity.

low-concentrated industries, such statistical significance disappeared. As represented by Table 4.17, those estimation results remained the same, except for the fact that the statistical significance of the market concentration variable was somewhat improved, even when we assumed that the market concentration is the only variable vulnerable to the endogeneity problem.

Table 4.18 summarizes the results of estimating Equation (4.8) through a fixed-effect model under the assumption that any explanatory variables are not susceptible to the endogeneity problem. These estimation results can be interpreted in the same manner as those in Table 4.16 or Table 4.17. That is, the import penetration does not have any statistically significant effects on the profitability of domestic firms industry, whereas the market concentration has a positive and statistically significant effect on the profitability of the industry. Different from the previous estimations, however, the statistical significance of the market-concentration coefficient was maintained in some models even after the sample was divided into two groups.

Table 4.17   *Estimation results on actual competitive pressure in Korea: endogenous variables CR*

	Dependent variable PM_t		
	Total sample	$CR_3 \leq 50$ percentile	$CR_3 > 50$ percentile
IP_t	0.1856	−0.3891	−0.0298
A	(0.3908)	(0.3007)	(1.0725)
CR_t	0.0041**	0.0008	0.0028
A	(0.0020)	(0.0038)	(0.0022)
AB test statistic	−0.94	1.12	−1.09
B	<0.345>	<0.263>	<0.276>
Hansen text statistic	27.69	11.78	8.95
C	[$\chi^2(27)$]	[$\chi^2(11)$]	[$\chi^2(11)$]
	0.427	0.380	0.626
Group	54	27	27
IV	39	23	23
Number of observations	535	267	268

Notes: A = heteroscedasticity and autocorrelation adjusted standard errors.
B = p-value of the test statistic.
C = the probability distribution of the test statistic.
**   indicates that the estimated coefficient is statistically different from 0 with the significance level of 5%. Estimation results for the year dummies are not shown for brevity.

The empirical results in this subsection indicate that increased import penetration did not tend to significantly reduce the profitability of the domestic industry over the time period from 1999 to 2009 in Korea. As mentioned earlier, these results are in stark contrast to previous studies showing the existence of an import-discipline effect.

However, in order to derive a conclusion from these conflicting results that actual competitive pressure from the foreign sector did not exist in the case of Korea, the following two prerequisites must be met. First, the estimation model and the estimation process must not have any errors. Second, our assumption that domestic firms correspond to increased imports with price cuts must be realistic.

In conjunction with the first prerequisite, the empirical analysis carried out in this subsection may be vulnerable to small-sample bias occurring from a rather small number of observations. Also, the estimation model may be constrained. For example, in Equation (4.8), any industry-specific characteristics except the market concentration and import penetration

Table 4.18   *Estimation results on actual competitive pressure in Korea: no endogenous variable*

	Dependent variable PM_t		
	Total sample	$CR_3 \leq 50$ percentile	$CR_3 > 50$ percentile
IP_t	−0.1138	−0.0372	−0.2132
A	(0.1156)	(0.0634)	(0.2362)
CR_t	0.0012*	0.0016*	0.0011
A	(0.0007)	(0.0008)	(0.0010)
R^2			
Within	0.0779	0.2063	0.0781
Between	0.0610	0.1087	0.2612
Overall	0.0673	0.0071	0.1798
Number of observations	590	294	296

Notes: A = heteroscedasticity and autocorrelation adjusted standard errors.
*   indicates that the estimated coefficient is statistically different from 0 with the significance level of 10%. Estimation results for the year dummies are not shown for brevity.

were assumed to be captured by ω_i and fixed throughout the analysis period. This assumption, however, can be criticized as unrealistic. There are technical factors that affect the profitability of an industry such as the minimum efficient scale of production, the rate of depreciation of capital and capital intensity. Even though these factors do not fluctuate greatly over time, it is difficult to assume that these are fixed for long periods of time. In this case, the estimation of Equation (4.8) may be vulnerable to problems from omitted variables. Being related to the second prerequisite, depending on how domestic firms respond to the changes in the import penetration, the profitability of the domestic industry may not be lowered even if significant competitive pressures from the foreign sector do exist. Thus, the assumptions about the response of domestic firms to increased imports must be realistic in order to draw conclusions about the existence of actual competitive pressures from the foreign sector from the empirical analysis carried out in this subsection.

SUMMARY AND CONCLUSION

In this chapter, in order to identify the importance of the foreign sector in investigating the degree of competition in the domestic market, we analysed the import-penetration ratio and domestic market-concentration ratio and carried out empirical analyses on the relationship between the profitability of the domestic industry and the degree of import penetration.

The main results and their implications can be summarized as follows:

First, related to the import penetration, in Korea there has been a very big cross-industry difference in the level and variability of import penetration over the analysis period. There are also a number of industries of which the level of import penetration is very high or showing very severe volatility. When we changed the market-concentration calculation method from CR_3 to $DMCR_3$, we found a number of industries where the decrease in the value of index is very large or the annual volatility of index changes significantly. These results mean that an attempt to infer the degree of competition in the domestic market through CR_3 may result in a distortion, depending on industry.

Second, the results of empirical analyses on the reaction of import penetration to changes in the profit margin of domestic firms indicate potential competition from the foreign sector has existed in Korea in the 2000s and occurred with a lag of one year. However, a tendency that increased import penetration reduces the profitability of the domestic industry was not found in the empirical analyses. Under specific preconditions, this result suggests that actual competitive pressure from the foreign sector did not exist during the analysis period in Korea. Combining these findings on the potential and actual competitive pressures, it is possible to make an interpretation that imports increase in response to an increase in the profitability of the domestic industry, but importers who increase imports may try to enjoy a higher profit rate stringing along with domestic firms rather than fiercely competing with the domestic firms. This interpretation provides a policy implication that promoting competition in the imports sector is required to remove entry barriers for import or to change the competitive behavior of existing importers.

If imports are mainly carried by domestic producers rather than independent importers, this can also be a reason for increased imports not to exercise competitive pressure to domestic producers. In countries with extremely high trade dependence, like Korea, the question "Who imports?" can have even greater implications in terms of competition policy.

This chapter has obvious limitations in that it is not a study of specific industries but a cross-industry analysis based on fairly broadly defined industries. Above all, industry specificity, such as international production networks that may affect the relationships between the degree of import penetration and the profitability of the domestic industry, was not fully considered in the analysis process. In this case, the statistically insignificant coefficient estimates of IP_t in tables 4.16, 4.17 and 4.18 may suggest that, rather than indicating that the import-penetration ratio does not affect the profitability of domestic industry, the industry-specific data used in this chapter are not very informative because of the existence of very large heterogeneity among industries. Considering this limitation of analysis, this chapter can be regarded as providing context and guidance for further industry-specific studies rather than presenting decisive conclusions.

NOTES

1. According to the 2010 European Commission "Guidelines on Vertical Restraints," two companies are treated as actual competitors if they are active in the same relevant market. Alternatively, a company is defined as a potential competitor of another company if, absent an agreement, in cases of a small but permanent increase in relative prices it is likely that this first company, within a short period of time normally not longer than a year, would undertake the necessary additional investments or other necessary switching costs to enter the relevant market in which the other company is active.
2. There are also empirical studies investigating the effect of potential competition limiting the scope of competition to the domestic market, such as Cool et al. (1999), Bergman and Rudholm (2003), Hall et al. (2003) and Savage and Wirth (2005).
3. Even though there is an error associated with the connection of the mining and manufacturing statistics and the trade statistics, if such a linkage structure is consistently maintained through the analysis period, the presence of an error may not be a big problem in analysing changes in import penetration in accordance with changes in the profit margin of the domestic industry. As a result, in "Empirical Analyses" we will include those six industries excluded in this section in the analysis. Depending on the inclusion of the six industries, the results of the analysis do not change significantly.
4. Here, import penetration was calculated according to the formula of [imports / (shipments − exports + imports)]. The import penetration rate can also be calculated as [imports / (shipments + imports)]. We used the former formula in this section because excluding exports in the denominator would be conceptually more appropriate as an indirect indicator of actual competitive pressures from the foreign sector.
5. Choi and Jo (2006) pointed out that market-concentration ratio variables can also be vulnerable to the endogeneity problem. As a result, they used the lag variables of market-concentration ratio as instrumental variables by adding another orthogonality condition $E(CR_{is} \mu_{it} = 0)$ to Equation (4.7). However, unlike the profit margin, it may be unrealistic to assume that the market-concentration ratio that is calculated based on the shipment of domestic firms is directly affected by unobserved variables affecting the import penetration. Also, using too many instrumental variables can fail to remove the endogeneity problem by over-fitting in the estimation process. In particular, the empirical estimation methods proposed in Arellano and Bond (1991), which are used in this section, are known to be vulnerable to these risks (Roodman 2006). Reflecting these realistic and econometric considerations, only the profit-margin variables are assumed to be vulnerable to the endogeneity problem in the empirical analyses of this section.
6. As mentioned earlier, the estimation method proposed in Arellano and Bond (1991) is known to be particularly vulnerable to the risk of failure to remove the endogeneity property of explanatory variables if too many instrumental variables are used in the estimation process. If a Hansen statistic of 1 is reported after the estimation, it indicates that such estimates have been exposed very highly to such a risk (Roodman 2006). The usual way to prevent this risk is to consciously control the number of instrumental variables so as not to exceed the number of groups in the estimation process.
7. The estimation method proposed in Arellano and Bond (1991) uses the lag variables of dependent variables and explanatory variables as instrumental variables. So, in order for

the endogeneity problem to be properly controlled in the estimation process, the number of groups should be large enough when compared to the number of instrumental variables. If we divide the sample into two groups, the number of groups becomes too small compared to the number of instrumental variables, as shown in Table 4.14 and Table 4.15, and the endogeneity property of explanatory variables might not be properly removed from the estimation process.

8. The reason for the differences between industries in respect to the time lag of market concentration affecting import penetration could also be explained theoretically. For example, if there exist structural factors that lead to highly concentrated markets and if those factors act as barriers for import penetration, it might be possible that in the low-concentrated industries the import penetration is affected by the same year's market-concentration ratio whereas in the high-concentrated industries it is affected by the previous year's market-concentration ratio.

REFERENCES

Arellano, M. and S. Bond (1991), "Some tests of specification for panel data: Monte Carlo evidence and an application to employment equations," *Review of Economic Studies*, **58**(2), 277–97.

Bain, J.S. (1951), "Relation of profit rate to industry concentration: American manufacturing, 1936–1940," *Quarterly Journal of Economics*, **65**(3), 293–324.

Bergman, M.A. and N. Rudholm (2003), "The relative importance of actual and potential competition: empirical evidence from pharmaceuticals market," *Journal of Industrial Economics*, **51**(4), 455–67.

Choi, Y. and S. Jo (2006), *An Empirical Analysis on Potential Competition and Market Structure with Overseas Sectors*, Seoul, Korea: Korea Development Institute.

Cool, K., L. Röller and B. Leleux (1999), "The relative impact of actual and potential rivalry on firm profitability in the pharmaceutical industry," *Strategic Management Journal*, **20**(1), 1–14.

Esposito, L. and F.F. Esposito (1971), "Foreign competition and domestic industry profitability," *The Review of Economics and Statistics*, **53**(4), 343–53.

European Commission (2010), "Guidelines on Vertical Restraints," at https://ec.eur opa.eu/competition/antitrust/legislation/guidelines_vertical_en.pdf (accessed on 29 November 2019).

Ghosal, V. (2002), "Potential foreign competition in US manufacturing," *International Journal of Industrial Organization*, **20**(10), 1461–89.

Hall, R.E., J. Moyer and M. van Audenrode (2003), "Potential competition and the prices of network goods: desktop software," working paper.

Jones, J.C.H., L. Laudadio and M. Percy (1973), "Market structure and profitability in Canadian manufacturing industry: some cross-section results," *Canadian Journal of Economics*, **6**(3), 356–68.

Katics, M.M. and B.C. Petersen (1994), "The effect of rising import competition on market power: a panel data study of US manufacturing," *Journal of Industrial Economics*, **62**(3), 277–86.

Khondker, B.H. (1996), "Foreign competition, industrial concentration and profitability in manufacturing sectors in Bangladesh," *The Bangladesh Development Studies*, **24**(1/2), 165–88.

Landes, W.M. and R.A. Posner (1980/81), "Market power in antitrust cases," *Harvard Law Review*, **94**, 937–96.

Lee, J. (2002), *Market Concentration Analysis in Korea: For the Mining and Manufacturing Industries*, Seoul, Korea: Korea Development Institute.

Lee, J. (2007), *An Analysis on Competitive Structure and Market Concentration in Korean Industries: For the Mining, Manufacturing and Service Industries*, Seoul, Korea: Korea Development Institute.

Lee, J., J. Yang and S. Lee (2011), *Market Structure Research*, Seoul, Korea: Korea Development Institute.

Levinsohn, J. (1993), "Testing the import-as-market-discipline hypothesis," *Journal of International Economics*, **35**, 1–22.

Pagoulatos, E. and R. Sorensen (1976), "Foreign trade, concentration and profitability in open economies," *European Economic Review*, **8**, 255–67.

Pugel, T.A. (1980), "Foreign trade and US market performance," *Journal of Industrial Economics*, **29**(2), 119–29.

Roodman, D. (2006), "How to do xtabond2: an introduction to 'difference' and 'system' GMM in Stata," Center for Global Development Working Paper No. 13.

Sabido, A.C. and D. Mulato (2006), "Market structure: concentration and imports as determinants of industry margins," *Estudios Economicos*, **21**(2), 177–202.

Savage, S.J. and M. Wirth (2005), "Price, programming and potential competition in US cable TV markets," *Journal of Regulatory Economics*, **27**(1), 25–46.

Schwartzman, D. (1959), "The effect of monopoly on price," *Journal of Political Economy*, **67**(3), 352–62.

Turner, P.P. (1980), "Import competition and the profitability of United Kingdom manufacturing industry," *The Journal of Industrial Economics*, **29**(2), 155–66.

PART III

Abuse of dominance

5. Structured rule of reason analysis of tying arrangements

Yong Hyeon Yang

INTRODUCTION

The regulation of monopolies is a central issue for competition authorities. Many abusive behaviors of a monopolist have been *per se* illegal, but the paradigm is changing: especially on exclusionary behaviors, it is claimed that their effects on efficiency must be considered. Such a view is now broadly accepted in many countries including the Republic of Korea. Accordingly, it becomes necessary to prove the anticompetitive effects of monopolistic behaviors in the Republic of Korea and, in 2007, that burden of proof was placed on the Fair Trade Commission by the Korean Supreme Court. Since then, the number of abusive behaviors condemned has decreased (see Table 5.1). One reason is that there is no clear rule on which the assessment of abusive behaviors is to be based.

This chapter suggests a rule that both the Fair Trade Commission and defendant firms might rely on in investigations. I focus on "tying arrangements," in particular, because tying may have exploitative or exclusionary effects or both. It is also claimed that tying may enhance efficiency. Hence a rule on the assessment of tying arrangements can be useful for assessment of other abusive behaviors of monopolists as well. The establishment of such a rule would then serve to guide firms to take into account the potential anticompetitive effects of abusive behaviors when choosing their strategies.

A "structured rule of reason" approach is necessary for all the possible effects, positive or negative, to be considered. One may think at first that the Fair Trade Commission often has difficulties in obtaining relevant data, so that it would be efficient in terms of the social cost to let the defendant firm prove the effects. It is ineffective or unfair, however, to have the firm prove anticompetitive effects of its abusive behavior, since, if the behavior is presumed legal without proof, the firm does not have an incentive to prove its anticompetitive effects and, if presumed unlawful, it would be very hard to prove a passive claim that the behavior is not harmful.

Table 5.1   Number of abusive cases, 1983–2012

Year	Begin investigation	Corrective measures	Surcharge	File to prosecutor
1983–89	5	5	0	0
1990	1	1	0	0
1991	3	0	0	0
1992	0	3	0	0
1993	2	2	0	0
1994	1	1	0	0
1995	3	3	0	0
1996	2	1	1	0
1997	1	2	0	0
1998	3	3	3	3
1999	1	1	1	0
2000	1	0	0	0
2001	2	3	2	0
2002	1	0	0	0
2003	1	1	0	0
2004	0	0	0	0
2005	1	0	0	0
2006	23	2	1	0
2007	15	34	22	0
2008	1	4	2	0
2009	6	2	2	0
2010	0	5	4	2
2011	1	0	0	0
2012	0	1	1	0
Total	74	74	39	5

Therefore, it would be better to have the Fair Trade Commission prove the anticompetitive effects, if any, of the behavior using available data and then to give the defendant firm a chance to make a counterargument.

The rest of the chapter is organized as follows. "Issues on Monopoly Regulation" points out two issues, among others, related to a rule on regulation of abusive behaviors in the Republic of Korea: one is how far to depart from the *per se* rule and the other is which article to apply on abusive behaviors. Solutions to these issues are identified in "Proposed Remedies." The solutions are applied to investigation of tying arrangements in "Investigation Procedures: Tying Cases," which suggests a set of procedures in detail to investigate tying. "Concluding Remarks" ends this chapter.

ISSUES ON MONOPOLY REGULATION

Rule of Reason or *per se* Rule

Many potentially anticompetitive behaviors are not *per se* illegal any more. The United States (US) is leading such a regulatory trend. According to the US Department of Justice (2008), in 1977 the Supreme Court overturned the *per se* rule for non-price vertical restraints. In 1997 the Court overturned a *per se* rule for maximum resale price maintenance. And in 2007 the Court overturned the *per se* rule against minimum resale price maintenance. The European Commission (2009) declared that, in the enforcement of Article 102 of the Treaty on the Functioning of the European Union (TFEU) (which is the same as Article 82 of the Treaty Establishing the European Community), it will examine claims put forward by a dominant undertaking that its conduct is justified.

The Republic of Korea is also following this trend. The Monopoly Regulation and Fair Trade Act (Fair Trade Act or MRFTA hereafter) regards potentially abusive behaviors as unlawful only when they are unreasonable or unfair. The Korean Supreme Court also ruled in 2007 that the behaviors are deemed unlawful abuse of dominance when they reduce competition but not simply when they are done by dominant firms.

In departing from a *per se* rule, it remains unclear which approach should be taken for specific behaviors. Even in the US and the European Union (EU), no agreement has been made on the standard approach for tying, for example. On the one hand, Ahlborn et al. (2004) assert that a (modified) *per se* legal approach must be taken for tying. On the other hand, Kühn et al. (2005) argue that a laissez-faire approach to bundling cannot be justified and propose a set of rules in favor of a structured rule of reason approach. A quick-look approach blending *per se* and rule of reason analyses has also been taken in some cases. It is necessary to set up a standard approach for assessing potentially abusive behaviors to allow firms to better understand the rules and to form expectations on the consequences of their behaviors.

Competing Articles for Abusive Behaviors

Some abusive behaviors can be challenged under both Article 3-2 and Article 23 of the Fair Trade Act. For example, tying arrangements may violate Article 3-2 and Article 23 at the same time. It should not be surprising that a behavior may be challenged under two different articles if the articles focus on different anticompetitive effects. In the US, tying arrangements may violate Section 1 of the Sherman Act, Section 2 of the

Sherman Act, Section 3 of the Clayton Act and Section 5 of the Federal Trade Commission Act, for different reasons.[1] In the Republic of Korea, however, the two articles noted above may be applied to the same anticompetitive effects. The difference is that one may be applied to a larger set of firms than the other.

Article 3-2 (in Chapter 2) prohibits abuse of dominance. If firms are in a dominant position, they may not engage in behaviors that exploit consumers or exclude competitors. Exploitative behaviors include exploitative price setting, quantity restraint and other behaviors that extract consumer surplus. Exclusionary behaviors include interrupting a competitor's market activity, deterring entry and other behaviors excluding competitors from markets. Table 5.2 shows how often each type of abusive behavior was regulated. The main purpose of Article 3-2 is to regulate behaviors of dominant firms so that they will not abuse their market power, which is similar to that of Article 102 of the TFEU.

Article 23 (in Chapter 5) prohibits unfair trade practices. Its application is not restricted to firms in a dominant position. Unfair trade practices that

Table 5.2   Number of abusive cases by type of behavior

Type of behavior	1983–2005	2006–12
Exploitative abuse		
Exploitative pricing	5	0
Quantity restraint	3	0
Elimination of the cheapest bundle	0	19[b]
Other exploitative behavior	2	0
Subtotal	10	19
Exclusionary abuse		
Predatory pricing	1	0
Refusal to supply	2	2
Exclusive dealing	8[a]	8
Conditional rebate	0	2[c]
Other exclusionary behavior	4	13[b]
Subtotal	15	25
Both exploitative and exclusionary abuse		
Price discrimination	1[a]	1
Tying	1	4[c]
Total cases	27	49

Notes: [a] Regulated for both exclusive dealing and price discrimination in the broadcasting commercial case.
[b] In total, 19 exploitative and 11 exclusionary cases are in the cable TV industry.
[c] Regulated for both conditional rebate and tying in the Qualcomm case.

are prohibited under this article include refusal to supply, discrimination in supply conditions, exclusion of competitors, coercion of trade, abuse of bargaining power, restriction in trade terms and unfair support of firms or persons in a special relationship.[2] The main purpose of Article 23 is to protect consumers and firms from unfair terms and conditions imposed by some firms in trade with those consumers and firms. Another purpose of the article is to prevent anticompetitive behaviors.[3]

The two articles are competing when a dominant firm makes a deal with consumers or other firms leading to anticompetitive effects by restricting their behaviors. Tying arrangements, for example, may reduce competition when a dominant firm tries to leverage their market power to another market. This violates not only Article 3-2 but also Article 23, as tying reduces competition by imposing unfair trade terms to consumers. The problem is that tying can be challenged by Article 23 whether or not the firm is in a dominant position, which makes Article 3-2 play an insignificant role in accusing dominant firms of their anticompetitive behaviors. Article 23 is used to prove anticompetitiveness and to impose corrective measures, while Article 3-2 penalizes the dominant firm more severely if successfully imposed.

PROPOSED REMEDIES

"Structured Rule of Reason" as a Standard Approach

I suggest that a "structured rule of reason" approach be taken for abuse-of-dominance cases. The Fair Trade Act states that potentially abusive behaviors of dominant firms are deemed unlawful only when they are unreasonable or unfair. This means that the behaviors must be regarded lawful unless they have been proven to be unreasonable or unfair. The Supreme Court ruled that the Fair Trade Commission must prove that competition is reduced by the behaviors. It does not imply that these behaviors can be deemed *per se* legal but that the anticompetitiveness and the procompetitiveness of the behaviors must be compared to reach a conclusion. Beginning with this proposition, a structured rule of reason approach leads to the following investigation procedures.

The behaviors—tying arrangements, for example—are presumed lawful until they are proven to have anticompetitive effects by the Fair Trade Commission. The following four steps may be used to prove anticompetitive effects. First, identify tying and tied products. This involves market definition and, if necessary, a separate product test.[4] Second, show the existence of market power or, more clearly, of market dominance. Third, identify a theory of harm. This requires an evaluation of whether the tying arrangements have exploitative or exclusionary effects or both. Lastly, provide empirical evidence of the harm. For exploitative abuse, it suffices to show that prior consumer surplus has decreased. For exclusionary abuse, it is necessary to show that competitors have exited the market or may exit in the near future or that potential entrants have given up on entering.

Behaviors are presumed unlawful at this stage unless defendant firms successfully disprove the charges. Counterarguments may consist of two distinct assertions. One is to falsify the arguments of the Fair Trade Commission. Firms may refute the logic on market definitions, dominance, theories of harm and others or provide different empirical results. When firms contest the empirical evidence, they must provide more concrete data to estimate a more developed regression model. The other assertion is to claim that the firm's behaviors enhance efficiency, thereby cancelling any harm. To succeed, firms need to estimate, using concrete data and a regression model, the increase in consumer surplus created by the efficiency enhancements. The Fair Trade Commission, or the court, makes a decision on whether the counterarguments can be justified or not and then compares the procompetitive and the anticompetitive effects of the behaviors to reach a conclusion.

Classifying Behaviors and Differentiating Articles

I suggest one of the following two rules be adopted. One is to apply Article 3-2 to anticompetitive behaviors that can be successfully implemented only by dominant firms and to apply Article 23 to other anticompetitive behaviors. Tying arrangements are a typical example of behaviors that may not reduce competition if the firm has little market power. Hence tying must be challenged under Article 3-2, not under Article 23. The other suggested rule offers a small variation. For this, Article 3-2 must be applied to those behaviors in principle, but Article 23 is exceptionally applied to cases where existence of market power is very likely but may be difficult to prove. An example of such cases would be funeral services—for which the demand appears and disappears over very short terms. The market power of funeral service providers may exist only over very short terms and thus its existence would not be easy to prove.[5] In such exceptional cases, Article 23 may be used to challenge tying.

The former remedy is clear and simple. It is also consistent with the proposition that behaviors that cannot be anticompetitive without market power must be punished only when the existence of market power is proven. The Fair Trade Act should be amended to implement this remedy. First of all, the Enforcement Decree of the Fair Trade Act defines tying, for example, as one of the unfair trade practices and thus tying may be challenged under Article 23. The latter remedy is easier to implement. Tying may be an unfair trade practice, but it is only in the exceptional markets for which it is preannounced that market power likely exists. If a market does not fall in the listed markets, tying in the market must be challenged under Article 3-2 so that existence of market power has to be proven.

INVESTIGATION PROCEDURES: TYING CASES

Identify Tying and Tied Products

Tying arrangements may reduce competition only when there is a separate demand for each product. If two (or more) products are always used together, tying is not likely to reduce competition.[6] To begin investigation of possible tying arrangements, one needs to verify that there are two separate products. It is presumed that the two products are separate if each has been individually sold. If they have been sold as a bundle only, the two products are separate only when there is a sufficient demand for at least one of them.[7] In any case, it is important to make sure that the bundled products cannot be separated and then sold separately. If the individual products may be separately sold in the resale market, consumers are not forced to choose an undesirable bundle over a desirable combination of products.[8] The burden of proof is levied on the plaintiff—the Fair Trade Commission or the competitors or the consumers of the defendant firms. The arguments may be refuted by the defendant firms.

Tying and tied products need to be identified to proceed to the next stage. This is required so that a theory of harm can be established. In general, market power in the tying goods market forces consumers to switch away from products of the competitors in the tied goods market. Thus the good for which the defendant firm has market power is usually regarded as the tying good. If the defendant firm makes an assertion that the other good must be regarded as the tying good, it has to prove the assertion. In rare cases, it is not required to identify tying and tied products when the defendant firm has market power in both markets and tying has only exploitative effects.

The two markets need to be defined at this stage, considering how to show the anticompetitive effects as well as the existence of market power. How the market may be defined is crucial to proving anticompetitive effects. Tying can be more anticompetitive when there are more consumers willing to purchase both products. In particular, the more consumers of tied products are willing to purchase tying products, the more anticompetitive tying is.

I suggest that the main purpose of defining the market is the assessment of how anticompetitive tying is, rather than limited to the examination of whether market power exists. This does not mean that markets need to be defined against the defendant firm's interest, but that market definition must be helpful in understanding the effects of tying on consumers as precisely as possible. A market in which tying has anticompetitive effects must first be defined and then the other market is defined correspondingly. Markets can be defined very narrowly regarding the scope of products, location and time if it helps identify the precise effects of tying. The definition can be further refined when identifying a theory of harm.

Market definition must be consistent with the usual standards but specific methods, such as the "small but significant and nontransitory increase in price" (SSNIP) test, may not be able to capture proper substitutability triggered by tying. The SSNIP test searches for a set of products within which consumers switch upon price changes, while tying arrangements change demands for fewer alternatives. For example, a consumer who wants to buy an iPhone would not give up buying a smartphone even if an iPhone is tied up with its own map system. Then it would be appropriate to define the relevant market as that of smartphones for the analysis of tying cases, while the SSNIP test is more likely to define the market as that of mobile phones as many consumers may switch to a feature phone at a 5 percent increase in the price of smartphones.

Note also that tying may have asymmetric effects on the tying good and the tied good. Tying is more likely to make consumers of competing goods in the tied good market switch to a bundle rather than to make consumers switch out from a bundle of the dominant firm. Therefore, the criterion of market definition could be differently applied to the two markets.

Show the Existence of Market Power

Tying is potentially anticompetitive only when it forces consumers to stay with the tying good of the defendant firm.[9] Consumers cannot switch to other products if switching is infeasible due to lack of alternatives. They also stay if switching is costly due to a quality differential, transaction costs, lock-in effects or incompatibility issues. The defendant firm is said to have market power in the tying case if consumers are forced, in the above sense, to avoid products of competitors. Hence tying is potentially anticompetitive only when the defendant firm has market power.

The Fair Trade Commission has to show that the defendant firm has market power, in this sense, if it wants to challenge tying arrangements.

Ideally it suffices to show that consumers are forced to purchase the tying good of the defendant firm—but it is seldom feasible to measure and empirically test how much consumers are "forced." Instead, one may observe indicators of market power to reach a decision. Such indicators include, as mentioned in the above paragraph, a lack of alternatives, a quality differential, transaction costs, lock-in effects and incompatibility issues. The defendant firm is more likely to have market power in the tying good market when there are fewer alternatives, the quality gap is larger, transaction costs are higher, lock-in effects are bigger and products are less compatible with each other.

In general, a firm is said to have market power if it can profitably raise its price above the competitive level for a significant period of time (European Commission [2009]).[10] Several factors may be used for assessing whether a firm has market power. The firm's market share is the most important factor to consider. Entry barriers, or the likelihood of expansion or entry, are other important factors. The market shares of the competitors, the existence of close substitutes, financial ability and other factors can also be considered. These measures indicate the lack of alternatives, that is, whether competitive alternatives in the market exist or not. They also reflect quality gaps, transaction costs and lock-in effects. Hence the general sense of market power, and thus the criteria for assessing the degree of market power, apply to tying cases as well.

There are additional factors to consider, however, in tying cases. One of the factors is compatibility. At least two complementary products must be involved in tying cases, while there is usually only one product in question for other cases of abusive behaviors. A product in the tying good market that is less compatible with tied goods is less substitutable for other tying goods. In this sense, the less compatible those competing products are, the more likely that consumers will stay with the tying good of the dominant firm. Such effects are more significant when consumers are uncertain about compatibility of the products, since fewer people will take a risk to switch to a substitute due to the possibility of a necessary costly switch back to the bundled product. The existence of switching costs and network externalities also amplifies these effects. Hence it is likely that the dominant firm's product has higher market power in tying cases, *ceteris paribus*, than in other cases.

Taking the above factors into consideration, the Fair Trade Commission can make a judgment on whether the defendant firm has market power in the tying good market. If the firm does not have market power, the tying is not likely to have anticompetitive effects, so that it is not necessary to investigate the case.

It is questionable, however, whether tying must always be deemed lawful, simply because it may be hard to show the existence of market power due

Table 5.3 *Types and numbers of tying cases to which Article 23 was applied, 1983–2005 and 2006–12*

Bundled products	1983–2005	2006–12
Funeral services with flowers and others	16	0
Wedding services with flowers and others	79	1
Cemetery plots with tombstones	6	0
Beer or soju with blended whiskey	5	0
Cars with expensive options	1	1
Offline lectures with online lecture	0	5
Other products[a]	3	1
Total	110	8

Note: [a] Other cases are tying popular lands for construction with unpopular lands, popular cosmetics with unpopular cosmetics and hotel rooms with meals.

to difficulties with market definition, data acquisition or other issues. There are markets that exist for very short periods in limited areas. Firms may have market power in such markets even when there may be many firms in these markets.

Funeral services are a good example of such markets. In that case, market power can be presumed to exist without proof. If such a case is not investigated at all, one may make an error of false negative. If market power is presumed in too many of such cases, one may make an error of false positive. Under the constraint that the second type of error is minimized, the Fair Trade Commission must list the exceptional cases in which market power is very likely to exist and thus is presumed without proof. The exceptions must be specific regarding the types of products and, if necessary, the consumers. Previous enforcement cases will provide a reference (Table 5.3).

Identify a Theory of Harm

The Fair Trade Commission has to identify the theory of harm that best explains the effects of the tying arrangements under investigation. Tying arrangements may have exploitative or exclusionary effects or both, while many other abusive behaviors may have only exploitative or only exclusionary effects.[11] A dominant firm ties its two products to make more profits. It pays to exploit consumer surplus by setting higher prices on bundled products or to exclude its competitors by forcing consumers to buy its bundled products. Neither of the above effects may exist or both effects may exist.

Depending on which effects the tying has, different clauses will be applied. Item 5 of Clause (1), Article 3-2 is applied to exploitative effects, and Items 3, 4 and 5 of Clause (1), Article 3-2 are applied to exclusionary effects.[12]

There are few theories on exploitative effects of tying. Several papers discuss the effects of tying on consumer surplus, but they mainly focus on social surplus and conclude that the overall effects are indeterminate. Competition authorities should aim at preserving the consumer surplus from dominant firms' behaviors, so I focus on consumer surplus in this chapter.[13] Consumers are worse off when prices of bundled products increase. If the products are sold separately and the individual price of each product does not rise, consumers are not worse off—so that tying has no exploitative effects.

Tying could be exploitative only in the following three cases. One is when the individual price of each product increases or the quality decreases. Another is when the tying good of the dominant firm becomes less compatible with the competing products of its tied good. The other is when the products are not separately sold. Two of the above three cases may apply simultaneously.

McAfee et al. (1989) discuss the first case. If a firm is a single supplier of two independent goods, the profit-maximizing prices of individual goods are higher under the mixed bundling scheme than under the non-bundling scheme.[14] The same applies to the cases where a firm has market power in one of the markets or where two goods are complementary. It is clear that increases in individual prices reduce consumer surplus unless the price of a bundle is lower than the sum of the old prices of individual goods. If there are consumers who are better off by purchasing a bundle at a price lower than before the two goods were bundled, the total change in consumer surplus is indeterminate so that the Fair Trade Commission needs to compare the changes in consumer surplus of the better-off and the worse-off.

The second case of a decrease in compatibility is similar to the case where the quality of the tying good is reduced. The difference is that the quality of a bundle is the same as before the tying good becomes less compatible, while it is not the case when the quality indeed decreases. This leads consumers to choose a bundle of the dominant firm over a combination of goods produced by different firms. None of the consumers is better off and, thus, this type of tying always reduces consumer surplus unless prices decrease. If the prices of individual goods and a bundle go down due to competition and cost reduction, the total change in consumer surplus needs to be computed more thoroughly.

The pure bundling case, which is the third case, has been studied in several papers. On the one hand, Nalebuff (2004) shows that, when two goods are independent, a dominant firm sets a lower price under the pure bundling scheme than under the non-bundling scheme regardless of whether there are competitors in the tied good market. On the other hand, Carbajo et al. (1990) show that, when two goods are independent, with one sold in a monopoly and the other in a duopoly, the equilibrium prices of a bundle and a tied good are higher under the pure bundling scheme than under the non-bundling scheme. The two papers reach different conclusions because they use different assumptions on the correlation of utilities from each good across consumers.[15] This implies that the price of a bundle can be higher or lower under the pure bundling scheme depending on the joint distribution of consumer's willingness to pay for two goods. When the price of a bundle goes up or does not change, it is always the case that consumer surplus is reduced. Some consumers will still purchase the same set of products at an equal or higher price, while other consumers will choose a less desirable alternative that had not been their best choice under the non-bundling scheme. When the price of a bundle goes down, consumer surplus may not be reduced.

There are relatively more studies on exclusionary effects of tying. Exclusion means that opportunities to reach a market are not given to (potential) competitors who would have been competitive if there were no tying. Tying may foreclose the tied good market so that the existing competitors or potential entrants may be excluded from the market. This may in turn foreclose the tying good market so that potential entrants may not profitably enter the market. Such effects lessen competition in the corresponding market, which is, without exception, deemed unlawful by competition authorities. Exclusionary effects can be made through the following four mechanisms: direct foreclosure, predatory pricing, network externalities or innovation incentives. Leverage theory says that tying directly forecloses the tied good market and thus is unlawful. But this conclusion has been criticized by Posner (1976) and his followers. Beginning with Whinston (1990), modified leverage theory shows possibilities of foreclosure that Posner's criticism may not apply to.

Whinston (1990) and Nalebuff (2004) show that a commitment to tying by a monopolist makes the competitor stay out of the tied good market, which gives more profits to the monopolist. When the commitment is credible, entry of a competitor into the tied good market leads to severe price competition so that, when taking entry costs into consideration, the competitor ends up with negative pay-off. Hence the competitor does not enter the market and the incumbent becomes a monopolist in both markets to make more profits.[16] In Whinston (1990), a commitment to tying becomes credible through physical tying, which makes the incumbent unable to unbundle. In Nalebuff (2004), a tying strategy is credible without physical tying, since pure bundling is more profitable than selling separately even after entry occurs.[17] A potential entrant may enter or stay out of the market depending on the equilibrium profit at entry and the entry cost. Although "innocent" pricing, by which the incumbent maximizes its profit presuming entry of competitors, may also deter entry, the incumbent, to maximize profits, may intentionally foreclose the market by setting the bundle price lower than the innocent price. Innocent pricing would not be illegal, but intentional foreclosure could be unlawful.

Carlton and Waldman (2002), Kim et al. (2011) and Genakos et al. (2006) show that monopolists can profitably foreclose the tied good market when network externalities exist. The first two papers discuss the case where there are two goods complementary of each other and direct network externalities exist in the tied good market. Genakos et al. (2006) considers a model in which two goods are demanded by distinct groups of consumers, but there are indirect network externalities due to availability of applications working on both goods. When there are network externalities, tying by a dominant firm is more likely anticompetitive and less likely procompetitive.

Choi and Stefanadis (2001) and Choi (2004) show that a dominant firm can tie its products to discourage the competitor's research and development (R&D) investment and innovation incentives. Choi and Stefanadis (2001) show that, when a success probability of R&D investment is low, tying by an incumbent monopolist always reduces the R&D investment by the rival firms, which in turn discourages their entry. Choi (2004) shows that the same holds true for the independent goods case. In both models, a dominant firm has an incentive to tie its products and the tying reduces consumer surplus and even social welfare.

The literature introduced above is a selection of work on theory of harm by tying arrangements. There are many other theories on the mechanism through which tying has anticompetitive effects. The Fair Trade Commission should identify the theories that best explain the tying under investigation or develop new theories if there are no such theories among those that have already been established. Models and assumptions of the theories must be falsifiable in order for the theories to be qualified, since it would be impossible to prove that the harm indeed occurs if it were not falsifiable. Whether the theories are supported by empirical evidence or not is investigated in the next stage.

Provide Empirical Evidence of the Harm

Once the theories of harm have been posed, empirical evidence supporting the theories must be suggested. The burden of proof is levied on the plaintiff—the Fair Trade Commission, consumers or the competitors of the defendant firm. The plaintiff must show that empirical data are consistent with the market structures modeled, the assumptions made and, more importantly, the harm to the market asserted by the theories. The market structures and the assumptions may be taken as plausible by the court without proof if reasonable, but the harm must be proven. Once the plaintiff successfully proves their claim, the defendant firm can make counterarguments. The burden of proof is now placed on the defendant firm, which can disprove the market structures, the assumptions or the harm to the market using supplementary data.

To be specific, the Fair Trade Commission has to provide an estimate of the decrease in consumer surplus in the exploitative tying cases. As discussed in the previous subsection, tying may have different effects on different groups of consumers depending on changes in the price, the quality and other factors. There are some cases in which all consumers are worse off or at least not better off, and thus it is presumed that consumer surplus is reduced. It is recommended that, even in such cases, the estimate is provided so that the anticompetitive effects may be compared to the efficiency-enhancing effects. If there is no efficiency effect, it would be clear that the tying is anticompetitive, but if the tying is shown to enhance efficiency, it would be difficult to reach such a conclusion without the estimate.

The Fair Trade Commission needs to compute the number of consumers who continue to purchase the same products, those who switch to other products and those who stop buying such products. Each group of consumers may be divided into subgroups depending on whether they switch from or to a bundle, which brands they switch to or which products they have purchased. Then changes in the consumer surplus of each subgroup need to be estimated considering the changes in price, quality, compatibility and, if possible, complementarity.

It will not be an easy task to construct such data, even for the price. In the first step, the Fair Trade Commission can simply estimate a change in the consumer surplus of a representative agent in a set of subgroups or, ideally, each subgroup. Consumers may be grouped by availability of sales data, price information, quality evaluation and other factors. When qualitative variables are not available, the first estimates are likely to depend on quantitative variables only. The total change in consumer surplus is the sum of the crude estimates. If it appears to be negative, the defendant firm must refine the estimation using supplementary data in order to make a counterargument. The data include sales by subgroups of consumers, prices of products and, if necessary, variables from which quality of products and compatibility and complementarity between products can be inferred. The firm may use a sophisticated model to estimate the total change in consumer surplus, the assumptions of which must be falsifiable.[18]

In the exclusionary cases, the Fair Trade Commission has to prove that competition is reduced due to tying. The Supreme Court ruled in 2007 that abusive behaviors are presumed to lessen competition when competitors exit the market or the entry of potential entrants is deterred. On the one hand, there can be exceptional cases in which exit or entry deterrence may occur for other reasons than tying. On the other hand, it can be the case that tying may not foreclose the market completely, although it has exclusionary anticompetitive effects. Hence, the Fair Trade Commission can pose the presumption that competition has been lessened due to tying when exit or entry deterrence is detected and must prove that such effects are very likely when exit or entry deterrence does not indeed occur. If such an assertion is accepted, the defendant firm can now make a counterargument that exit or entry deterrence is not due to the tying or that such effects are unlikely.

More specifically, when there is no competitor who exits or is deterred from entry, it has to be proven that the defendant firm's market share has risen in the tied good market due to tying or that it is very likely. The Fair Trade Commission needs to compute the change, from tying, in the defendant firm's market share in the tied good market. Then it needs to be shown that the tying led such effects to take place. Since it is confirmed in the previous stage that the firm has market power in the tying good market and that the market power can be leveraged into the tied good market through some mechanism, the increase in the market share can be attributed to the effects of the tying. One question is whether or not there can be other factors leading to the same result.[19] Regression can be useful for analyzing this question. The Fair Trade Commission may regress other factors out as long as data are available. If the defendant firm does not agree with the commission, it may provide a refined regression result using supplementary data.

Models and assumptions of the suggested theories of harm also need to be verified. For example, some theories assume that two products are independent, while others assume perfectly complementary products. One can verify the assumptions by estimating the utility function or the system of demand functions. In the exclusionary cases, it may be an important issue whether the defendant firm's decision to tie two products is irreversible or not. It is verifiable by investigating how costly the investment to tie was, how much of the cost is sunk and how costly it would be to unbundle.

It is also important to empirically examine the mechanism of market foreclosure implied in the theories—predatory pricing, network externalities or innovation discouraging. The Fair Trade Commission needs to prove that the price of the bundle is significantly lower than the "innocent" competitive price, that there exist non-trivial network externalities on the demand side or that innovation by competitors has been reduced. Proof may be challenging, mainly due to data availability, but such a procedure is necessary to verify the anticompetitiveness of the tying. Once it is proven using available data by the Fair Trade Commission, the defendant firm has a chance to make a counterargument using supplementary data and a more sophisticated model.

Efficiency Claims

Tying may enhance efficiency in various ways. A bundle can be a new product that has not been found useful before, and thus its market will be created and extended. Tying can reduce production costs as well as transaction costs to increase social efficiency. Efficiency enhancement may be claimed by the defendant firm and the burden of proof is also placed on the firm. The firm needs to show that, for example, the production cost has significantly decreased due to the tying using their cost data. It has to be verifiable and falsifiable. The same applies to market extension and transaction cost reduction.

Once it is shown by the firm, the Fair Trade Commission has a duty to review the claim and, if necessary, to make a counterargument. Review of the claim involves two procedures. One is to verify that the claim is proven without an error. The empirical evidence must be consistent with the facts and there must not be logical errors in the claim. The other is to check whether the efficiencies claimed can, or cannot, be achieved in other ways than tying. Tying may be said to enhance efficiency only when there does not exist any less anticompetitive method that achieves the same efficiency. If there exists such a method, the Fair Trade Commission needs to make a counterargument that the tying does not contribute to efficiency enhancement. The Fair Trade Commission has to search for the methods that may achieve the claimed efficiencies of the tying. If one is found, it will be compared to the tying in efficiency and anticompetitiveness. The commission has to prove that the method is less anticompetitive than and as efficient as the tying. The defendant firm may make a counterargument that the tying is the best way to achieve efficiency.

CONCLUDING REMARKS

The investigation procedures explained above are efficient in the following senses. First, the Fair Trade Commission can proceed step by step, with an option to drop a case at any stage. A case of a potentially abusive behavior is identified with the definition of a relevant market. If market power is not shown to exist, the case will be dropped and it will not be challenged any more. Once existence of market power is proven, a theory of harm is sought by the plaintiff. If a relevant theory of harm is not identified, the behavior will be deemed lawful. When a theory suggests that the behavior may be anticompetitive, the plaintiff provides empirical evidence that proves the anticompetitive effects. Such a step-by-step investigation enables, under their resource constraints, the Fair Trade Commission to deal with more cases. Second, the defendant firm has a chance to refute the plaintiff's logic and evidence at each stage as well as an option to claim efficiency-enhancing effects of the behavior. It is incentive compatible for both agents that the plaintiff proves anticompetitive effects first and the defendant makes counterarguments. It is cost efficient to let the defendant, who has access to the relevant data, prove efficiency-enhancing effects.

There are some practical issues with implementing this rule. One of the issues is how to deal with the case in which more than one effect exists at the same time. When both exploitative and exclusionary effects exist, the behavior will be deemed unlawful for anticompetitiveness of both effects. What if, however, the behavior increases surplus of current consumers and lessens competition in the future at the same time? Comparison of the two effects requires an expectation of how competitive the market will be in the future with and without the behavior. Hence it may be difficult to compute a decrease in consumer surplus by lessened competition. One solution would be to refer to a case of predatory pricing that has long been deemed unlawful due to lessening competition in spite of a decrease in the current price.

Another issue would concern which abusive cases Article 23 may be applied to without proving the existence of market power. For example, tying has anticompetitive effects only when market power exists and, thus, it is basically unlawful only when market power is shown to exist. That said, there are cases in which market power exists but is hard to prove. If potentially abusive behaviors are deemed lawful in all such cases, it is likely that too many such behaviors will be tried.

However, if abusive behaviors can be ruled anticompetitive by Article 23 without proof of market power, as they have been in the Republic of Korea, lawful behaviors of non-dominant firms will be prevented and thus competitors will be protected from effective competition. Therefore, Article 23 must be applied only exceptionally to cases in which market power is very likely to exist but is hard to prove due to data availability, market definition or other issues. It is recommended that the list of such cases be announced so that firms are less uncertain about the results of their strategy. For this purpose, the list must be stated as clearly and concretely as possible.

NOTES

1. See US Department of Justice (2008), 78.
2. Unfair support is banned for two different reasons. One is to prevent tunneling the profit to the firms or persons in a special relationship. The other is to protect effective competition in the market in which unfair support may take place.
3. The implementation document announced by the Fair Trade Commission that supplements Article 23 declares that a trade shall be deemed unlawful when it lessens competition or is unfair.
4. A separate product test was introduced first in *Jefferson Parish v. Hyde* (1984).
5. There are many funeral service providers, but it might be hard to buy such services at the moment it is urgently necessary.
6. Even when two products are always used together, there is also a separate demand for each if parts for replacement are demanded.
7. See *Jefferson Parish v. Hyde* (1984) for a separate-product test.
8. If the resale is very costly, though possible, or if the resale price is too low, one may conclude that the bundle cannot be detached.
9. Driving consumers out of both the markets is a side effect that the firm has not intended, but it can also be included in the anticompetitive effects of tying.
10. See European Commission (2009), paragraph 11. This also states, "the expression 'increases prices' includes the power to maintain prices above the competitive level and is used as shorthand for the various ways in which the parameters of competition—such as prices, output, innovation, the variety or quality of goods or services—can be influenced to the advantage of the dominant undertaking and to the detriment of consumers."
11. For example, predatory pricing, refusal to supply and exclusive dealing have exclusionary effects, while exploitative price setting and quantity restraint have exploitative effects only. Price discrimination may be exploitative when employed to final consumers, and exclusionary when carried out to intermediary producers, but it cannot be exploitative and exclusionary at the same time.
12. Tying can be challenged by Item 5 of Clause (1), Article 3-2 only after the enforcement decree is amended, since "unreasonable transaction to exclude competitors" in Item 5 is currently limited to predatory pricing and exclusive dealing in the enforcement decree.
13. The competition authorities may not consider profits when trying to prove anticompetitive effects. As efficiency-enhancing effects will be claimed by the defendant firm, it is only the effects on consumer surplus that should be claimed by the competition authorities. Also, when comparing the two effects, one may put more weight on consumer surplus than overall efficiency. If otherwise weighted, consumer surplus can be exploited by the firm in the end. Such a conduct that a firm simply transfers surplus from consumers to the firm but hardly improves social welfare would be better prevented to the interest of consumers, so that innovations increasing both consumer surplus and profits are encouraged.
14. Two goods are said to be independent when consumption of one does not affect the utility of the other. Goods are independent when they enter the utility function in an additively separable form. Independent goods are neither net substitutes nor net complements of each other.
15. Nalebuff (2004) assumes that willingness to pay for one is independently distributed

with that for the other across consumers, while Carbajo et al. (1990) assume that they are perfectly correlated.

16. Posner (1976) points out that a monopolist cannot earn more profits by tying two goods than by selling separately when the two goods are perfect complements. This is not the case when the two goods are not perfect complements. Whinston (1990) assumes two goods are independent.

17. A credible commitment to the price of the bundle is required.

18. It may lead to a different estimate whether or not to consider the reaction of competing firms. If the price of competing products increases, consumer surplus will be estimated to decrease further when the reaction is considered, but the result will be the opposite in the other case. The equilibrium reaction would be better considered in principle, but the Fair Trade Commission may not take it into account when data are not available. The defendant firm must include the effect of its choice on the reaction of competitors in the estimation model. If the expectation for the reaction is different from the realization, the firm must explain why such an expectation is reasonable.

19. There are many other possible explanations. Some examples include cost reduction or quality improvement by innovation. Note that cost reduction without price cut is not likely to increase the market share of the firm. High supply substitutability may lead to a similar result, since competitors can move to more profitable markets in which the same facilities can be used in production.

REFERENCES

Ahlborn, C., D. Evans and J. Padilla (2004), "The antitrust economics of tying: a farewell to per se illegality," *Antitrust Bulletin* **49**, 287–341.

Carbajo, J., D. de Meza and D. Seidmann (1990), "A strategic motivation for commodity bundling," *Journal of Industrial Economics* **38**(3), 283–98.

Carlton, D., and M. Waldman (2002), "The strategic use of tying to preserve and create market power in evolving industries," *Rand Journal of Economics* **33**(2), 194–220.

Choi, J. (2004), "Tying and innovation: a dynamic analysis of tying arrangements," *Economic Journal* **114**(492), 83–101.

Choi, J., and C. Stefanadis (2001), "Tying, investment, and the dynamic leverage theory," *Rand Journal of Economics* **32**(1), 52–71.

European Commission (2009), "Communication from the commission—guidance on the commission's enforcement priorities in applying article 82 of the EC Treaty to abusive exclusionary conduct by dominant undertakings," *Official Journal of the European Union*, available via https://eur-lex.europa.eu/legal-content/EN/ALL/?uri=CELEX%3A52009XC0224%2801%29 (accessed on November 29, 2019).

Genakos, C., K.-U. Kühn and J. Reenen (2006), "The incentives of a monopoly to degrade interoperability: theory and evidence from PCs and servers," working paper.

Jefferson Parish Hospital District No. 2 et al. v. Hyde, 466 U.S. 2, 1984.

Kim, J., S. Bang and S. Hwang (2011), "Anti-competitiveness of instant messenger tying by Microsoft," *Hitotsubashi Journal of Economics* **52**(2), 185–98.

Kühn, K.-U., R. Stillman and C. Caffarra (2005), "Economic theories of bundling and their policy implications in abuse cases: an assessment in light of the Microsoft case," *European Competition Journal* **1**, 85–121.

McAfee, P., J. McMillan and M. Whinston (1989), "Multiproduct monopoly, commodity bundling, and correlation of values," *Quarterly Journal of Economics* **104**(2), 371–83.

Nalebuff, B. (2004), "Bundling as an entry barrier," *Quarterly Journal of Economics* **119**(1), 159–87.

Posner, R. (1976), *Antitrust Law: An Economic Perspective*, Chicago, IL: University of Chicago Press.

US Department of Justice (2008; withdrawn in 2009), "Competition and Monopoly: Single-Firm Conduct under Section 2 of the Sherman Act."

Whinston, M. (1990), "Tying, foreclosure, and exclusion," *American Economic Review* **80**(4), 837–59.

APPENDIX 1: ARTICLES 3-2 AND 23 OF THE MONOPOLY REGULATION AND FAIR TRADE ACT

Article 3-2 (Prohibition of Abuse of Market-Dominating Position)

(1)   No market-dominating entrepreneur shall commit acts falling under the following subparagraphs (hereinafter referred to as the "abusive acts"): <Amended by Act No. 5813, Feb. 5, 1999>
 1.   An act of determining, maintaining or changing unreasonably the price of commodities or services (hereinafter referred to as the "price");
 2.   An act of unreasonably controlling the sale of commodities or provision of services;
 3.   An act of unreasonably interfering with the business activities of other entrepreneurs;
 4.   An act of unreasonably impeding the participation of new competitors; and
 5.   An act of unfairly excluding competitive entrepreneurs, or of doing considerable harm to the interests of consumers.
(2)   Categories or standards for abusive acts shall be determined by Presidential Decree. <Newly Inserted by Act No. 5335, Dec. 30, 1996; Act No. 5813, Feb. 5, 1999>

Article 23 (Prohibition of Unfair Trade Practices)

(1)   No entrepreneur shall commit any act which falls under any one of the following subparagraphs, and which is likely to impede fair trade (hereinafter referred to as "unfair trade practices"), or make an affiliated company or other entrepreneurs perform such an act: <Amended by Act No. 5335, Dec. 30, 1996; Act No. 5813, Feb. 5, 1999; Act No. 8382, Apr. 13, 2007>
 1.   An act of unfairly refusing any transaction, or discriminating against a certain transacting partner;
 2.   An act of unfairly excluding competitors;
 3.   An act of unfairly coercing or inducing customers of competitors to deal with oneself;
 4.   An act of making a trade with a certain transacting partner by unfairly taking advantage of his position in trade;
 5.   An act of trade under terms and conditions which unfairly restrict or disrupt business activities;
 6.   Deleted; <by Act No. 5814, Feb. 5, 1999>
 7.   An act of assisting a person with a special interest, or other

companies by providing advanced payment, loans, manpower, immovable assets, securities, goods, services, right on intangible properties, etc. thereto, or by transacting under substantially favorable terms therewith; and

8. An act which threatens to impair fair trade other than those listed in subparagraphs 1 through 7.

(2) The categories or standards for unfair trade practices shall be determined by Presidential Decree. <Amended by Act No. 5335, Dec. 30, 1996>

(3) If it is necessary to prevent acts of violation of the provisions of paragraph (1), the Fair Trade Commission may make and publicly announce the guidelines to be observed by entrepreneurs.

(4) In order to prevent unreasonable inducement of customers, the entrepreneurs or entrepreneurs' organization may voluntarily make a fair competition code (hereinafter referred to as the "fair competition code"). <Amended by Act No. 5814, Feb. 5, 1999>

(5) Entrepreneurs or an entrepreneurs' organization may request that the Fair Trade Commission examine whether or not the fair competition code as referred to in paragraph (4) is in violation of the provisions of paragraph (1) 3 or 6.

APPENDIX 2: RELEVANT ARTICLES IN ENFORCEMENT DECREE OF THE MONOPOLY REGULATION AND FAIR TRADE ACT

Article 5 (Types of and Criteria for Abusive Acts)

(1) "Unreasonable fixing, maintenance, or alteration of price" as per Item 1, Clause (1), Article 3-2 (Prohibition on the Abuse of Market Dominance) of the Act pertains to a sharp increase or insignificant decrease in the price/cost of goods or services relative to the changes in the supply and demand or in the supply cost without justifiable reason (limited to general or similar businesses).

(2) "Unreasonable control of the sale of goods or provision of services" as per Item 2, Clause (1), Article 3-2 (Prohibition on the Abuse of Market Dominance) of the Act refers to the following:

1. Significantly decreasing the supply of goods or services without justifiable reason and considering the recent trends

2. Decreasing the supply of goods or services despite a supply shortage in distribution without justifiable reason

(3) "Unreasonably hampering another enterpriser's business activities"

as per Item 3, Clause 1, Article 3-2 (Prohibition on the Abuse of Market Dominance) of the Act involves hindering another enterpriser's business activities by directly or indirectly engaging in any of the following acts: <Amended on March 27, 2001>

1. Hindering the purchase of raw materials required for the production of the other enterprise without justifiable reason
2. Employing human capital indispensable to the business activities of another firm by granting or promising excessive economic compensation compared to normal practices
3. Refusing, discontinuing, or limiting the use of or access to essential facilities for the manufacture, provision, or sale of products or services of other enterprisers without justifiable reason
4. Engaging in unreasonable acts other than those in Items 1, 2, and 3 and deemed by the Fair Trade Commission to hinder the business activities of other enterprisers

(4) "Unreasonably hindering the entry of a new competitor" as per Item 4, Clause (1), Article 3-2 (Prohibition on the Abuse of Market Dominance) of the Act involves obstructing the entry of new competitors by directly or indirectly engaging in any of the following acts: <Amended on March 27, 2001>

1. Entering into an exclusive contract with a transaction partner without justifiable reason
2. Purchasing the rights, etc., required for the continued business activities of an established enterprise without justifiable reason
3. Refusing or limiting the use of or access to essential facilities for the manufacture, provision, or sale of products or services of new competitors without justifiable reason
4. Engaging in unreasonable acts other than those in Items 1, 2, and 3 and deemed by the Fair Trade Commission to hinder the entry of new competitors

(5) "Unreasonable transaction to exclude competitors" as per Item 5, Clause (1), Article 3-2 (Prohibition on the Abuse of Market Dominance) of the Act pertains to any of the following:

1. Where there is a possibility of excluding a competitor by supplying goods or services at unreasonably low prices or purchasing goods or services at unreasonably high prices compared to the normal transaction price
2. Unreasonably transacting with a partner under the condition that the partner does not transact with a competing enterprise

(6) The Fair Trade Commission may determine and announce the specific types of and criteria for Abusive Acts as referred to in Clauses (1)~(5). <Amended on March 31, 1999>

Article 36 (Designation of Unfair Business Practices)

(1) The types of and criteria for Unfair Business Practices as per Clause (2), Article 23 (Prohibition on Unfair Business Practices) of the Act are listed in Appendix 1.

(2) When deemed necessary, the Fair Trade Commission may establish and announce the detailed standards for the types of and criteria for Unfair Business Practices as per Clause (1) for purposes of applying them to a particular area or act. In this case, the Fair Trade Commission shall hear the opinions of the heads of the relevant administrative agencies in advance. <Amended on March 31, 1997>

Types of and Criteria for Unfair Business Practices [related to Clause (1), Article 36] <Amended on March 30, 2002>

1. Refusal to deal
   "Unreasonably refusing to transact" as stipulated in Item 1, Clause (1), Article 23 (Prohibition on Unfair Business Practices) of the Act pertains to the following:
   A. Collective refusal to deal
   Refusing to initiate business with a certain enterpriser or suspending transaction or significantly restricting the quantity or nature of commodities or service in a transaction with a certain enterpriser with which you have forged a continuous transaction relation without justifiable reason and in collusion with your competitors
   B. Other types of refusal to deal
   Unreasonably refusing to initiate business with a certain enterpriser or suspending transaction or significantly restricting the quantity or nature of commodities or services in a transaction with a certain enterpriser with which you have forged a continuous transaction relation

2. Discriminatory treatment
   "Unreasonable discrimination against certain transacting partners" as stipulated in Item 1, Clause 1, Article 23 (Prohibition on Unfair Business Practices) of the Act refers to the following:
   A. Price discrimination
   Depending on the transacting partner or transaction territory, unreasonably transacting at a highly favorable or unfavorable price
   B. Discrimination in the terms and conditions of transaction

Unreasonable discrimination in the terms and conditions, e.g., quantity or quality in favor of or against a certain enterpriser

C. Discrimination in favor of affiliated corporations

Discrimination in trading terms and conditions such as price, quantity, or quality in favor of or against certain partners without justifiable reasons for the benefit of your affiliated corporations

D. Collective discrimination

A group unreasonably discriminates in favor of or against a certain enterpriser, thereby putting such enterpriser at a considerable advantage or disadvantage

3. Elimination of competitors

"Unreasonably excluding competitors" as stipulated in Item 1, Clause 2, Article 23 (Prohibition on Unfair Business Practices) refers to the following:

A. Unjustifiable discounts

Continuing to supply your commodities or services at a price that is considerably lower than the supply cost without justifiable reason or to supply such commodities or services at an unduly lower price, thereby threatening the viable existence of your competitors or those of your affiliated corporations

B. Unjustifiably high-priced purchase

Purchasing commodities or services at an unjustifiably higher cost than the normal transaction price, thereby threatening the viable existence of your competitors or those of your affiliated corporations

4. Unfairly luring customers

"Unreasonably luring customers of your competitors to deal with you" as stipulated in Item 1, Clause 3, Article 23 (Prohibition on Unfair Business Practices) of the Act pertains to the following:

A. Luring customers by promising unjustifiable gains

Providing or promising to provide unjust or excessive gains in violation of normal business practices, thereby luring your competitor's customers

B. Luring customers using fraudulent means

Other than through labeling or advertising as provided for in Item 9, misleading your competitors' customers by falsely claiming that the content, terms and conditions, or other transaction matters involving your commodities or services are considerably superior to or much more advantageous than they actually are compared to those of your competitors, or that the content, terms and conditions, or other transaction matters involving your competitor's commodities or services are considerably less advantageous than or inferior to what they actually are compared to your commodities or services, thereby luring your competitors' customers

C. Luring customers through other methods
Unduly hindering transactions between your competitor and its customers by impeding the execution of contracts or by encouraging such customers to breach their contracts, thereby luring them

5. Coercion in dealing
"Unreasonably coercing the customers of your competitors to deal with you" as stipulated in Item (1), Item 3, Article 23 (Prohibition on Unfair Business Practices) of the Act refers to the following:

A. Tie-in sales
Wrongfully forcing the transaction partner to purchase another commodity or service from you or an enterpriser you designated when supplying commodities or services in violation of normal business practices

B. Forcing employees to purchase or make a sale
Wrongfully forcing your officers or employees or those of your affiliated corporation to purchase or sell your commodities or services or those of your affiliated corporation

C. Other types of coercion
Offering the transaction partner undue terms and conditions and other disadvantages in violation of normal business practices, thereby forcing the transaction partner to transact with you or the enterpriser you designated

6. Abuse of superior position
"Unreasonably taking advantage of your superior position when transacting with others" as stipulated in Item (1), Clause 4, Article 23 (Prohibition on Unfair Business Practices) of the Act pertains to the following:

A. Coercion to purchase
Forcing the transacting partner to purchase commodities or services that the transaction partner does not wish to purchase

B. Coercion to provide benefits
Forcing the transacting partner to provide economic benefits such as money, commodities, or services

C. Imposing a sales target
Imposing a target on the transacting partner for transactions involving the commodities or services you supply and forcing the transaction partner to meet the target

D. Offering disadvantages
    Establishing or modifying the transaction conditions to the
    disadvantage of the transacting partner or placing the partner
    at a disadvantage in the course of carrying out the transaction
    using methods other than those described in Items 1~3

E. Interference in management
    Interfering in the management activities of transaction partners
    by requiring them to obtain approval or directions from you
    when they hire or fire officers or employees or by restricting the
    manufacturing articles, scale of facilities, production quantity,
    or details of transaction

7. Transaction based on restrictive conditions
    "Transacting with others under terms and conditions that unreason-
    ably restrict business activities" as stipulated in Item (1), Clause 5,
    Article 23 (Prohibition on Unfair Business Practices) of the Act
    refers to the following:

    A. Exclusive dealings
        Wrongfully transacting with an enterpriser on the condition that
        the enterpriser does not deal with your competitor or those of
        your affiliated corporation

    B. Restriction on the transaction area or partner
        Transacting with a transaction partner on the undue condition
        that the partner limits its transaction area or partner(s)

8. Interference in the business activities of other enterprisers
    "Acts that unreasonably disrupt the business activities of other enter-
    prisers" as stipulated in Item (1), Clause 5, Article 23 (Prohibition on
    Unfair Business Practices) of the Act refer to any of the following acts:

    A. Unfair use of technology
        Unduly using the technology of the other enterpriser such that
        its business activities are seriously hampered

    B. Unfairly luring or hiring personnel
        Unreasonably luring or hiring the personnel of the other enter-
        priser such that its business activities are seriously hampered

    C. Interference in the change of transacting partner
        Unreasonably interfering in the change of transaction counter-
        part of the other enterpriser such that its business activities are
        seriously hampered

    D. Interference through other methods
        Interfering with the business activities of other enterprisers
        through unreasonable means other than those specified in Items
        1~3 such that their business activities are seriously hampered

9. Deleted <June 30, 1999>

10. Undue financial, asset, and manpower support

The following acts constitute the act of unreasonably "providing specially related persons or other corporations with temporary payment, loan, manpower, real estate, securities, intangible property rights, etc., or aiding a special related person or other corporations by trading under extremely favorable terms" as per Item (1), Clause 7, Article 23 (Prohibition on Unfair Business Practices) of the Act:

A. Undue financial support

Aiding a specially related person or other corporations through the provision of excessive economic benefits by providing or transacting funds, e.g., temporary payment, loan, etc., at substantially high or low costs or by providing or transacting such funds in substantial amounts.

B. Undue asset support

Aiding a specially related person or other corporations through the provision of excessive economic benefits by providing or transacting assets such as real estate, securities, intangible property rights, etc., at substantially high or low costs or by providing or transacting such assets in substantial volumes.

PART IV

Merger and collusion

6.   Comments on merger guidelines

Joseph Farrell

In 2009–10 I was privileged to be part of the six-person United States (US) Federal Trade Commission–Department of Justice (FTC–DOJ) team that drafted the 2010 revision of the then 18-year-old US *Horizontal Merger Guidelines* (HMG; US Department of Justice and Federal Trade Commission 1992). As it happened, the UK competition agencies were revising their guidelines at about the same time and, working with the two UK agencies' then chief economists Amelia Fletcher and Alison Oldale, I was privileged to offer input into that revision as well.[1] Of course, this chapter does not claim to represent official views of any of these agencies. Rather, I comment on the role of guidelines and on some of the many economic issues in horizontal merger guidelines.

WHAT ARE MERGER GUIDELINES? WHOM DO THEY GUIDE?

Merger guidelines serve multiple purposes and disparate audiences. An outsider might naturally expect that a key audience would be business-people who don't have expert advisors. Some government guidelines are directed at such audiences, and one of our goals in the 2010 revision was to put things in plainer language where possible, but to some degree modern merger analysis is a technical and, in certain ways, an arcane task. Thus I reluctantly suspect that most non-specialists would find it challenging to digest any recent version of the HMG (US Department of Justice and Federal Trade Commission 2010).

Another audience is internal—within the antitrust agencies. Guidelines can help the senior officials (or "front office") guide the staff to emphasize or weigh evidence in this way or that. Or longtime career staff might use guidelines as an internal memo to communicate institutional memory to the sometimes less experienced front office. Or both.

Guidelines can also be a language in which the agencies communicate with courts: as an official and relatively long-lived document describing merger analysis in general, not arguing a case of a specific merger, guidelines can gain credibility with a sometimes skeptical audience. To be sure, recent editions of the HMG have stated that they do not constrain how the agencies may argue a case in court, but some courts have seen fit to override such a disclaimer and to hold the agencies to what (the court believed) the guidelines say. Hillary Greene (2006) has discussed how the guidelines have been "institutionalized."

Guidelines also do not live in isolation. They occupy a rich world of other commentary and discussion including litigation documents such as briefs and complaints, as well as court decisions; "competitive impact statements" (DOJ) or "analyses to aid public comment" (US FTC) for negotiated settlements, a much more common intervention than actual litigation; and speeches and articles by officials and staff. In 2006 the DOJ and the FTC issued a *Commentary on the Horizontal Merger Guidelines* (US Department of Justice and Federal Trade Commission 2006), an important stepping stone from the 1992 HMG to the 2010 HMG. I don't know why the agencies chose to issue a commentary rather than to revise the guidelines at that time.

GUIDELINES AND ECONOMICS

As a field of study, economics, including the study of competition and the effects of mergers, has made progress, some of which I will touch on below. In a legal system set up to defer to precedent, and whose decision-makers often learned their own economics many years ago, there can be some push and pull—even tension!—between progress and precedent. Guidelines mirror this: they seek to describe how agencies actually analyse mergers, which normally involves both some institutional traditions and at least one eye on how courts will analyse a disputed case; but they also seek to describe best, not merely typical, practices in merger analysis.

In US merger control, one such push–pull has been on or near the surface for decades: that is, attitudes to the Supreme Court's *Philadelphia National Bank* (PNB) decision fifty years ago, cementing a presumption that mergers creating "undue concentration" in a market are harmful. A recent symposium in the *Antitrust Law Journal* expressed a range of those attitudes.[2] But, to my mind, it is a mistake to cast this simply as an "ancient versus modern" debate or, despite my framing above, simply as progress versus precedent. The issues are more subtle.

First, inferences from concentration depend on how markets are defined. This is a commonplace in antitrust litigation where parties try to convince courts to adopt market definitions that would, under PNB, cause their side to win. A separate question would be, what approach to market definition would make inferences based on concentration as informative and reliable as possible? Moreover, the approach to market definition that would make the PNB inference (high concentration, substantially increased by a merger, tends to mean trouble) reliable needn't be the same as the approach to market definition that would make the reverse-PNB inferences (low concentration post-merger tends to mean no trouble) reliable. Courts have sometimes been tempted to economize on analysis by using the same approach for both inferences; the extent to which this works is, of course, also an issue for indicators other than concentration.

Second, as Salinger (1990) put it, modern economics students are often taught "contempt" for the econometric literature that sought to correlate concentration and price-cost margins or profits and that emerged with mixed and uncertain results. However, many of the criticisms of the profit-concentration studies point out flaws that one would expect to lead to false negatives. More importantly, perhaps, as Schmalensee (1989) noted, the results of intra-industry price-concentration studies are stronger and less equivocal. Thus it is not right to say that economic science no longer credits a PNB link.

Rather, one would really want to know more about the source and dynamics of concentration. In some markets, it is intense competition that ensures high concentration, as the winner takes all; in others, barriers protect incompetent or greedy incumbents against incursion. One wouldn't expect those different kinds of highly concentrated markets to have the same implications for economic performance and consumer welfare (see the 2010 HMG, section 5.3). Similarly, some markets have many similar-sized rivals running as hard as they can and barely keeping up with each other; others are fragmented because of barriers to expansion, as in "monopolistic competition."

Consistent (I think) with a relatively nuanced understanding along such lines, the 2010 US HMG retain the PNB logic, especially for coordinated effects, contrary to speculation among some at the time that the guidelines would "abandon" or "downplay" market definition and the use of market shares and concentration measures. In fact, sections 4 and 5 of the guidelines—in my printed copy, approximately 18 pages out of 46—focus on those topics. But the guidelines also recognize other analytical techniques, more explicitly and in more detail than did their 1992 precursor. Shapiro (2010) compellingly paints this as a long-term trend toward recognizing multiple techniques and sources of evidence.

Third, one probably cannot evaluate a diagnostic tool in isolation: they are not primarily used that way and, anyway, one would have to ask, "Compared to what?" If the PNB presumption and/or the reverse-PNB presumption were sharply discounted, would they be replaced by some other logic or presumptions or would courts and decision-makers merely be advised that concentration evidence is no longer to be relied on? If the latter, what would be the effect on enforcement? Since the default position (both legal and statistical) is that mergers are permitted to proceed, context-free skepticism about inferences is apt to reduce enforcement and the retrospectives literature, if anything, suggests that enforcement has become somewhat too weak overall. That's no reason to cover up legitimate caveats, but we should keep in mind the difference between replacing one mode of analysis with a better one, on the one hand, and merely removing an imperfect but useful mode of analysis, on the other hand.

With this background, let me offer some comments on how more modern and flexible economic analysis complements the still-prominent market definition and concentration analysis in the 2010 US HMG.

SUBSTANTIVE CENTRAL QUESTION AND TYPES OF EVIDENCE

As the preamble in section 2 of the 2010 HMG notes, the agencies "consider any reasonably available and reliable evidence to address the central question of whether a merger may substantially lessen competition."

That anodyne phrasing actually takes the non-trivial position that the task is a search for "evidence to address the central question." This framing opposes a more procedural approach—a distinction sometimes described as "standards versus rules." For instance, some courts have held that certain kinds of evidence on entry barriers shouldn't count and, while one can interpret such a position as a bold venture by those courts into economic analysis, a more sympathetic interpretation is as an insistence on reformulating the flexible enquiry guided by the "substantial lessening of competition" standard into a procedurally more predictable process involving rules that echo that enquiry but do not incorporate all of its subtleties.

In line with this preference for substance over procedure, the 2010 HMG depart from the single mode of analysis (market definition and concentration) that dominated earlier guidelines. They include, and even stress, that mode of analysis, but they don't grant it either substantive or procedural monopoly power. Instead, as Shapiro (2010) argued, they are like a fox that "knows many things." The HMG recognize that the agencies use many sources of information and types of analysis.

UNILATERAL EFFECTS

Much of the discussion of the 2010 HMG in the US antitrust community—especially during the public consultations in 2009–10—focused on the HMG's identification of modern economic methods for gauging the risks of unilateral effects.

What is a "unilateral effect"? One arcane but conceptually clean definition is that it is the effect that the merger would have on equilibrium, holding fixed the reaction functions of non-merging firms, and thus changing conduct only (a) through changes to the merging firms' conduct and (b) through re-equilibration by non-merging firms in the same way as they would have re-equilibrated to the same change in the merging firms' conduct without a merger. This definition goes with the focus on changes in the merging firms' incentives when competition ceases between them, given their joint competitive environment, which is assumed not to change with the merger. In practice, however, very many analyses of unilateral effects address only a narrower question: how a simultaneous-move (static) quantity or price-setting oligopoly equilibrium shifts with the merger.

In the context of a Cournot or quantity-setting oligopoly equilibrium, Farrell and Shapiro (1990) studied how static equilibrium shifts with a merger. Technically the analysis introduced the construct of an "infinitesimal merger," enabling the use of calculus techniques and introducing (though not by name) the concept of critical compensating marginal-cost efficiencies. The results showed that, although the level of the Herfindahl concentration index[3] is related to a weighted average of price-cost margins (the Cowling–Waterson formula), the Herfindahl does not cleanly predict (at the theoretical level) the effect of a merger on price and output. Nor does the so-called change in the Herfindahl, meaning twice the product of the merging firms' market shares—this would be the change in the Herfindahl if outputs did not change, which is of course not an assumption sustained throughout a Cournot merger analysis.

Subsequently, during his first period of service as chief economist at the DOJ, Shapiro (1996) offered simple calculations for unilateral-effect shifts in the static differentiated-product Bertrand equilibrium, with specific functional forms for demand. In line with Farrell and Shapiro (1990) but more starkly, Shapiro noted that he was "keenly aware" how importantly the predicted price effect depends on the assumed functional form for demand.

With the rise of computer technology, economists began to use more ambitious "merger simulations," calibrating parameters of a pre-merger equilibrium (almost always a static equilibrium) from pre-merger data and using those parameter estimates to predict post-merger prices and

quantities, often reporting more than one significant digit in their estimates. The sensitivity to functional form infected, of course, the numbers
that emerged. Froeb et al. (2005) and Slade (2009) illustrated in specific
cases how econometric demand estimation and merger simulation gave
dramatically different results depending on the assumed functional form
for demand (notwithstanding that the parameters of each demand system
were not assumed but estimated on the same data).

This situation is unsatisfactory in itself, and has plausibly contributed to
a tendency for some to conclude that economists can't agree and, thus, that
economic evidence cancels itself out. What to do?

A "technocratic" response might seek more data and put more econometric firepower into estimating a flexible demand system with fewer
a priori assumptions about functional form. Perhaps, in the era of "big
data," we may sometimes be able to do this informatively, but I am not
optimistic. We are most concerned with long-run or at least medium-run
competitive consequences, and longer-term demand responses to a semi-
permanent price change are often quite different from responses to very
short-term changes, especially to price changes expected to be temporary.
For instance, in supermarket scanner data, price changes for paper towels
are likely dominated by occasions when paper towels go on sale and the
corresponding demand changes are likely dominated by stocking-up
or time-shifting of purchases—not by substitution to sponges or cloth
towels, which is what would count more for a merger effect.[4] If we do have
longer-run price variation in the data, it can hardly all be recent—unless it
is in varying geographic markets, for instance, which raises its own issues.
Moreover, while slopes (elasticities) and cross-elasticities of a demand
system may be reasonably stable over the medium term, curvature of
demand may well be more sensitive to modest changes in some customers'
willingness to pay.

To my mind, a better response in our present state of knowledge is not
to stress those labile price predictions but to focus on the more robust
elements of our analysis. Two approaches that have been used in recent
years are measures of upward pricing pressure (UPP) and the illustrative
price rise (IPR).

UPP is a simple and robust idea. In the perhaps complex balancing that
drives pre-merger pricing, many factors may play a role—not only single-
product demand elasticity but also cross-product effects, cost effects such
as learning by doing, the long-run value of customer relationships and
demand inertia and so on. Such factors, if equally present post-merger
and pre-merger, would complicate and perhaps obstruct estimation of
pre-merger parameters but needn't be problematic for evaluating the
change in incentives caused by the merger. That change in incentives

consists of newly taking into account the effect on the merger partner's profits, which were of no concern before the merger. To quantify this, consider the effect of selling one more unit of a product. The effect on the merger partner's profits is calibrated by the extent to which that unit sale cannibalizes (or induces) sales by the merger partner and by the incremental profits of those affected sales. This is UPP, expressed as a virtual new marginal cost of the additional unit sold. One can then see that the merger's effect on price will be very closely related to the pass-through of this new marginal cost: this intuition is described in Farrell and Shapiro (2010) and made more precise and rigorous by Jaffe and Weyl (2013). Because we already knew that pass-through of marginal-cost changes for a single firm is complex and labile, this clarifies not only why merger simulation price predictions vary widely across demand specifications but also why they vary (as Froeb et al. 2005 pointed out) with pass-through rates. To my mind, this argues for discussing our results at the more robust level of changes in virtual marginal cost—an approach that also simplifies comparison of these competitive effects against plausible merger efficiencies. This is what UPP does.[5]

The IPR is superficially framed as a price prediction but, in my view, is best interpreted as a different tack for avoiding the sensitivity of price predictions to demand specifications: it simply and explicitly assumes a "for-instance" demand specification, rather than claiming accuracy for the specification used. In practice I understand that the UK competition authorities have used the iso-elastic specification, which yields high pass-through rates and thus high IPR numbers, partly with an eye to cautiously clearing mergers (if the predicted effect without efficiencies, even under iso-elastic demand, is small enough then the merger is probably harmless). In that usage, it seeks to complement or replace the "inverse PNB" inference described above.[6] More broadly I think it is better seen as a simple and consciously back-of-the-envelope way of translating the UPP measure into familiar price terms—but not one that should be treated as a "real" prediction of price, let alone a highly precise one.

I won't resist a final piquant comment. These forms of unilateral-effect analysis offer a modern economic alternative to market definition and concentration for evaluating mergers. But while this is real progress, it also echoes long-established ideas: in particular, since the 1980s, merger guidelines have called for market definition via the economic analysis of what a hypothetical monopolist over a group of products would find it profitable to do. When one takes seriously the quantitative hypothetical-monopolist test for market definition, for instance by engaging in critical-loss analysis, one is led to much the same considerations as arise when one bypasses market definition and goes directly to calibration of unilateral effects.

COORDINATED EFFECTS

In many oligopolies, competing firms react to one another's competitive moves, such as price changes, and anticipate such reactions in evaluating whether such moves are likely to be profitable. Indeed, observers often view reactions as indicating substantial competition between those firms and failure to react as suggesting the absence of such competition. Characteristically firms consider whether to match a price change, stay pat or offer something in between.

In the economics literature this is sometimes described as "conjectural variation" (CV). In that phrase, the variation is in price or quantity; the conjectures have to do with how equilibrium is affected not by actual reactions—in a static equilibrium there is no change to react to[7]—but by anticipated or conjectural reactions. For example, in a quantity-setting framework, Cournot equilibrium involves each firm choosing quantity as if its rivals' quantities would not respond (as indeed they couldn't, if it were literally a one-shot simultaneous-move game). With positive CV, each firm is modeled as believing that, if it expands its output, its rivals will expand theirs by some amount calibrated by the CV parameter(s). This makes expanding output less attractive, or reducing output more attractive, and so will lead to an equilibrium with lower output than Cournot equilibrium.

Clearly, this framework begs some questions. Is it a simultaneous-move game or isn't it? Where does the CV parameter come from? Is it limited by some kind of consistency or credibility requirements? In the literature, this cluster of questions is summarized by questioning whether the CV approach has good micro-foundations. Largely for that reason, and because the theory's predictions depend importantly on the CV parameter (that's the whole point) and that parameter sometimes seems to appear out of thin air, the approach has been relatively neglected in theoretical work, although it is sometimes used in econometric studies where (part of) the goal is to estimate the CV parameter rather than to justify it based on theory and logic.

Instead, the bulk of the economics theory literature on oligopoly conduct has bifurcated into two strands. The first strand studies static Nash equilibria, such as Cournot or (usually differentiated-product) Bertrand equilibria. The second strand studies dynamic subgame-perfect Nash equilibria, using the powerful techniques of the "folk theorems" concerning infinitely repeated games.

In principle the repeated-game strand should encompass CV to the extent that it's consistent with equilibrium behavior (both on and off the equilibrium path).[8] In practice, however, as I explain below, the usual discussions of the repeated-game strand distract from the important concerns captured under CV; and this fact about the literature and about the education of economists (and indirectly of lawyers) creates a practical problem for merger review. It is not entirely helpful to say that all forms of oligopoly are in principle encompassed in an approach that, in practice, directs attention away from forms of conduct that are widely pervasive in oligopoly.

The repeated-game strand of the oligopoly literature asks in what circumstances there exists a subgame-perfect equilibrium whose equilibrium path includes (for instance) high prices. Fundamental "folk theorem" results in this (and the game theory) literature give necessary and sufficient conditions for such existence. High-enough prices give players an incentive to deviate or "cheat" by cutting price to attract more customers, and so a high-price equilibrium logically must involve responses or consequences for deviating that will, on balance, seem unattractive to a player contemplating deviation. As a powerful analytical tool, the literature observes that, if a price path is a subgame-perfect equilibrium path at all, it is the price path of such an equilibrium supported by certain sometimes highly artificial, most-draconian, credible "punishments" that would be triggered in response to any "deviation."

So far, so technical. But it does not follow that every subgame-perfect equilibrium will in fact use (or threaten) those, or any explicit, "punishments." That was just an analytical tool to diagnose when (for instance) certain prices might be too high to be sustained in any equilibrium. When prices are not too high, in that sense, they might be sustained in many different equilibrium ways, including some that are much more natural and less redolent of *ex-ante* negotiated incentives. CV-type equilibria may exist (and even be subgame-perfect) when trigger-strategy equilibria are behaviorally implausible. Consequently, doing a reality check on the idea that oligopolists in X industry would reach agreement on prices and on punishments for deviation could easily lead one astray. For example, if there is so much hostility that it's hard to imagine them agreeing on anything, does that mean that they can't sustain high prices? Careful logic says no; intuition based on phrasing like "agreement, detection and punishment" risks saying yes.

In short, while it is central to the game-theory approach to consider what would happen following a deviation and to check that it does not clearly appeal to the deviating player, I think that looking for "punishments" can guide the brain to an unduly narrow set of possibilities and encourages us to look for (perhaps tacitly) collusive actions, or circumstances, that can allow players to negotiate their way to such a highly profitable but highly artificial equilibrium. This may well be the most challenging hurdle in running a cartel. But failure to negotiate detailed common expectations and agree on well-structured punishments doesn't have to bring an oligopoly to an approximation of static competition. Natural responses can make a big difference.

The 1992 guidelines discussed factors making coordination more likely, introducing the topic in a way that was, in principle, entirely consistent with that focus. But the overarching stress quickly turned to (a) reaching agreement, with (b) detection and punishment as key necessities and with (c) the framework being one where firms seek to coordinate and face difficulties that they may or may not be able to overcome.

Focusing on maximally deterrent responses to "deviations" also contributes to another pervasive problem with the repeated-oligopoly literature. Those punishments are analytically chosen to be as powerful as possible (that is, as harsh as can be made credible), so the threat of them "supports" high prices as often as is game-theoretically possible (in principle, outcomes inconsistent with subgame-perfect equilibrium are not consistent with incentives[9]). But this approach predicts (the potential for) "collusive" pricing far more widely than informed observers believe actually happens. A subgame-perfect equilibrium with fully collusive pricing exists even for startlingly large numbers of symmetrically placed firms (see, for instance, Shapiro 1989). Occasionally this might mean we are surprised by large-numbers collusion; but most of the time it likely means that the condition for existence of a collusive subgame-perfect equilibrium is not the key to whether collusion happens.

These seem to me important problems for the antitrust economics discussion of oligopoly conduct. They are generally not flat-out errors, but, in my experience, they guide many participants, much of the time, toward an unduly rigid discussion and, in particular, toward putting undue weight on whether an industry can plausibly feel its way to something like a trigger-strategy equilibrium without actually meeting in a smoke-filled room.

In contrast, a branch of the economic theory literature, notably Maskin and Tirole (for example, 1987), derives CV-type equilibria as Markov-perfect equilibria in the repeated game. In this framework, as I believe is often the case in reality, firms do not so much punish their rivals for departing from an agreed-upon price pattern but rather simply respond to how their own environment has changed with their rivals' new prices. This does not mean responding as if their rivals' recent initiatives are the last word; on the contrary, firms in the model predict how rivals will respond to their responses. But it is (technically) driven by the state of the industry rather than by history or (very non-technically) it is pragmatic rather than punitive.

It remains to be seen how case-specific analysis of parallel accommodating conduct will play out. In particular, increased observability of rivals' competitive moves plays a key role both in the vigor of CV reactions and in the ability to sustain a conscious and purposive coordination; similarly, each firm's vulnerability to reactions by its rivals is key in both classes of analysis. I believe, however, that (at least as interpreted by all but the most subtle experts) the purposive coordination framing omitted so much oligopoly conduct, or described it in such an artificial framework, that it created an undue risk of confusion. I regard it as a significant conceptual improvement for the 2010 HMG to be explicit in recognizing this widespread kind of oligopoly behavior. The authors did so through a discussion in section 7, "Coordinated Effects," that offers a home for analysis recognizing CV and the potential for a merger to affect the strength of CV. This logic does not rely on a purposive analysis of repeated play in oligopoly; its recognition of what is sometimes called "parallel accommodating conduct" has been criticized.[10] Some commentators have recognized this but expressed a preference to view CV-type conduct as unilateral. This would fit into the formal definition of unilateral effects above if and only if rivals' reaction functions did not change; thus it would not capture a move to sharper and more vigorous CV. But in the end I don't think it should matter in what box one puts it; the important point is to dissipate any impression that the guidelines authoritatively divide oligopoly conduct or merger effects into two forms and that CV is in neither box.

LEARNING FROM EXPERIENCE: MERGER RETROSPECTIVES

US antitrust agencies review, on average, over a thousand mergers per year, accumulating a great deal of experience generally, with the application of specific techniques and in specific industries. A great deal of learning results. But the learning opportunities are not fully exploited because few of the predictions about what will happen with or without a merger are explicitly (let alone systematically) compared with actual experience. I agree with those who believe it would be well worth while to follow up on, say, all mergers that draw a second request (a few percent of mergers notified under the Hart–Scott–Rodino Act—or, very roughly, 50 per year[11]). If this were done internally, however, as might be necessary if relevant data are confidential, it would require a large expansion of the FTC's Bureau of Economics and/or the DOJ's Economic Analysis Group. Some resource savings might be achievable if we were willing to take advantage of a statistical tradeoff: with many more merger retrospectives ("observations"), it would become less important to minimize random errors (though no less important to minimize systematic errors or bias) in each. The fiscal challenge would also be simpler if it were possible to recruit outside (for example, academic) effort into the task; I believe that doing an intelligent merger retrospective or two would be a good addition to the profession's customs for the training of micro-economists.

Absent such a program, we are left with an increasingly rich but not necessarily representative set of studies: see Kwoka (2015). As this chapter is about guidelines rather than all of merger analysis, I'll close by echoing footnote 1 of the 2010 HMG, urging that guidelines remain living documents, subject to updating and improvement in the light of continued learning.

NOTES

1. Dr. Fletcher was chief economist at the Office of Fair Trading (OFT) and Dr. Oldale was chief economist at the Competition Commission. Subsequently those two UK agencies were replaced by the new Competition and Markets Authority (CMA).
2. *Antitrust Law Journal* (2015), **80**(2); the articles by Salop (2015) and by Ginsburg and Wright (2015), between them, frame this tension clearly.
3. This widely used index of market concentration is the sum of the squares of firms' market shares.
4. See Hendel and Nevo (2006), for instance.
5. UPP is sometimes referred to as GUPPI (gross upward pricing pressure index). Some treatments distinguish the two terms according to whether and at what stage estimates of efficiencies are counted.
6. Similarly, the increasing use of UPP has raised the question of whether, and how strongly, an inverse inference can be drawn if the UPP is relatively small—some have suggested 5 percent of the price as a threshold. I am generally skeptical that one index should create too strong an inference in either direction. More technically, the construction of UPP creates a risk in using it as a safe harbor: when two firms compete primarily with one another, under undifferentiated Bertrand competition, the UPP index can be zero (high diversion ratios but zero margins!), and these are circumstances where it may be especially important to preserve their competition. (The issue is that the initial "infinitesimal merger" would indeed be harmless, but it would then grow strongly as one edged toward a full merger; in less stark cases, the initial infinitesimal merger is better aligned with the overall merger.)
7. One should not be confused by the fact that static Nash equilibrium analysis uses a theoretical construct called a "reaction function" or "best-response function." Despite the name, that is not normally anyone's reaction in a dynamic game (except for Stackelberg followers), and Nash equilibrium involves optimization by each player against others' expected strategies, not against their "reaction functions." The static best-response function is simply a technical device that can be used to solve for the static Nash equilibrium.
8. Indeed; as playing a static Nash equilibrium each period is always a subgame-perfect equilibrium of the infinitely repeated game, it should also encompass the static strand!
9. In passing, I will note that experiments and other experiences with, for instance, finitely repeated games suggest that inconsistency with subgame-perfect equilibrium does not always prevent an outcome from happening.

10. Harrington (2013) is a thoughtful (although in my view problematic, as I explain in the text) example.
11. The FTC and the DOJ annually publish a Hart–Scott–Rodino report that gives these and many other descriptive statistics and that describes the agencies' enforcement actions.

REFERENCES

Farrell, Joseph and Carl Shapiro (1990), "Horizontal mergers: an equilibrium analysis," *American Economic Review*, **80**(1), 107–26.

Farrell, Joseph and Carl Shapiro (2010), "Antitrust evaluation of horizontal mergers: an economic alternative to market definition," *Berkeley Electronic Journal of Theoretical Economics: Policies and Perspectives, Volume 10*, Berkeley Electronic Press, article 9.

Froeb, Luke, Steven Tschantz and Gregory Werden (2005), "Pass-through rates and the price effects of mergers," *International Journal of Industrial Organization*, **23**(9), 703–15.

Ginsburg, Douglas and Joshua Wright (2015), "Philadelphia National Bank: bad economics, bad law, good riddance" (part of Symposium on Philadelphia National Bank), *Antitrust Law Journal*, **80**(2), 377–96.

Greene, Hillary (2006), "Guideline institutionalization: the role of merger guidelines in antitrust discourse," *William and Mary Law Review*, **48**, 771–857.

Harrington, Joseph (2013), "Evaluating mergers for coordinated effects and the role of 'parallel accommodating conduct,'" *Antitrust Law Journal*, **78**(3), 651–56.

Hendel, Igal and Aviv Nevo (2006), "Measuring the implications of sales and consumer inventory behavior," *Econometrica*, **74**(6), 1637–73.

Jaffe, Sonia and Glen Weyl (2013), "The first-order approach to merger analysis," *American Economic Journal: Microeconomics*, **5**(4), 188–218.

Kwoka, John (2015), *Mergers, Merger Control, and Remedies*, Cambridge, MA: The MIT Press.

Maskin, Eric and Jean Tirole (1987), "A theory of dynamic oligopoly, III: Cournot competition," *European Economic Review*, **32**(7), 1567–68.

Salinger, Michael (1990), "The concentration-margins relationship reconsidered," *Brookings Papers on Microeconomic Activity*, **21**(1990), 287–335.

Salop, Steven (2015), "The evolution and vitality of merger presumptions: a decision-theoretic approach," *Antitrust Law Journal*, **80**(2), 269–306.

Schmalensee, Richard (1989), "Inter-industry studies of structure and performance," in Richard Schmalensee and Robert D. Willig (eds), *Handbook of Industrial Organization, Volume 2*, Amsterdam: North Holland Publishing Co., 951–1009.

Shapiro, Carl (1989), "Theories of oligopoly pricing," in Richard Schmalensee and Robert D. Willig (eds), *Handbook of Industrial Organization, Volume 1*, Amsterdam: North Holland Publishing Co., 329–414.

Shapiro, Carl (1996), "Mergers with differentiated products," *Antitrust*, **10**(2), 23–30.

Shapiro, Carl (2010), "The 2010 merger guidelines: from hedgehog to fox in forty years," *Antitrust Law Journal*, **77**(1), 49–107.

Slade, Margaret (2009), "Merger simulations of unilateral effects," in B. Lyons (ed.), *Cases in European Competition Policy*, Cambridge: Cambridge University Press, 312–46.

US Department of Justice and Federal Trade Commission (1992), *Horizontal Merger Guidelines*, at www.justice.gov/atr/horizontal-merger-guidelines-0 (accessed on December 2, 2019).

US Department of Justice and Federal Trade Commission (2006), *Commentary on the Horizontal Merger Guidelines*, at www.justice.gov/atr/file/801216/download (accessed on December 2, 2019).

US Department of Justice and Federal Trade Commission (2010), *Horizontal Merger Guidelines*, at www.justice.gov/sites/default/files/atr/legacy/2010/08/19/hmg-2010.pdf (accessed on December 2, 2019).

7. What next? Cartel strategy after getting caught

Robert C. Marshall, Leslie M. Marx and Claudio Mezzetti

Once firms are being prosecuted for collusion, strategies remain available to them that have the potential to reduce the penalties they face. Settlement negotiations offer opportunities to negotiate restricted pleas that limit penalties from follow-on litigation and leniency programs such as Amnesty Plus offer opportunities to reduce fines associated with collusion in one product by revealing collusion in another. We offer the implications for antitrust policy.

INTRODUCTION

As stated by the US Department of Justice (DOJ), "When competitors collude, prices are inflated and the customer is cheated. Price fixing, bid rigging, and other forms of collusion are illegal and are subject to criminal prosecution by the Antitrust Division of the United States Department of Justice."[1] Furthermore, according to the DOJ, "In recent years, the Antitrust Division has successfully prosecuted regional, national, and international conspiracies affecting construction, agricultural products, manufacturing, service industries, consumer products, and many other sectors of our economy."[2]

In many cases, the prosecution of a cartel is facilitated by the information provided by a leniency applicant. According to the DOJ website: "The Antitrust Division's Leniency Program is its most important investigative tool for detecting cartel activity. Corporations and individuals who report their cartel activity and cooperate in the Division's investigation of the cartel reported can avoid criminal conviction, fines, and prison sentences if they meet the requirements of the program."[3] In a 2001 speech, while he was the director of criminal enforcement of the Antitrust Division at the DOJ, Scott D. Hammond asserted that: "Since we expanded our Amnesty

Program in 1993, there has been more than a ten-fold increase in amnesty applications. In the last two years, cooperation from amnesty applicants has resulted in scores of convictions and well over $1 billion in fines."[4]

Once a firm is being prosecuted for participation in a cartel, a number of things can affect the penalties ultimately imposed on the firm. In many jurisdictions, firms being prosecuted for collusion may negotiate a settlement with the government.[5] There appears to be some flexibility for cartels to negotiate settlement terms that favor them in terms of limiting future penalties, for example from civil litigation, in exchange for concessions to the competition authority, which may include the amount of criminal fines, the number of individuals receiving prison terms or the total length of prison terms.[6] In addition, programs such as the DOJ's Amnesty Plus,[7] which was implemented in 1999 in response to concerns about offending firms being involved in price-fixing conspiracies in multiple product markets, allow a firm being prosecuted for collusion to qualify for reduced fines by applying for leniency in a separate product in which it is also engaged in collusion.

In this chapter, we consider firms' strategies related to settlement negotiation and leniency applications once they are being prosecuted for collusion. Our focus is on the implications for antitrust policy.

In "Settlement Terms Affect Follow-On Litigation" we discuss the effects of settlement negotiations on deterrence through their impact on follow-on litigation. In "Model" we present a simple model of settlement negotiation. In "Leniency for Multi-Product Colluders" we discuss how leniency programs can affect incentives for multi-product colluders, potentially decreasing deterrence and creating incentives for the formation of sacrificial cartels. "Conclusion" ends this chapter.

SETTLEMENT TERMS AFFECT FOLLOW-ON LITIGATION

Many corporate crimes damage individuals or other purchasers. For example, fraud and price fixing hurt purchasers, while insider trading damages shareholders. When purchasers are damaged, criminal penalties are just one part of deterrence. In addition to criminal penalties, there is often civil litigation by either a class, opt-out plaintiffs or both. The civil litigation can be a substantial part of the financial penalty and thus a substantial part of deterrence. In the US, the absence of a criminal finding can complicate plaintiffs' efforts in civil litigation and potentially reduce plaintiffs' expected recoveries. Even when there is a criminal finding, civil litigation can be significantly affected by the scope of the criminal finding in dimensions such as the time period, products, geography, suppliers' behavior and affected purchasers. Generally, more limited criminal findings can reduce a supplier's potential exposure in civil litigation.

The parameters of the plea agreement also matter to enforcement authorities, but it appears that some parameters are given more attention than others. A review of recent DOJ press releases in cartel cases reveals an emphasis, in terms of what is reported, on the amounts of fines and the extent to which individuals received prison sentences.[8] These press releases do not appear to emphasize the comprehensiveness of the plea parameters, including the extent to which they encompass all relevant time periods, products, buyers and geographies. This is natural since the public has no information about a given cartel matter and will be unable to determine whether, say, a plea length is small or large given the evidence—but the public will be able to observe that a criminal fine of hundreds of millions of dollars seems to be quite punitive and indicative that antitrust enforcement authorities are "doing a good job."

The true parameters describing the conduct may be hard to infer from the documentary evidence. For example, whether a price-fixing conspiracy had a duration of eight or ten years may be difficult for enforcement authorities to establish from the discovery record. Alternatively, the enforcement authorities may perceive differences in the cost and likely success associated with pursuing more expansive claims regarding the extent of the conduct, including factors such as the length of the conduct, the set of products, geographic scope and purchasers affected.

In such an environment, there are tradeoffs to be considered in settlement negotiations. An enforcement authority might view the marginal gains from documenting all the fine details of a conspiracy as small relative to the expected resources required to accomplish that. For example, when considering such tradeoffs, an enforcement authority might look favorably upon pleadings that involve relatively shorter plea periods but relatively higher criminal penalties.

This is consistent with the Canadian experience:

> Canada added that in its experience in negotiations of plea agreements and fines the competition authority might be willing to narrow the scope of the guilty plea in light of possible subsequent civil action, and might seek a relatively higher fine to compensate for the reduce[d] charge to ensure that the fine was adequate in light of the volume of affected commerce. In the consent agreement the level of the fine might appear distorted because the trade off struck between lesser charge and higher fine might not be apparent to the outside observer.[9]

At the risk of redundancy, but to be clear, we are aware of no evidence that antitrust enforcement authorities restrict pleas when they have "bulletproof" evidence in exchange for larger criminal fines. For example, if the DOJ has hard evidence that a cartel was in place from at least January 2005 through at least December 2008, we are unaware of any evidence to suggest that the DOJ would "sell" a reduced plea period, say, January 2006 through December 2007, for a larger criminal fine. However, it may be the case that the DOJ has good but softer evidence that the conspiracy started by at least January 2004 and yet even softer evidence that it began as early as January 2000. Similarly there may be good but softer evidence that the cartel continued until at least June 2009 and, again, even softer evidence that it lasted until December 2011. Furthermore, the DOJ may have hard evidence that the cartel affected ten related products, while the evidence is good but weaker that the cartel affected an additional five products beyond the ten. The DOJ could pour scarce enforcement funds into shoring up the most expansive time period and entire set of products in preparation for a trial, but, given the limited resources of the DOJ, the costs and risk of trial, and numerous other cartel cases that need the attention of the DOJ's scarce enforcement resources, the DOJ will naturally be drawn towards accepting a conspiracy plea for "from at least January 2005 through at least December 2008" and affecting "at least ten products" in exchange for a criminal fine that is large and perhaps more commensurate with the longer periods and extended set of products. Counsel for cartel firms negotiate such pleas, gladly paying larger fines for the restricted pleas, because such pleas reduce expected civil damages and reduce the overall penalties—criminal plus expected civil penalties—faced by the cartel firms.

In what follows, we review two cases that raise questions as to whether the criminal pleading understated the full extent of the conspiracy. In the next section, we discuss the results of a simple model that illustrates the incentives at play.

Example: Vitamins Cartel

The primary manufacturers of vitamins admitted to participating in an international price-fixing conspiracy for much of the 1990s.[10] However, for the individual vitamin products affected by the conspiracy, there are differences in the beginning and ending dates of the conspiratorial activity as identified in US plea agreements versus the European Commission (EC) decision in *Vitamins*. For a summary of US plea agreements, see the Expert Report of B. Douglas Bernheim (Bernheim 2002, Table 6) in the Vitamins Antitrust Litigation.[11] For example, US plea agreements in vitamin A for cartel members Roche and BASF identify a plea period from January 1990 until February 1999, but the EC decision finding begins in September 1989, four months earlier. Similarly, US plea agreements in vitamin B5 for cartel members Roche and BASF identify a plea period from January 1991 until December 1998, but the EC decision finding does not end until February 1999, two months later.

In addition, although there were no guilty pleas dating as far back as 1985, economic evidence related to coordinated price announcements suggests that the conspiracy may have begun in 1985 (Marshall et al. 2008).

We can illustrate the effect on overcharge estimates of this difference in the collusive period based on analysis provided in the Bernheim Report, which estimates overcharges to the associated plaintiffs to be approximately 33 percent greater when one views the conspiracy as starting in 1985 rather than only during the period to which the defendants pled guilty (Bernheim 2002, Table 1).

Figure 7.1 shows the estimated "but-for" price for a particular vitamin product, Vitamin A Acetate 650 Feed Grade. As you can see from the figure, the "but-for" price line (that is, the price series that would have been observed in the absence of collusion) is estimated under the assumption that the period prior to 1990 is non-collusive.

We can contrast this to the "but-for" price line that would result if one assumes that the conspiracy began instead in 1985. As shown in Figure 7.2, substantial incremental overcharges result from this change.

If, in fact, the conspiracy began in 1985, the restricted plea in the criminal case may have substantially reduced civil penalties if civil litigants based overcharge estimates only on the restricted plea period. The approach taken by the enforcement authorities may have been reasonable

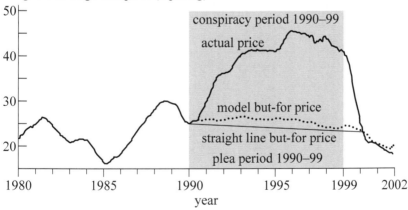

Figure 7.1   Vitamin A Acetate 650 feed grade price and but-for price: conspiracy period 1990–99

weighted average unit price ($ per kg)

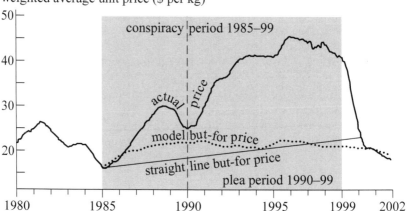

*Figure 7.2   Vitamin A Acetate 650 feed grade price and but-for price:
conspiracy period 1985–99*

given resource constraints and the tradeoffs they faced, including the
consideration of whether the burden of establishing the existence of
the conspiracy in the earlier time period was substantial; however, it is
important to note that limiting pleas in this way can lead to a substantial
reduction in deterrence.

Example: DRAM Cartel

In the dynamic random-access memory (DRAM) conspiracy, firms pled
guilty to a conspiracy that affected only "certain original equipment
manufacturers (OEM) of personal computers and servers."[12] According
to the plea agreements, "The conspiracy directly affected these OEMs
in the United States: Dell Inc., Hewlett-Packard Company, Compaq
Computer Corporation, International Business Machines Corporation,
Apple Computer Inc., and Gateway, Inc." (Samsung Plea Agreement,
p. 4). (The same sentence appears in the Hynix Plea Agreement[13] and in
the Infineon Plea Agreement.[14]) In addition, the Elpida Plea Agreement
identifies Sun Microsystems as having been affected by the conspiracy.[15]

These plea agreements are striking in light of evidence that DRAM
is largely a commodity product. For example, testimony before the US
International Trade Commission stated that, "DRAMs are a global commodity product and, in fact, all of the major DRAM customers insist that
their DRAM suppliers offer a single worldwide price."[16] Given the commodity nature of the product and the "single worldwide price," it seems

unlikely that the conspiracy's effects could have been limited to only seven OEMs in the US; indeed, it is likely that the conspiracy affected prices more generally.

This restriction on the plea creates an incremental burden on purchasers of DRAM other than the seven named OEMs in order for them to recover damages, to the benefit of the colluding firms.

MODEL

In this section, we provide a model of settlement negotiation between an enforcement authority and a firm that has engaged in collusion. We assume that the enforcement authority behaves so as to maximize criminal fines net of enforcement costs (as opposed to minimizing anticompetitive behavior). We assume that the firm behaves so as to minimize the sum of criminal and civil penalties.[17] We allow the possibility that a firm could agree not to contest a criminal fine in exchange for adjustments by the enforcement authority of the parameters on which the fine is based.

For simplicity, we focus on plea length as the key parameter of the plea agreement.

Setup

We model the criminal fine as being calculated as follows:

We assume that $\underline{t}$ is the earliest date and that $\bar{t}$ is the latest date for the conspiracy that can be argued given the evidence. The enforcement authority must choose a defensible plea period, defined by a starting date $t_0 \in [\underline{t}, \bar{t}]$ and an ending date $t_1 \in [\underline{t}, \bar{t}]$, with $t_0 < t_1$. Given the plea period, the volume of affected commerce is $\sum_{t=t_0}^{t_1} \pi^t$, where π^t is the volume of affected commerce in period t. The enforcement authority must assign a culpability score $s \in S$ to the firm,[18] where S is the set of culpability scores that can be argued credibly given the evidence. Finally, the enforcement authority must select a fine from within the allowable range, given the volume of affected commerce and the culpability score. We let $\lambda \in [0,1]$ denote the scale factor determining the fine's distance between the minimum and maximum fine. For example, if the enforcement authority selects a scale factor of λ and if the minimum fine given the plea period and culpability score is a and the maximum is b, the amount of the fine is $a + \lambda(b - a)$. We let the function $f(t_0, t_1, s, \lambda)$ denote the fine; it is a strictly decreasing function of the starting period t_0 and a strictly increasing function of the ending period t_1, the culpability score s and the scale factor λ.

We let $c(s,\lambda)$ denote the cost of enforcing the fine combined with any expected reductions in the fine. We assume that it is a strictly increasing function of both s and λ, taking into account the increased workload associated with a more aggressive fine. In general, one would expect c to increase as s approaches the upper bound for the culpability score that can be argued given the evidence and to increase as λ approaches one, indicating that the fine approaches the maximum amount given the volume of affected commerce and the culpability score. The cost may also depend on t_0 and t_1, for example if the burden of proving existence of a conspiracy increases with the time period; however, we focus on the case in which c is independent of the plea period. While our model incorporates the effect on cost of the culpability score, capturing the increased complexity associated with further incorporating the effects of the plea period on costs to the enforcement authority is beyond the scope of this chapter.

To summarize, an enforcement authority interested in maximizing the amount of the fine it collects net of enforcement costs chooses the plea period, culpability score and scale factor to solve

$$\max_{t_0 \in [\underline{t},\overline{t}], t_1 \in [\underline{t},\overline{t}], t_0 < t_1, s \in S, \lambda \in [0,1]} f(t_0, t_1, s, \lambda) - c(s,\lambda). \qquad (7.1)$$

Let $t_0^N, t_1^N, s^N, \lambda^N$ be the solution of (Equation 7.1), $F^N = f(t_0^N, t_1^N, s^N, \lambda^N)$ be the fine, $C^N = c(s^N, \lambda^N)$ the enforcement cost and $F^N - C^N$ the value of the difference between the fine and the enforcement cost at the solution.

The firm's objective function is to minimize the sum of criminal and civil penalties. For simplicity, we assume that civil penalties depend only on damages during the plea period, and not on the culpability score, scale factor or the amount of the criminal fine. Specifically, let $d(t_0, t_1)$ be damages defined based on a plea period from t_0 to t_1, where $d(t_0, t_1)$ is less than or equal to the amount of affected commerce during the plea period. Civil penalties can be up to triple the damages amount. To avoid introducing additional parameters, we write the penalties as equal to triple damages; however, a scale factor can also be introduced to account for less-than-triple damages with no effect on the qualitative results:

$$p(t_0, t_1) = 3d(t_0, t_1).$$

Thus, the firm's payoff related to the enforcement action is

$$-f(t_0, t_1, s, \lambda) - p(t_0, t_1).$$

We assume that d and hence p are strictly decreasing in t_0 and strictly increasing in t_1. Letting $P^N = p(t_0^N, t_1^N)$, the firm's payoff in the absence of negotiation with the enforcement authority is $-F^N - P^N$.

Results

It is immediately apparent from Equation 7.1 and the fact that f decreases with t_0 and increases with t_1 that, absent any negotiation with the firm, it is optimal for the enforcement authority to set $t_0^N = \underline{t}$ and $t_1^N = \bar{t}$ (recall that we assume the cost to the enforcement authority is not affected by the length of the plea period).

Claim 1: In the absence of negotiations with the firm, the enforcement authority maximizes the criminal fine by basing it on the maximum justifiable plea period, $t_0^N = \underline{t}$ and $t_1^N = \bar{t}$.

Now consider the possibility of negotiations between the enforcement authority and the firm being prosecuted. The enforcement authority has no incentive to accept a payoff that is less than the maximum value $F^N - C^N$, defined as the solution of Equation 7.1. We assume that the firm can reduce the enforcement agency's costs to zero (our results continue to hold if costs are reduced but remain positive) by accepting the fine imposed on it. By refusing to negotiate with the firm, the enforcement authority obtains $F^N - C^N$. Thus, we can think of $f(t_0, t_1, s, \lambda) - F^N + C^N$ as the enforcement authority's gain over the status quo of no negotiation from an agreement to settlement parameters (t_0, t_1, s, λ). Similarly, we can think of $F^N + P^N - f(t_0, t_1, s, \lambda) - p(t_0, t_1)$ as the firm's gain over no negotiation from agreeing to settlement parameters (t_0, t_1, s, λ). We use the asymmetric Nash bargaining solution, with a bargaining power equal to $\beta \in (0,1)$ for the enforcement authority, as our solution concept. (A value of $\beta = \frac{1}{2}$ corresponds to the standard Nash bargaining model.) That is, we assume that the bargaining outcome is given by the solution of the following problem:

$$\max_{t_0 \in [\underline{t}, \bar{t}], t_1 \in [\underline{t}, \bar{t}], t_0 < t_1, s \in S, \lambda \in [0,1]} \{\beta \ln (f(t_0, t_1, s, \lambda) - F^N - C^N) +$$

$$(1 - \beta) \ln (F^N + P^N - f(t_0, t_1, s, \lambda) - p(t_0, t_1))\}. \quad (7.2)$$

At an interior solution, the first order condition with respect to t_h, $h = 0,1$, is:

$$\frac{\beta}{f(t_0, t_1, s, \lambda) - F^N + C^N} \frac{\partial f(t_0, t_1, s, \lambda)}{\partial t_h} -$$

$$\frac{1 - \beta}{F^N + P^N - f(t_0, t_1, s, \lambda) - p(t_0, t_1)} \left(\frac{\partial f(t_0, t_1, s, \lambda)}{\partial t_h} + \frac{\partial p(t_0, t)}{\partial t_h} \right) = 0. \quad (7.3)$$

Since f and p are both strictly decreasing in t_0 and strictly increasing in t_1, it must be that at the solution

$$\frac{\beta}{f(t_0, t_1, s, \lambda) - F^N + C^N} > \frac{1 - \beta}{F^N + P^N - f(t_0, t_1, s, \lambda) - p(t_0, t_1)}. \qquad (7.4)$$

Differentiating (7.2) with respect to $\theta = s, \lambda$ gives:

$$\left(\frac{\beta}{f(t_0, t_1, s, \lambda) - F^N + C^N} - \frac{1 - \beta}{F^N + P^N - f(t_0, t_1, s, \lambda) - p(t_0, t_1)} \right) \frac{\partial f(t_0, t_1, s, \lambda)}{\partial \theta} > 0$$

where the inequality follows from Equation 7.4 and the fact that f is strictly increasing in both s and λ. It is thus immediate that the solution to Equation 7.2 is $s^* = \max_{s \in S} s$ and $\lambda^* = 1$. In addition, the negotiations involve the selection of interior values of t_0 and t_1, so that the plea period is reduced below the maximum period.

Claim 2: At an interior solution, the bargaining outcome is for the enforcement authority and the firm to negotiate a settlement that maximizes the culpability score and scale factor, $s^* = \max_{s \in S} s$ and $\lambda^* = 1$, and reduces the plea period, $t_0^* > t_0^N = \underline{t}$ and $t_1^* < t_1^N = \bar{t}$.

In addition, since $-f(t_0^*, t_1^*, s^*, \lambda^*) - p(t_0^*, t_1^*) > -F^N - P^N$, the firm's payoff increases as a result of settlement negotiation and hence deterrence is reduced by the presence of such settlement negotiation relative to its absence.

Claim 3: Settlement negotiation that generates restricted pleas reduces deterrence by increasing the colluding firms' payoffs.

Example

Consider the following example. Assume the volume of affected commerce is the same in each period and equal to π. Define the base fine as 20 percent of the amount of affected commerce; that is, the base fine is $0.2\pi(t_1 - t_0)$. Let $S = [0,1]$, so that the culpability score is between zero and one. Given the plea period, culpability score and scale factor, define the fine to be the following function of the start and end dates, culpability score and scale factor:

$$f(t_0, t_1, s, \lambda) = 0.2\pi(t_1 - t_0)(0.75 + 1.25s)(1 + \lambda).$$

As we have defined this function, the minimum fine (the fine when $\lambda = 0$) can be as little as 75 percent of the base fine and the maximum fine (the fine when $\lambda = 1$) can be as much as four times the base fine, depending on the culpability score. Given the culpability score, the minimum and maximum fines differ by a factor of 2, with the final amount of the fine depending on the scale factor.

Define the cost function so that a culpability score or scale factor close to the upper bound for its range imposes costs on the enforcement agency and/or may lead to later reductions in the level of the fine. Specifically, we let

$$c(s,\lambda) = 8\pi s\lambda.$$

This cost function is chosen so that the cost of choosing $s = 1$ and $\lambda = 1$ offsets any payoff to the enforcement authority from collecting a fine.

To model the firm's payoff, assume damages are a factor α times the volume of affected commerce, so that civil penalties are

$$p(t_0, t_1) = 3\alpha\pi(t_1 - t_0).$$

In the absence of negotiations with the firm, the enforcement authority solves Equation 7.1. Letting $\underline{t} = 0$ and $\bar{t} = 10$, the solution is $t_0^N = 0$, $t_1^N = 10$, $\lambda^N = 0.45$, and $s^N = 0.27$, with $F^N = 3.17\pi$, $C^N = 0.99\pi$ and $P^N = 30\alpha\pi$. In general, as stated in Claim 1, the plea length will always be chosen at its maximum, but the culpability score and scale factor will not necessarily be chosen at their maxima. Without negotiations, the enforcement authority's payoff is $F^N - C^N = 2.18\pi$, and the firm's payoff is $-3.17\pi - 30\alpha\pi$.

When the enforcement authority and the firm negotiate, they set $s^* = 1$ and $\lambda^* = 1$, and the solution to the first order condition (Equation 7.3) of the bargaining problem (Equation 7.2) can be easily computed. Letting $\alpha = 0.3$, the optimal plea length is $t_1 - t_0 = 7.16\beta + 2.73(1-\beta)$, which is about 27 percent of its original length if the firm has all the bargaining power and 49 percent of its original length with equal bargaining power, $\beta = 0.5$. Indeed, even if the enforcement authority has all the bargaining power, $\beta = 1$, it finds it advantageous to reduce the plea length to 71 percent of its original length, as this allows it to substantially increase the fine paid by the firm.

Recall that the original penalty without negotiation is 3.17π, while with negotiation it is 2.18π if the firm has all the bargaining power, 3.96π with equal bargaining power and 5.73π when the enforcement authority has all the bargaining power. When the firm has all the bargaining power, it is able to reduce the fine in exchange for eliminating the enforcement authority's enforcement cost. As the bargaining power of the enforcement authority increases, the firm is willing to pay a higher fine in order to reduce the plea length and hence civil penalties.

LENIENCY FOR MULTI-PRODUCT COLLUDERS

We now turn to a different set of strategies that colluding firms face after getting caught, namely strategies related to leniency applications. These strategies differ from the strategies surrounding settlement negotiation discussed above in that they suggest actions that colluding firms might take prior to getting caught that can reduce the probability of detection.

The theoretical economics literature on antitrust leniency has mostly focused on models of tacit collusion. For surveys, see Rey (2003) and Spagnolo (2008).[19] The general conclusion of these models is that the presence of a leniency program makes collusion more difficult. The literature has also addressed the potential for the strategic use of leniency by cartels; in particular, it has recognized that, by reducing expected fines, a leniency program may reduce deterrence—for example, see Chen and Rey (2012), Chen and Harrington (2007), Spagnolo (2004) and Motta and Polo (2003).

To the extent that the presence of leniency programs makes it harder for firms to sustain collusion, leniency programs may cause the cartels that do form to invest in more extensive preparatory work or more sophisticated concealment. This more sophisticated preparatory work might include reorganizing the corporate hierarchies of the firms in the cartel in order to limit the number of individuals in the firms that would need to know about the conspiracy. More sophisticated concealment might involve hiring an external consulting firm to organize meetings and maintain sensitive cartel documents in a location out of reach of authorities.[20]

In some cases, however, leniency can potentially provide incentives for firms that are colluding in one product to extend the conspiracy to include another product. Given the ability of cartels to adapt in response to changing enforcement regimes, the possible existence of this or other "perverse effects" from leniency programs is a concern that has been raised in the literature. As stated in Wils (2008a):

> [S]uccessful cartels tend to be sophisticated organisations, capable of learning. It is thus safe to assume that cartel participants will try to adapt their organisation to leniency policies, not only so as to minimise the destabilising effect, but also, where possible, to exploit leniency policies to facilitate the creation and maintenance of cartels. This raises the question whether there could be features of leniency programmes that risk being exploited to perverse effects. (137)

There are many examples of firms engaged in collusion in more than one product and even many examples of firms applying for leniency in more than one product. Table 7.1 from Marx et al. (2015) considers EC decisions in cartel cases for 2001–12 and shows that 21 multi-product colluders have

Table 7.1   *Multi-product colluders that received a complete fine reduction in at least one product in EC cartel cases, 2001–12*

Firm	Number of Products	No fine reduction	Incomplete fine reduction	Complete fine reduction
Akzo Nobel	9	2	4	3
Takeda	6	4	1	1
Aventis	5	—	2	3
William Prym	5	1	3	1
Bayer	4	—	2	2
KONE	4	1	1	2
Otis	4	—	3	1
Degussa	3	—	1	2
Merck	3	1	1	1
Samsung	3	—	1	2
Shell	3	2	—	1
ABB Ltd.	2	1	—	1
Boliden	2	—	1	1
BP	2	—	—	2
Chemtura	2	—	—	2
Chiquita	2	—	—	2
DHL and Exel	2	—	—	2
GrafTech International	2	—	—	2
Kemira Oyj	2	1	—	1
Mueller	2	—	—	2
Siemens	2	1	—	1

Source: Marx et al. (2015).

received a 100 percent fine reduction through the leniency program in at least one of the products in which they were prosecuted.[21]

Table 7.1 reflects a concern that has been raised regarding leniency—that it is often the large firms that are the ones applying for leniency, again raising the concern that leniency programs are being exploited.

We review two papers, Choi and Gerlach (2012a) and Marx et al. (2015), that address the potential exploitation of leniency by multi-product colluders.

In the model of Choi and Gerlach (2012a), firms operate in a repeated oligopoly in each of two product markets.[22] For certain parameter values, when the firms engage in collusion in only one product, collusive equilibria may not exist or it may be that the only collusive equilibrium involves both firms applying for leniency whenever the antitrust authority opens an investigation. For such parameter values, a leniency program is effective at deterring collusion or at increasing the probability that a single-product cartel that comes under investigation will be successfully prosecuted and penalized.

However, if firms engage in collusion in multiple products, additional equilibria exist in which a leniency program is less effective. As shown in Choi and Gerlach (2012a, Propositions 2 and 5), equilibria exist in which multi-product firms do not apply for leniency at all if there is an investigation in only one of the products affected by the conspiracy and they only apply for leniency in one product when both products come under investigation. This type of collusive strategy increases the expected per-product profit for the multi-product cartel. For some parameter values, collusive equilibria exist only when firms collude in multiple products and not otherwise. Thus, leniency can provide an incentive for firms to extend collusive conduct to a larger number of products.

Some antitrust leniency programs explicitly link fine reductions across products for multi-product cartels. For example, in the US, under the DOJ's Amnesty Plus program, a firm that is being prosecuted for collusion in one product but that is not the leniency applicant can still potentially receive treatment as if it were the leniency applicant by applying for leniency and thereby turning in another product. According to the DOJ:

> The size of the Amnesty Plus discount depends on a number of factors, including: (1) the strength of the evidence provided by the cooperating company in the leniency product; (2) the potential significance of the violation reported in the leniency application, measured in such terms as the volume of commerce involved, the geographic scope, and the number of co-conspirator companies and individuals; and (3) the likelihood the Division would have uncovered the additional violation absent the self-reporting, i.e., if there were little or no overlap in the corporate participants and/or the culpable executives involved in the original cartel under investigation and the Amnesty Plus matter, then the credit for the disclosure would be greater. Of these three factors, the first two are given the most weight.[23]

Marx et. al. (2015) provide a model of the effects on multi-product colluders of different implementations of an antitrust leniency program by a competition authority. First, they show that an antitrust leniency program that requires convicted firms to attest to whether or not they are colluding in any other product markets can increase leniency applications in the first product investigated but reduce the probability of prosecution in the other products. This linkage can create incentives for firms to extend collusion to sacrificial products or markets. By applying for leniency in products where penalties would be limited, firms may be able to reduce the probability of conviction in more valuable products.

Marx et al. (2015) also study the Amnesty Plus program. They model Amnesty Plus by assuming that each of two firms colluding on a main product has the option to collude with some other firm in a separate, minor, product with limited antitrust liability. In this environment, Amnesty Plus can create both additional incentives for collusion in the main product and incentives for firms to collude in other products. To see why, note that collusion in the minor product gives each firm the ability to obtain reduced fines in the main product should the firm be prosecuted, even if it is not the leniency applicant. In turn, this reduces the incentives for firms to apply for leniency in the main product, which reduces detection and deterrence. As noted in Marx et al. (2015), the negative effect of Amnesty Plus on detection and deterrence occurs because Amnesty Plus reduces the preemption effect. A firm has less incentive to apply for leniency if it can obtain a similar fine reduction through Amnesty Plus in the event that its co-conspirator applies for leniency. A similar reduction in the preemption effect occurs when the competition authority offers fine discounts for cooperating firms other than the first firm to apply for leniency.

In this way, leniency programs that link fine reductions across markets or products can create opportunities for strategic reactions that ultimately result in reduced detection and deterrence. In particular, Amnesty Plus, as well as other cooperation discounts, reduces concerns by colluding firms that they will lose the race to be first to apply for leniency, because these programs allow them to obtain discounts even if they are not first. When conspirators do not have a strong incentive to be first to apply for leniency, it may be that in equilibrium no firm applies at all. In this way, Amnesty Plus and cooperation discounts more generally reduce the incentive of firms to apply for leniency, dampening the effectiveness of a leniency program.

CONCLUSION

There appears to be some flexibility for cartels to negotiate settlement terms that favor them in terms of limiting expected future penalties, for example from civil litigation, in exchange for concessions to competition authority, which may include the amount of criminal fines, the number of individuals receiving prison terms or the total length of prison terms.

Our model suggests that limited criminal pleas, for example in terms of plea length, customers affected or geography, can handicap the ability of civil litigants to pursue damages and hence reduce deterrence. From an empirical research viewpoint, pleas must be viewed as identifying only a subset of the conspiratorial conduct and not as a description of the full extent and exact nature of the conspiracy.

Furthermore, there are ways in which leniency policies can potentially create incentives for colluding firms to engage in collusion in additional products. As shown in Choi and Gerlach (2012a), firms colluding in multiple products may be able to coordinate their strategies across products, thereby insulating one of the products from the threat of leniency applications. Marx et al. (2015) show that the Amnesty Plus program, which provides fine reductions to colluding firms that reveal collusion in other products, also provides incentives for firms to engage in collusion in additional products. Extending collusion to other products provides the benefit of reducing the threat of leniency applications in the original product; colluding firms know they can obtain fine reductions through Amnesty Plus even if they are not the first to apply for leniency.

The results and discussion of this chapter suggest that antitrust enforcement authorities should ensure that incentives for settlement negotiations recognize that deterrence relies on civil as well as criminal penalties and that antitrust enforcement authorities should consider the possibility of strategic abuse of leniency programs—especially the possibilities that arise when collusion in one product affects incentives for leniency applications in another product. The analysis presented here suggests value in additional case studies of cartel conduct, including internal studies conducted by enforcement agencies such as the DOJ. In addition, this analysis points to the need for enforcement agencies to continue to adjust and enhance the tools available to them including, potentially, such changes as encouraging whistleblowers for collusive conduct (see Aubert et al. 2006) or expanding the opportunities and benefits for individual leniency applicants.

ACKNOWLEDGMENTS

We thank Don Klawiter, Bill Kovacic, Chip Miller, George Rozanski, Steve Schulenberg and Wouter Wils for helpful conversations. We thank the participants in the East-West Center and Korea Development Institute project on Competition Law and Economics: Beyond Monopoly Regulation for valuable comments. We thank Gustavo Gudiño and Hoël Wiesner for valuable research assistance. Marshall and Marx thank the Human Capital Foundation (www.hcfoundation.ru/en/), and especially Andrey Vavilov, for financial support. Mezzetti's work was funded in part by Australian Research Council grant DP120102697.

NOTES

1. "Preventing and detecting bid rigging, price fixing, and market allocation in post-disaster rebuilding projects: an antitrust primer for agents and procurement officials," available at www.justice.gov/atr/public/guidelines/disaster_primer.pdf (accessed 31 July 2013).
2. "Price fixing, bid rigging, and market allocation schemes: what they are and what to look for: an antitrust primer," available at www.justice.gov/atr/public/guidelines/211578.pdf (accessed 31 July 2013).
3. United States (US) DOJ website, www.justice.gov/atr/public/criminal/leniency.html (accessed 22 October 2012). In Australia, Chairman of the Australian Competition and Consumer Commission (ACCC) Graeme Samuel stated that the ACCC's Immunity Policy for Cartel Conduct was "absolutely vital" in the Australian government's efforts to crack cartels and he credited it with exposing potential cases at the rate of about one a month (Beaton-Wells and Fisse 2011, 379). See also Beaton-Wells (2008a, b) and Wils (2007).
4. "When calculating the costs and benefits of applying for corporate amnesty, how do you put a price tag on an individual's freedom?" presented at the American Bar Association's Criminal Justice Section's Fifteenth Annual National Institute on White Collar Crime, 8 March 2001, available at www.justice.gov/atr/public/speeches/7647.pdf (accessed 30 October 2012).
5. See Beaton-Wells (2008b) and Wils (2008b).
6. Policies vary in terms of the flexibility for settlement terms. For example, the Australian Director of Public Prosecutions (DPP)'s Prosecution Policy states that the charges should bear a reasonable relationship to the nature of the criminal conduct of the accused.
7. See Marx et al. (2015) and Lefouili and Roux (2012) for discussion and theoretical models of Amnesty Plus. See also Wils (2008a, chapter 5.4.4).
8. DOJ press releases are available at www.justice.gov/atr/public/press_releases/2013/ (accessed 31 July 2013). This emphasis is echoed in the press, with statements such as: "With this win under its belt, including the huge fines and the jail times sought and imposed, expect the DOJ going forward to seek bigger and bigger criminal fines and longer and longer sentences as a deterrent to future global price fixing conspiracies" (www.antitrustlawyerblog.com/2012/09/doj_nets_huge_fines_and_jail_t_1.html, accessed 31 July 2013).
9. Organisation for Economic Co-operation and Development, Working Party No. 3 on Co-operation and Enforcement, 13 October 2006, "Private remedies: class action/collective action; interface between private and public enforcement," summary record of the meeting held on 7 June 2006, at para. 45, DAF/COMP/WP3/M(2006)2/ANN3.
10. See, for example, the European Commission Decision in *Vitamins*, available at http://eur-lex.europa.eu/LexUriServ/LexUriServ.do?uri=OJ:L:2003:006:0001:0089:EN:PDF (accessed 31 July 2013) and the DOJ press release "Two German Firms and Two U.S. Corporations Agree to Plead Guilty to Participating in International Vitamin Cartels," available at www.justice.gov/atr/public/press_releases/2000/4684.htm (accessed 31 July 2013).
11. The Expert Report of B. Douglas Bernheim, MDL No. 1285, In re: Vitamins Antitrust Litigation, Misc. No. 99–0197 (TFH), 24 May 2002, was submitted as exhibit number 243 in In re: Vitamins Antitrust Litigation, case No. 99–0197 (TFH) filed in the District Court of the District of Columbia. We obtained the document through a request to the law clerk of Chief Judge Thomas F. Hogan. The document was made available based on DC Local Civil Rule 79.2 and the United States District Court for the District of Columbia's policy of not retaining exhibits that are admitted into evidence at trial in civil cases.
12. See, for example, the Plea Agreement of Samsung Electronic Company, Ltd., and Samsung Semiconductor, Inc., US District Court, Northern District of California, San Francisco Division, Case No. CR05-0643PJH, 2 (Samsung Plea Agreement).

13. Plea Agreement of Hynix Semiconductor, Inc., US District Court, Northern District of California, San Francisco Division, Case No. CR 05-249 (PJH), 4 (Hynix Plea Agreement).
14. Plea Agreement of Infineon Technologies AG, US District Court, Northern District of California, San Francisco Division, Case No. 04-299 (PJH), 3–4 (Infineon Plea Agreement).
15. Plea Agreement of Elpida Memory, Inc., US District Court, Northern District of California, San Francisco Division, Case No. CR 06-0059 (PJH), 2–3, 4–5 (Elpida Plea Agreement). The Elpida Plea Agreement states: "For purposes of forming and carrying out the conspiracy charged in Count Two of the Information, Defendant's employees had discussions and reached agreements with employees of its coconspirator on how it would allocate and divide a bid offered by Sun Microsystems in an auction on or about March 26, 2002. The Defendant and its coconspirators submitted bid proposals to Sun Microsystems for a bid on a 1 GB NG DIMM lot to achieve that result, including submitting complementary bids to ensure the success of their agreement" (Elpida Plea Agreement, 4–5). However, the Infineon, Hynix and Samsung plea agreements make no mention of the conspiracy having an effect on Sun Microsystems.
16. US International Trade Commission Hearing in the Matter of DRAMs and DRAM Modules from Korea, Investigation No.: 701-TA-431, 32.
17. The threat of prison terms for individuals engaged in collusion also has a deterrent effect. A full analysis of this would require a model of agency issues within firms, the effects of individual versus corporate leniency and the deterrent effects of the threat of prison for white collar criminals, which is beyond the scope of this chapter. Thus, we focus on financial penalties.
18. See U.S.S.G. Section 8C2.5(g)(3).
19. See also Wils (2008a, chapter 5), Chen and Rey (2012), Choi and Gerlach (2012b), Lefouili and Roux (2012), Harrington (2008), Chen and Harrington (2007), Aubert et al. (2006), Buccirossi and Spagnolo (2005, 2006), Spagnolo (2004), Motta and Polo (2003) and Spagnolo (2000). Sokol (2012), Zhou (2012), Miller (2009) and Stephan (2009) contain empirical investigations of leniency; for experimental analyses, see Bigoni et al. (2012a, b) and Hinloopen and Soetevent (2008).
20. For example, the Organic Peroxides Cartel hired a consulting firm, AC Treuhand, that maintained certain cartel documents in Switzerland: "AC Treuhand produced, distributed and recollected the so called 'pink' and 'red' papers with the agreed market shares which were, because of their colour, easily distinguishable from other meeting documents and were not allowed to be taken outside the AC Treuhand premises" (EC Decision in *Organic Peroxides* at para. 92(b)).
21. Some EC decisions apply to more than one product. For example, the EC decision in *Vitamins* covers multiple vitamin products, with a separate application of the leniency program for each product.
22. See Choi and Gerlach (2012b) on the effects on multi-product cartels of demand linkages among products.
23. The US DOJ's *Frequently Asked Questions Regarding the Antitrust Division's Leniency Program and Model Leniency Letters* (2008, 9; available at www.justice.gov/atr/public/criminal/239583.htm, accessed 23 October 2012).

REFERENCES

Aubert, Cécile, Patrick Rey and William E. Kovacic (2006), "The impact of leniency and whistle-blowing programs on cartels," *International Journal of Industrial Organization* **24**(6), 1241–66.
Beaton-Wells, Caron (2008a), "Forks in the road: challenges facing the ACCC's

immunity policy for cartel conduct: part 1," *Competition & Consumer Law Journal* **16**, 71–113.

Beaton-Wells, Caron (2008b), "Forks in the road: challenges facing the ACCC's immunity policy for cartel conduct: part 2," *Competition & Consumer Law Journal* **16**, 246–85.

Beaton-Wells, Caron and Brent Fisse (2011), *Australian Cartel Regulation: Law, Policy and Practice in an International Context*, Cambridge, UK: Cambridge University Press.

Bernheim, B. Douglas (2002), The Expert Report of B. Douglas Bernheim, MDL No. 1285, submitted as exhibit number 243 in re: Vitamins Antitrust Litigation, case No. 99-0197 (TFH) filed in the District Court of the District of Columbia.

Bigoni, Maria, Sven-Olof Fridolisson, Chloé Le Coq and Giancarlo Spagnolo (2012a), "Fines, leniency, and rewards in antitrust," *RAND Journal of Economics* **43**(2), 368–90.

Bigoni, Maria, Sven-Olof Fridolisson, Chloé Le Coq and Giancarlo Spagnolo (2012b), "Trust, leniency and deterrence: evidence from an antitrust experiment," unpublished working paper, University of Bologna.

Buccirossi, Paolo and Giancarlo Spagnolo (2005), "Optimal fines in the era of whistleblowers: should price fixers still go to prison?" Lear Research Paper No. 05-01.

Buccirossi, Paolo and Giancarlo Spagnolo (2006), "Leniency policies and illegal transactions," *Journal of Public Economics* **90**, 1281–97.

Chen, Joe and Joseph E. Harrington, Jr. (2007), "The impact of the corporate leniency program on cartel formation and the cartel price path," in Vivek Ghosal and Johan Stennek (eds), *The Political Economy of Antitrust*, New York: Elsevier, pp. 59–80.

Chen, Zhijun and Patrick Rey (2012), "On the design of leniency programs," unpublished working paper, University of Auckland.

Choi, Jay Pil and Heiko Gerlach (2012a), "Global cartels, leniency programs and international antitrust cooperation," *International Journal of Industrial Organization* **30**(6), 528–40.

Choi, Jay Pil and Heiko Gerlach (2012b), "Multi-market collusion with demand linkages and antitrust enforcement," unpublished working paper, University of New South Wales.

Harrington, Joseph E., Jr. (2008), "Optimal corporate leniency programs," *Journal of Industrial Economics* **56**, 215–46.

Hinloopen, Jeroen and Adriaan R. Soetevent (2008), "Laboratory evidence on the effectiveness of corporate leniency programs," *RAND Journal of Economics* **39**, 607–16.

Lefouili, Yassine and Catherine Roux (2012), "Leniency programs for multimarket firms: the effect of amnesty plus on cartel formation," *International Journal of Industrial Organization* **30**, 624–40.

Marshall, Robert C., Leslie M. Marx and Matthew E. Raiff (2008), "Cartel price announcements: the vitamins industry," *International Journal of Industrial Organization* **26**, 762–802.

Marx, Leslie M., Claudio Mezzetti and Robert C. Marshall (2015), "Antitrust leniency with multi-product colluders," *American Economic Journal: Microeconomics* **7**(3), 205–40.

Miller, Nathan H. (2009), "Strategic leniency and cartel enforcement," *American Economic Review* **99**(3), 750–68.

Motta, Massimo and Michele Polo (2003), "Leniency programs and cartel prosecution," *Journal of Industrial Organization* **21**, 347–79.

Rey, Patrick (2003), "Towards a theory of competition policy," in M. Dewatripont, L.P. Hansen and S.J. Turnovsky (eds), *Advances in Economics and Econometrics: Theory and Applications*, Cambridge, UK: Cambridge University Press, pp. 82–132.

Sokol, Daniel D. (2012), "Cartels, corporate compliance and what practitioners really think about enforcement," *Antitrust Law Journal* **78**, 201–40.

Spagnolo, Giancarlo (2000), "Self-defeating antitrust laws: how leniency programs solve Bertrand's paradox and enforce collusion in auctions," *FEEM Working Paper 52.00*, Milano, Italy: Fondazione Eni Enrico Mattei.

Spagnolo, Giancarlo (2004), "Divide et impera: optimal leniency programs," *CEPR Discussion Paper 4840*, London: Centre for Economic Policy Research.

Spagnolo, Giancarlo (2008), "Leniency and whistleblowers in antitrust," ch. 7 of P. Buccirossi (ed.), *Handbook of Antitrust Economics*, Cambridge, MA: MIT Press.

Stephan, Andreas (2009), "An empirical assessment of the European leniency notice," *Journal of Competition Law & Economics* **5**, 537–61.

Wils, Wouter P.J. (2007), "Leniency in antitrust enforcement: theory and practice," *World Competition* **30**(1), 25–64.

Wils, Wouter P.J. (2008a), *Efficiency and Justice in European Antitrust Enforcement*, Portland, OR: Hart Publishing.

Wils, Wouter P.J. (2008b), "The use of settlements in public antitrust enforcement: objectives and principles," *World Competition* **31**(3), 335–52.

Zhou, Jun (2012), "Evaluating leniency with missing information on undetected cartels: exploring time-varying policy impacts on cartel duration," unpublished working paper, Bonn University.

PART V

Vertical restraints

8. Competition policy and the economics of vertical restraints

Ralph A. Winter

INTRODUCTION

Competition policy regulates firms' decisions or conduct in three main areas: mergers, cartels and single-firm decisions. The basis for regulating mergers and certainly the basis for prohibiting cartels are well understood. High levels of concentration brought about by a merger can lessen competition to the detriment of consumers—and cartels are obviously anticompetitive.

In contrast, competition policy towards single-firm decisions, especially the adoption of vertical restraints, is an area of much disagreement.[1] Vertical restraints are restrictions placed on retailer or distributor decisions in contracts entered between retailers and upstream manufacturers. Vertical restraints constrain prices that retailers set, territories into which retailers sell, the products that retailers sell and in general restrict the ways in which retailers can compete. A traditional view is that restrictions on retailer competition are anticompetitive almost by definition. Others argue that there is little or no basis for regulating vertical agreements.

The interventionist side of this debate traditionally had more influence on policy. Competition law has a long history of placing limits on the use of vertical restraints in manufacturer–retailer contracts. As economics has become more influential, however, the law in this area has changed. In the US, vertical restraints on territories have been essentially legal since *Sylvania*;[2] vertical price ceilings have been legal since *State Oil v. Khan*;[3] and the century-old *per se* rule against vertical price floors (resale price maintenance, RPM) was replaced by a "rule of reason" approach in *Leegin*.[4] The trend in this law in the US is having influence internationally. In South Korea, for example, maximum price restraints have been treated under a rule of reason in the sense that they are permitted "if reasonably justified" (Article 29(1) of the *Monopoly Regulation and Fair Trade Act* [MRFTA]). This law reflects the same understanding of the economic benefits of vertical price ceilings that motivated the change in the US law with *State Oil v. Khan* overturning *Albrecht v. Herald*[5] in 1997. The MRFTA prohibits the implementation of minimum RPM without mention of possible benefits of the practice. The Korean Supreme Court decided, in a recent case, however, that minimum RPM can be justified in certain circumstances—although that decision ruled against the use of RPM in the particular case.[6]

This chapter reviews the economic foundations of competition policy towards vertical restraints, arguing for the potential of still-greater movement in the law on vertical restraints towards strong economic foundations.

A complete analysis of vertical restraints would arrive at an optimal policy towards each restraint under a range of market structures and market conditions. I do not offer a complete delineation of optimal competition policy in this short chapter. Instead, with the perspective offered by the most basic principle of competition policy, I offer a high-level overview of optimal policy towards vertical restraints. This principle is that agreements among producers of complementary products and services—for example, vertically linked suppliers—should be *prima facie* legal. Antitrust scrutiny of vertical agreements should be focused on the extent to which the agreements have horizontal effects in competition among substitute producers. A necessary condition for the legal prohibition of a vertical restraint should be that the restraint reduce interbrand competition by facilitating collusive pricing or that the restraint facilitate the exclusion of entry into upstream manufacturing or the exclusion of low-cost entrants into the downstream retailing sector.

On the one hand, where a manufacturer adopts vertical restraints in order to increase profit without regard to the lessening of competition with other manufacturers, the practice should be allowed. On the other hand, where evidence indicates that manufacturers are employing RPM to facilitate a cartel, it should not be allowed. Nor should it be allowed where a manufacturer lessens competition by using a vertical restraint to exclude a rival from a market or when a retailer cartel imposes the obligation to enforce minimum resale prices across a set of manufacturers in order to exclude a class of retailers such as discount retailers.

Specifically, economic theory supports the following conditions as necessary for striking down an RPM agreement by a supplier. The agreement must:

- reduce interbrand competition by supporting a manufacturer cartel
- facilitate exclusion of a rival manufacturer by a dominant manufacturer or cartel of manufacturers

- along with RPM agreements by other suppliers, support high prices across products, coordinated by a cartel at the (multi-product) retail level
- be imposed, at the behest of a retailer cartel, to facilitate exclusion of discount retailers.

The principle that law should not intervene in supply-chain contracts without evidence that contracts have lessened interbrand competition sounds very simple, and I think reasonable, to most economists. But, even after the influence that economics has had to date, existing law is far from consistent with this principle. And policy discussion is often at odds with this principle. I critique below a set of arguments from policy discussions and legal rulings that represent alternative views.

I discuss briefly the roles of vertical restraints using cases including one involving cookware in the US. This case may be particularly interesting for a study co-sponsored by the Korea Development Institute because the South Korean MRFTA recently struck down the use of RPM by a cookware manufacturer.[7]

I start, in "Background: Vertical Restraints in Practice," with a review of the types of vertical restraints that we see in practice. Then, focusing on RPM, I offer a brief review of the economic theories of the restraint. These divide into theories under which the practice can lessen interbrand competition and theories of incentives for RPM by a single manufacturer.

BACKGROUND: VERTICAL RESTRAINTS IN PRACTICE

In the simplest of all supply-chain contracts, the seller sets a price and buyers choose quantities to purchase at the posted price. A manufacturer sells to any distributor or retailer wanting to purchase its product. No restrictions are placed on distributor pricing, territories, the other products that could be offered by distributors or on customers to whom the distributor can sell. The entire property rights to the product are transferred with the exchange of units of the product and it is up to the distributor of the product to decide on how and where to resell the product.

In reality, contracts struck by firms along a supply chain, from the providers of raw materials down to retailers selling to consumers, are more complex. Prices remain the principal means by which incentives are aligned along a supply chain, but we also observe more complex contract terms. The following types of payment terms are among those adopted in real-world contracts:

- general "non-linear pricing schedules," including quantity discounts, block pricing, two-part pricing, minimum-quantity contracts and take-or-pay contracts
- "royalty contracts," in which payment depends on quantity of a product resold by a downstream retailer, not the quantity purchased by the retailer
- "loyalty contracts," in which (in one form) the buyer's payment for an input depends on the proportion of the buyer's needs that are met by the input
- "slotting allowances," which are fixed payments by a manufacturer for the right to be represented in a retail outlet and which may include the rights to a specified amount of shelf space or floor space
- "buyback options" under which the retailer can return unsold inventory
- "consignment selling" arrangements.

We also see contracts that impose restraints on buyers' actions:

- "price floors" or "price ceilings" imposed on retailers of a product (RPM)
- "territorial restrictions" on where a dealer may sell, where a dealer may actively sell, or where a dealer may locate; territorial restrictions may also be placed on the upstream firm, such as a franchisor, in the location of future outlets
- "exclusivity clauses," either constraining the downstream buyer not to purchase from other suppliers or constraining the supplier not to deal with other outlets
- "tying restrictions," either in the form of "bundling" products for which separate markets could be or are established, or "requirements tying," which stipulates that the buyer must purchase all of its requirements of an input B from the seller if the buyer is to purchase input A from the seller.

As an empirical matter, vertical restraints are common and arise in many settings where market power is minimal. Evidence on the frequency of vertical restraints is available primarily for RPM, the most popular restraint during the times when it has been legal. Vertical price floors have been imposed on retailers of a wide cross-section of products: clothing, skis and other sports equipment, watches, jewelry, luxury goods of all kinds, candy, beer, bread, floor wax, furniture polish, milk, toilet paper, cereal, canned soup, books, shoes, mattresses, large appliances and automobiles, to name a few (Overstreet 1983; Ippolito 1988). Products in virtually every category have been subject to RPM at one time or another and estimates of the proportion of retail sales that have been subject to RPM range as high as 25 percent in the United Kingdom and 4 percent to 10 percent in the US (Scherer and Ross 1990, 549). In Canada, before the law prohibiting RPM was enacted in 1951, an estimated 20 percent of goods sold through grocery stores and 60 percent sold through drugstores were "fair-traded" (Overstreet 1983, 153, 155).

Information is also available on the extent of exclusivity. Of retail sales through independent retailers, more than one-third was found to be subject to some form of exclusive dealing in a recent study (Lafontaine and Slade 2005, citing a 1988 US Department of Commerce Study). Some exclusivity restraints are clearly efficient and would attract no attention from antitrust law. A McDonalds franchisee must sell exclusively McDonalds' hamburgers as opposed to Wendy's or Burger King's products. Any luxury jewelry retailer is restrained against placing cheap watches for sale in its store. Finally, tying, defined broadly, is ubiquitous. Shoelaces are sold with shoes. Gloves and shoes are sold in pairs. Cars are sold with tires. Tying presents potential anticompetitive concerns in only a very small percentage of cases where it is observed.

In the analysis below, I focus on vertical price restraints—specifically RPM, because this area has been by far the most important in the law. I then extend the discussion to vertical restraints in general.

THE ECONOMIC THEORIES OF RPM

Vertical price ceilings can be explained, in the simplest framework, as a response to the "double marginalization problem" (Spengler 1950). A downstream retailer of a single product, if facing little competition from other retailers of the same product, will set a price that is higher than the price that would maximize the combined profit of the retailer and the upstream manufacturer. The retailer marks the price up from the wholesale price rather than the "true" marginal cost because in setting the price it ignores the flow of profits to the upstream manufacturer through the wholesale margin. The simple price-only contract thus fails to achieve the privately efficient retailer pricing decision. A price ceiling imposed on the retailer resolves the problem and the lower price benefits consumers as well. Vertical price ceilings are not controversial as a matter of economics and, with the *State Oil* decision, this vertical restraint is effectively *per se* legal in the US.

Vertical price floors are controversial. Any agreement to set a floor on prices is, at first blush, anticompetitive simply because it prevents firms from competing by lowering prices. Vertical price floors were *per se* illegal in the US, as a conspiracy to raise prices, following *Dr. Miles Medical Co.*[8] in 1911. Section 2 of the US Sherman Act does not distinguish horizontal conspiracies from vertical conspiracies or agreements. However, if price were the only determinant of demand, a manufacturer acting alone would not want to see higher retail prices for its product. At any given wholesale price, any manufacturer gains from greater demand and therefore from lower retail prices, *ceteris paribus*. The observation of RPM, if a manufacturer is acting alone, means that *ceteris* are not *paribus*: the higher price means the elicitation of some other retailer decision affecting demand. Alternatively, the practice may be anticompetitive if it leads to higher prices across products. I review below the single-manufacturer theories of RPM and the anticompetitive theories.

RPM by a Single Manufacturer

An overview of the economic theories of RPM starts with two simple observations. First, retailers do more than set prices. Retailers offer convenience, specifically a low time cost of purchasing, by providing staff, well-organized inventory, clear information and even short cashier lines. Retailers invest in enthusiastic staff and sales efforts in providing accurate and complete point-of-sale information. Retailers choose the level of post-sale service of items that may need repair as well as return policies (not just the specific written return policies but the general sense of either willingness or reluctance that they exhibit in accepting returns). Retail activity is multi-dimensional, with prices being only one component of the set of decisions. Consumers purchasing a specific product end up with the same physical product wherever they shop—but the surplus gained from purchasing depends upon their entire retail purchase experience. This is especially true for luxury or fashion items where the consumer value is particularly sensitive to product image. Expensive perfume purchased from Walmart or Carrefour is simply not the same "product" as an identical bottle of chemicals purchased from a luxurious perfume counter in an up-market outlet with classical music playing in the background. Retailers add value to the final product purchased by consumers, whether by saving consumers' time on the purchase of a routine item or by investing in the enhancement of their customers' shopping experience.

The second observation is that consumers are heterogeneous in their preferences for convenience versus lower prices. Some care more about convenience than low prices, some less. And the consumers who care the most about convenience—busy consumers with high opportunity costs of time—are least likely to spend time searching among stores.

Given these two observations or assumptions, we have two propositions. First, a simple price contract may leave retailers with inadequate incentives to provide sales effort in its various dimensions. Second, contracts with vertical restraints can restore, or at least enhance, these incentives.

We begin by developing the first proposition: explaining why the price system alone may fail to coordinate incentives along a supply chain by leaving retailers with inadequate incentives to exert the level of sales effort that would be specified in a hypothetical, ideal, "complete" contract that restricted all of the actions of the retailers. This is the issue of market failure in the Williamsonian (Williamson 1983) sense. The failure of the price system to coordinate incentives, that is, to maximize the combined wealth of firms along the supply chain, opens up the potential for more complex contracts.

We restrict the discussion for the moment to one dimension of sales effort, that is, demand-enhancing activity, and measure investment in this activity in dollars.[9] Consider a manufacturer selling through a set of retailers that, for simplicity, adopt the same price and effort decisions in a symmetric retail equilibrium whatever the wholesale price set by the manufacturer. We denote the price and sales effort by p and e, respectively, and the wholesale price by w. The demand in the market, at a symmetric retail market equilibrium, is denoted by $Q(p,e)$. Finally, we denote the elasticity of demand with respect to price by ε_p and the demand elasticity with respect to sales effort by ε_e.

The price and sales effort that would be set in an ideal, complete contract are at the levels, denoted by (p^*, e^*), that would maximize the combined profit of all parties to the contract, that is, to the manufacturer and to the retailers.[10] In the setting in which a manufacturer has a fixed fee to collect profits from retailers, the wholesale price is freed from its role in collecting profits and is available to use as an instrument to elicit optimal decisions on the part of retailers—as in Mathewson and Winter (1984). The question is whether the single instrument, w, is enough to elicit the decisions (p^*, e^*). That is, as w is raised from marginal cost to the level w^* that elicits p^*, will the retailers offer the optimal sales effort, e^*, or some effort level below or above e^*? And if the optimum is not achieved, that is, there is a Williamsonian market failure, what are the sources of this market failure? As w is raised, p goes up, but (under normal assumptions) the retail margin, $(p - w)$, will fall. The retail margin represents the marginal benefit that a retailer obtains from attracting one more unit of demand through sales effort, so the incentive to provide effort drops as w is raised.

In addressing the market-failure question, a very useful result is the Dorfman–Steiner theorem (Dorfman and Steiner 1954). Dorfman and

Steiner considered a firm, facing demand $Q(p, e)$, that depends on price and sales effort (effort being, in their discussion, advertising or product quality). They showed that the firm will optimally devote a proportion of revenue to sales effort that is given by the ratio of the two elasticities of demand:

$$(\text{Dorfman}-\text{Steiner}) \qquad e / pQ = \varepsilon_e / \varepsilon_p \qquad (8.1)$$

In our context, the theorem describes the efficient (collective profit-maximizing) effort decision as determined in the hypothetical complete contract. But we can also use (8.1) to characterize the choice of effort and price by a single retailer, within a simple wholesale price contract, in exactly the same way—substituting the retailer's elasticities for the market elasticities in the right-hand side of (8.1). Thus the market-failure question reduces to the following: why would the ratio of advertising elasticity to price elasticity differ for an individual retailer than for the market as a whole?[11] The right-hand side of (8.1) is equal to the marginal rate of substitution between effort and price for the firm making the decision; the market-failure question is then why the marginal rate of substitution between prices and sales effort differs between an individual retailer and the market as a whole.

Our second proposition is that vertical restraint contracts can resolve the market failure or incentive distortions in retailers' decisions on prices and other demand-enhancing activities. This proposition can also be posed within the Dorfman–Steiner framework before we proceed to addressing the questions. When the ratio $\varepsilon_e / \varepsilon_p$ is smaller for the individual retailer than it is for the market as a whole (evaluated at the first best p and e), retailers are "biased" at the margin towards prices that are too low and effort levels that are too low. Retailers rely excessively (from the perspective of private efficiency) on attracting customers through low prices rather than high sales effort. In this case, to start with the most important vertical restraint, two different roles for vertical price floors arise. If the manufacturer maintains a price floor at p^* and lowers the wholesale price w, it is increasing the incentive to provide effort (since the marginal benefit of attracting demand, the retail margin, is expanding). It can do so until e^* is achieved. The price floor influences directly the incentives to exert sales effort under this mechanism. A second role for price floors arises when the manufacturer can implicitly contract for effort (for example, maintaining a sufficiently high level of freshness of the product or adequate servicing), but only at the cost of periodic monitoring of the level of effort. A price floor can act to protect retail profits against erosion from intensive price competition. Under this indirect mechanism, incentives for providing effort are improved because a retailer has more to lose in the event that it is caught shirking on effort (Klein and Murphy 1988).[12]

The economic explanation of why a manufacturer would benefit from imposing RPM in the form of a vertical price *floor* thus reduces to asking why retailer demand is relatively more sensitive to price, relative to sales effort, compared with market demand as a whole. We express this condition for the profitability of RPM below:

$$\varepsilon_e / \varepsilon_p \text{ (for retailer)} < \varepsilon_e / \varepsilon_p \text{ (for market)} \qquad (8.2)$$

We can now return to the question of why retailer incentives deviate from market incentives and apply the framework to explaining observed contracts. We offer, within the framework, five theories of the incentive for RPM, although many other theories are available. The first is a "correlation argument." Suppose that consumers most willing to shop among retail outlets for their preferred combination of price and sales effort are also those consumers for whom price matters relatively more than sales effort. This is a natural assumption because sales effort often reduces the time cost of purchasing; consumers end up with the same physical product wherever they purchase but at lower time cost when greater sales effort takes the form of shorter cashier lines and more highly trained sales staff and so on. Consumers willing to travel to shop at different stores are those with low costs of time and these consumers are also willing to tolerate long cashier lines in favor of lower prices. This structure yields individual-retailer demand that is relatively price elastic, with the inequality (8.2) being met. In other words, the consumers that a retailer attracts away from other retailers are relatively more influenced by low prices than by high sales effort. Retailers set their sales strategy to attract consumers not just into the market but, also, away from other retailers. Attracting consumers away from other retailers involves setting low prices, since this is what attracts shoppers, but it is a pure waste from the perspective of total market demand. The demand attracted away from other retailers does not increase demand for the product at all. Retailers are therefore biased in their strategies towards low prices and inadequate service. RPM counters this inefficiency, altering incentives towards higher sales effort and constraining prices against falling (Winter 1993).

A second theory is that retailer effort towards product promotion and greater product awareness may influence demand upwards in other outlets. Even prominent displays of a product on the store floor or in shop windows raises consumer awareness of the product and makes them more likely to purchase the product not just from the outlet undertaking the sales effort but from other outlets as well (if the consumer happens to find another outlet most convenient when the need for the product arises). This is particularly true if a retailer's decision to display (or simply carry) a product conveys information about the quality of the product (Marvel and McCafferty 1984). If even only some potential consumers of other outlets are affected this way, the market demand for the product is relatively more sensitive to sales effort as opposed to price than the individual retailer demand, that is, (8.2) is satisfied. RPM again counters the distortion in incentives.

The third theory is similar. The quality of a product—such as a photo-copier, an appliance or an automobile—may depend not only on the quality decisions of the manufacturer but also on the quality of post-sales service or installation by the dealer. If the consumer cannot perfectly distinguish between a failure of quality as between the dealer and the product itself, greater efforts by the dealer towards quality enhance the reputation not just of the dealer but of the product itself. Again, the market demand will be relatively more sensitive to the effort expended by the dealer (relative to price) than the dealer's own demand is. The condition (8.2) for the profitability of RPM is met.

A fourth theory is the classic "free-riding" story (Telser 1960). Suppose that stereo equipment requires detailed information and a listening-room experience for a consumer to decide which model of amplifier or speakers best fits her needs. Outlets provide this information. A new stereo store could open up selling equipment in boxes with very low prices but no information provided at the point of sale. Consumers could avail themselves of the information provided by the informing stores, which charge higher prices to cover the cost of the information provided, then make their purchases at the low-priced store. Demand for the product as a whole will suffer from this type of free-riding. RPM restores demand by preventing this kind of free-riding. Without the ability to attract consumers on the basis of low prices alone, outlets must provide the entire package of information and competitive prices.[13]

The free-riding story is far stronger than is necessary to explain RPM, as Klein (2009), Winter (1993) and a number of other authors have argued. Our framework makes this very clear. The free-riding story involves a positive impact of service by one retailer (the informing retailer) on the demand faced by another (the free-riding retailer). This is a positive cross-elasticity. This is sufficient for (8.2), but all that is necessary for the condition for RPM to be profitable is that demand cross-elasticity be relatively less sensitive for sales than it is for price. To generate an incentive for RPM by an individual manufacturer, it is not necessary that the sales cross-elasticity be positive (as it is in the classic free-riding story: greater information by the informing store increases demand at the free-riding store). That is, it is not necessary that some (non-informing) stores benefit from the sales effort supplied by other stores. If the sales cross-elasticity is negative but relatively low, RPM is profitable.

The theories of RPM that I have summarized are based on the lemma that, in the simplest of models, condition (8.2) is necessary and sufficient for the incentive for contractual price floors. In Winter (1993), this lemma is derived in a simple model from first principles rather than from reference to the Dorfman–Steiner theorem. For a fifth, and particularly important, theory of the incentive for RPM, it is helpful to review these principles. In any theory of contracts, a distortion in an agent's (retailer's) decision arises from externalities imposed by the decision on other participants in the contract or organization. An agent's decision to increase price by a dollar exerts a negative externality, in proportion to the wholesale margin, on the upstream supplier. It exerts an offsetting, positive, externality on competing retailers, since a higher price increases demand at competing retailers. The same two externalities flow from the retailer's decision on effort. A price system alone can elicit optimal retailer incentives only if there exists a wholesale price at which both the two externalities on price, and the two externalities on effort, are exactly offsetting. Consistent with the Dorfman–Steiner perspective, this yields, as a necessary condition for the success of the price system (without vertical restraints), that (8.2) hold with an equality instead of an inequality.

The fifth theory concerns demand uncertainty and the incentives for retailers to order adequate levels of inventory when retailers compete for final demand. I follow Krishnan and Winter (2007); Deneckere et al. (1996) were the first to show that the price system alone fails to convey adequate incentives for inventory investment by competitive retailers. Consider a market in which two retailers order inventory from a single manufacturer at a wholesale price, **w**, prior to the realization of uncertain demand. Demand is not perfectly correlated across retailers. If one retailer ends up with excessive demand, demand may spill over to the other retailer. The product is perishable, as in the classic "newsvendor" model of inventory.

In this type of model, there are "horizontal" externalities between the two retailers, positive for raising price and negative for raising inventory. There is a positive "vertical" inventory externality in that one more unit ordered increases the manufacturer's profit. But there is no vertical price externality: once inventory has been ordered, the prices set by the retailers are a matter of indifference to the manufacturer. As a result, externalities cannot balance under any wholesale price. Only the horizontal externality impacts price at the margin—and this externality causes prices to be too low.

The implication of this "missing externality theory" is that, in the absence of price restraints, retailers are biased towards decisions that involve too little inventory relative to the collective profit-maximizing decisions. RPM restores the first-best private optimum by protecting the retail margin and thus encouraging the order of additional inventory: when a price floor is set at p^*, the profit-maximizing price, the manufacturer can lower the wholesale price until the retail margin is high enough to elicit the optimal inventory decisions.

The implication of this theory, and the theory developed by Deneckere et al. (1996), is that the price system alone is fundamentally unable to elicit adequate inventory decisions. A vertical price floor will raise inventory levels, raise the expected volume of transactions and generally raise welfare.

RPM and inventory incentives: case evidence

Case studies provide direct evidence of the role of RPM in correcting distortions in inventory incentives. The "fair trade" state laws that allowed RPM were repealed in the early 1970s, allowing economists to study the impact of a sudden elimination of RPM from the feasible set of contracts. Anthony P. Hourihan and Jesse W. Markham (1974) conducted case studies of nine manufacturing companies that had been using the restraint. In five of the nine cases studied, prices were unaffected, consistent with the price restraint not binding retailer decisions. In three of the four cases where retail prices did decline, the availability of the product to consumers dropped because of a drop in inventory, a drop in the selection of items to carry within the product line and, in two cases, a drop in the number of outlets carrying the product. The products carried by the firms with decreases in inventory were house wares and tableware, both of which are products with a strong seasonal demand, so our assumptions of demand uncertainty and perishability are plausible. In other cases as well, the termination of RPM led to fewer outlets, to the detriment of the manufacturer.

Corning Glass Works used RPM from 1937 until it was prevented from doing so in a case brought by the FTC in 1975. Ippolito and Overstreet (1996) analyse this case in depth and conclude that the theories of RPM as anticompetitive are "convincingly rejected" by the evidence. The theory that Ippolito and Overstreet highlight as most consistent with the evidence is the "outlets" hypothesis, which is that, by encouraging more outlets to carry the product, RPM adds to the demand of a product. The outlets hypothesis is a special case of the inventory hypothesis, that RPM adds efficiently to the incentive for outlets to stock adequate inventory. In interviews ten years after the case, for example, Corning executives indicated that one of the most important effects of the case was the loss of many of its smaller outlets.

In another example, after legislation had ended an earlier era of fair trade pricing, the number of dealers selling Schick shavers fell from 35,000 to 7,000 in one year; P.W.S. Andrews and Frank A. Friday (1960) suggest a causal connection between the prohibition of RPM and this extraordinary drop in outlets.

Theories of RPM as Anticompetitive

RPM can serve to facilitate an upstream cartel among manufacturers. Coordinating wholesale prices would be difficult for members of an upstream cartel because these prices are not posted and may be part of more complicated contracts. Coordinating an upstream cartel via the monitoring of retail prices without vertical restraints would also be difficult because of the variation or "noise" that enters the relationship between a wholesale price and the set of retail prices charged in different locations. Retail price floors allow upstream cartel members to agree on prices and to monitor prices. Telser (1960) used this theory to explain the adoption of RPM by General Electric and Westinghouse in the market for large lamps. Jullien and Rey (2007) formalize this argument.

RPM can also be used to support a downstream retail cartel. When retailers sell multiple products and collectively require that all manufacturers in a product market engage in RPM, the retailer cartel can effectively implement cartel pricing across products. This explanation is of some historical importance in explaining, for example, the success, in North America, of traditional drug stores in delaying the development of discount drug stores (Overstreet 1983, 143).[14, 15]

The US Supreme Court, in *Leegin*, discussed a third potential anticompetitive theory of RPM: that the practice results in exclusion at the retail level. A manufacturer can use RPM to protect rents at the retail level, as in the Klein–Murphy theory, but the retailer "performance" that is contingent upon continued receipt of the rents is not provision of adequate service but rather agreeing to refrain from carrying the products of a new entrant. A dominant firm or small set of collectively dominant firms can thus protect their dominant position against entry by sharing the rents from the dominance with retailers. Retailers know that, once entry is allowed, rents will be much reduced in the market and, as agents who share in these rents, retailers will suffer. John Asker and Heski Bar-Isaac (2014) offer a thorough analysis of this theory.[16] The theory of RPM as exclusionary requires that there be a small number of distributors, as in the case of the American Sugar Refining Company discussed by Asker and Bar-Isaac (2014; see also Zerbe 1969; Marvel and McCafferty 1984). With many retailers, it is unlikely that a new entrant could not gain toehold entry by sharing profits from entry with one or a small number of retailers.

Empirical tests of the impact of RPM

A number of studies have attempted to distinguish anticompetitive theories of RPM from theories applicable to a single manufacturer or to study the impact of the practice on prices. These studies are reviewed in Marvel and McCafferty (1984), McKay and Smith (2016) and extensively in Overstreet (1983). Some of the studies take advantage of the differing laws on RPM across states to study the impact of RPM. The *per se* illegality of RPM following *Dr. Miles Medical Co.* (1911) applied to interstate commerce, but, beginning with California in 1933, a number of states adopted "fair-trade laws" that applied to intrastate commerce. These laws permitted RPM for some transactions. In 1937, the Miller–Tydings Act allowed states to legalize RPM even for interstate commerce within their border.[17] The Miller–Tydings and McGuire acts were repealed in 1975.

Comparison of prices between nearby markets with different RPM laws allowed estimates of the impact of RPM. As discussed in Overstreet (1983) and Marvel and McCafferty (1984), drug price comparisons found prices at stores in the same chain to be 23 percent higher in fair-trade Kansas City, Kansas, than across the river in no-RPM Missouri. Price differentials for appliances between Baltimore and free-trade Washington, DC, were even greater.

A positive impact of RPM on prices is consistent with both the single-manufacturer and anticompetitive theories of RPM. Attempts at testing between these two classes of theories have been based on the impact of the practice on quantities. Shepard (1978) found that the repeal in 1975 of state laws banning RPM in the US led to decreased sales. McKay and Smith (2016) undertakes an in-depth analysis of the impact of RPM.

Following the *Leegin* decision in the US, RPM is no longer *per se* illegal. But state-level laws in some states continue to prohibit the practice, whereas in other states the rule of reason applies. Newspaper articles suggest that RPM has increased in many product areas, including (as listed by McKay and Smith [2016]), childcare and maternity wear, light fixtures and home accessories, pet food and supplies, and rental cars. McKay and Smith use a difference-in-difference estimation technique to identify the impact of RPM by comparing the change in prices in a *control group*, consisting of those states in which RPM is not allowed, with the change in those in a *treatment group* of states in which RPM is allowed.[18] This study found a small impact on prices overall, with an average of 1.6 percent increase across product departments (with a **t** value of 2.42 percent). The test results were suggestive of a drop in quantity, though the levels were low. The average percentage of quantity change, that is, the economic significance of the estimated impact, is not reported.[19] Lambert and Sykuta (2013), however, set out a persuasive critique of McKay and Smith's study.

The McKay–Smith study does not examine particular cases or examples of RPM but rather the impact of differences in legal environments towards RPM. To prove anticompetitive harm from an RPM-permissive legal environment, one would have to show that the transition to the permissive environment (with the *Leegin* decision) lead to a significant price increase and a significant output decrease for the same product—and for a significant number of products. As Lambert and Sykuta point out, only 1.6 percent of the product categories examined by McKay and Smith showed both a price increase and quantity decrease; for individual products, the percentage may have been even lower.

In an important study, Pauline Ippolito (1991) investigated all 203 reported US RPM cases between 1975 and 1982, the period during which US antitrust law treated RPM most harshly. Ippolito assumed that, if the plaintiff in any case had evidence that RPM was supporting collusion, one would see horizontal price-fixing allegations as well as the allegation of RPM. Allegations of collusion appeared in only 13 percent of the sample of cases, suggesting that the collusion theories of RPM were less important than service and sales-enhancing theories. Ippolito's study did not, however, deal with the single-firm exclusion theories. And since RPM was *per se* illegal over the 1975–82 period, allegations of collusion may not have been necessary for the plaintiff to prevail even if collusion incentives were significant, thus understating the importance of collusion.

THE IMPLICATIONS FOR POLICY

Optimal Policy towards RPM

The economic theories support a competition policy towards RPM that allows the practice except if there is evidence that it (1) facilitates cartel interbrand pricing, (2) is the consequence of coordinated retailer pressure (for example, to exclude discounters) or (3) facilitates exclusion of entry by another brand. The burden of proof in placing restrictions on the use of RPM should rest on the side of intervention. Market conditions must be consistent with the existence of a cartel or exclusionary incentive in order for those theories to be entertained.

This hardly sounds like a profound conclusion to an economist. Collusion and exclusion are the two kinds of anticompetitive activity. That a practice should be legal unless evidence suggests either collusion or exclusion at a high level seems like an obvious conclusion. But the proposed approach differs in some respects from both existing law and many policy discussions. I discuss the differences below.

RPM Policy Fallacies

A sensible law would allow RPM when it is efficient but not when it is inefficient; the use of RPM by a single manufacturer may be inefficient and, where it is, it should be illegal

This rule would be unworkable. I propose allowing single-manufacturer use of RPM not because it is always efficient but because it "often" is efficient and it is impossible, as a matter of practice, to distinguish efficient uses of RPM by a single firm from inefficient uses. RPM is an instrument, when used by a single manufacturer to elicit some action on the part of retailers, that affects demand or is often used for that purpose. (Call this action "service.")

There is no guarantee that the social trade-off of greater service for higher price is the same for the monopolist. But we do not regulate individual firm decisions on the basis that intervention "might" improve welfare. Policy on intervening in market contracts cannot rest on the mere possibility of a welfare gain from intervention. The law governing price discrimination is parallel; welfare may go up or down with price discrimination, but the law makes no effort to distinguish carefully the cases where welfare rises from those in which it falls.

We do not regulate firm choices of price versus quality or service when a firm implements these choices directly. Nor should we when the choices are being implemented via RPM.

In a competition case involving RPM, the burden should lie on the side of the firm to demonstrate a free-riding justification of the practice

This way of thinking about policy towards RPM is ubiquitous. The point is contained in European Competition Law, as interpreted by the European Vertical Restraints Guidelines. And the argument was central to the dissent in the *Leegin* case. In his dissent, Mr. Justice Stephen Breyer (a justice with an excellent understanding of antitrust matters) writes:

> Petitioner and some amici have also presented us with newer studies that show that resale price maintenance sometimes brings consumer benefits. Overstreet (1983: 119–129) (describing numerous case studies). But the proponents of a per se rule have always conceded as much. What is remarkable about the majority's arguments is that nothing in this respect is new . . . .. The one arguable exception consists of the majority's claim that, even absent free riding, resale price maintenance may be the most efficient way to expand the manufacturer's market share by inducing the retailer's performance and allowing it to use its own initiative and experience in providing valuable services . . . . *I cannot count this as an exception, however, because I do not understand how, in the absence of free-riding (and assuming competitiveness), an established producer would need resale price maintenance.* Why, on these assumptions, would a dealer not expand

its market share as best that dealer sees fit, obtaining appropriate payment from consumers in the process? There may be an answer to this question. But I have not seen it. (551 U. S. (2007) 15 BREYER, J., dissenting [emphasis added])

Mr. Justice Breyer states quite explicitly that he does not understand how, in the absence of free-riding, there can be an incentive conflict between retailers and a manufacturer that requires remedy via RPM. Yet almost any action that a retailer supplies—convenience, a comfortable shopping environment, advice—is subject to possible under-provision from the perspective of the manufacturer. A retailer designs its strategy, that is, its mix of price and non-price instruments, not only to attract individuals into the product market but to attract individuals away from other retailers. The manufacturer would like the retailer to focus on the former goal. The retailer does not, because those shoppers willing to compare retailers are less sensitive to convenience comfort than they are to price. The manufacturer can use RPM to correct this distortion in retailer incentives. This is consistent with the very wide range of products that RPM is used for, relative to the predictions of the free-riding story.

The European Commission's "Guidelines on Vertical Restraints" also places undue emphasis on free-riding as an evidentiary "requirement" for the proposition that RPM is efficient for established firms.[20] In explaining why the practice may be used to induce retailers to provide additional presale service, the guidelines describe the traditional free-riding argument (involving consumers obtaining services at one outlet and then purchasing from a lower-price outlet), and then state (at paragraph 225):

> The parties will have to convincingly demonstrate that the RPM agreement can be expected to not only provide the means but also the incentive to overcome possible free riding between retailers on these services and that the pre-sales services overall benefit consumers as part of the demonstration that all the conditions of Article 101(3) are fulfilled.

The free-riding story presents a clear normative justification for RPM and any alternative theory is often met with the question, "But how do you know the manufacturer's use of RPM is efficient?"[21]

The likelihood of an anticompetitive use of RPM by a firm is greater the higher the degree of market power of the firm; the use by dominant firms is presumptively anticompetitive
This is the approach taken in European competition law, where practices by dominant firms are heavily scrutinized and subject to burdens of proof on the part of the firm. RPM is presumptively efficient when adopted in

a product market with a competitive structure. But at the other end of the spectrum of market power, a pure monopoly with neither close substitutes nor the threat of entry, RPM should also be legal. None of the anticompetitive theories applies for a pure monopolist. It is in the intermediate case, where there is some competition but not very much or where there is the potential of entry into a fixed set of available distributors, in which RPM should be subject to antitrust scrutiny. The concern over RPM is non-monotonic in the degree of market power.

A problem with RPM is the suppression of intrabrand competition and higher prices since, by definition, RPM prevents competition via lower retail prices; evidence shows that this effect can be strong

This view of RPM is not exactly wrong so much as unhelpful. It is true that higher prices with RPM are a cost of adopting the practice. But they are a cost to the manufacturer as well, and the manufacturer (in the single-firm theories) has voluntarily adopted RPM in exchange for benefits—increased service, for example. It is the potential difference between private and social marginal rates of substitution that is at issue for efficiency analysis. Does the willingness of the manufacturer to accept higher prices for greater service signal a positive net social value of the same trade-off? Or are there conditions under which one can be sure that the social value of the trade-off is negative?

Evidence from empirical studies of the impact of RPM shows that the practice generally increases price, reduces quantity and, therefore, reduces welfare; this favors prohibition of the practice

This is not a view that I ascribe to any scholar, but it is an implication that might be drawn by some from empirical studies. Three things are wrong with the proposition.

First, the most up-to-date empirical work does not show a strong and significant average effect on quantity (although more work needs to be done in this regard). Prices rise with RPM, not surprisingly, but quantities may or may not fall significantly. We do not know at this point.

Second, even if "on average" the impact of RPM is to reduce quantity, the cases where the quantity is reduced through cartel behavior (I take the exclusionary use of RPM to be less common) may be identifiable. The optimal policy would then be to identify, in a particular case, evidence for or against the cartel hypothesis. Empirical studies of the average impact can inform our "prior" probability about whether the use of RPM in a particular case is anticompetitive. As Cooper et al. (2005) argue, this is an important input into case decisions. But the main input into a legal decision should still be case-specific facts.

Third, quantity may decrease even with the use of RPM by a single manufacturer. Consider, for example, the use of RPM by a luxury-goods manufacturer to maintain the distribution of its products through high-end retailers so as to encourage the image of its product as luxurious. Forcing the manufacturer to sell through discount outlets or the Internet may well force prices down but would be interfering in the manufacturer's choice of high brand image versus low price in a way that would never be implemented as a constraint on the firm's choice if this choice were made directly rather than through vertical restraints.

Since we already have laws against cartels, there is no need for a rule-of-reason approach to RPM; the practice should be *per se* legal
This is a proposition that has been put forward by Judge Richard Posner (1981), among others. The counter-argument is that cartel laws are imperfect, in particular, in dealing with tacit collusion. Restriction of facilitating practices, which describes some instances of RPM, can be good policy because tacit collusion itself is not and cannot be made illegal.

EXTENDING THE POLICY CONCLUSIONS TO OTHER VERTICAL RESTRAINTS

Vertical restraints, apart from RPM, often include some form of exclusivity. These include vertical territorial restrictions, which have a number of variations: for some products and services (for example, home-furnace repair), distributors can be assigned all customers in a specified territory. For other products (fast food franchisees), this customer assignment may be impossible, but outlets can be offered guarantees that no competing outlet will be established within a specified area. Exclusivity restrictions can be imposed on downstream distributors, in the case of insurance markets, for example, where some agents are restricted to selling insurance from one company exclusively. Or they can be imposed on upstream input suppliers, restricting the suppliers against selling to other downstream firms. "Requirements tying" is a form of exclusivity in that it restricts downstream firms from purchasing any of its requirements of an input from a competing upstream firm. We see many variations of these restraints and other restraints discussed in the introduction. Sometimes the restraints are combined, as when a distributor is allowed to sell outside its designated territory but not below a specified price.

Many theories can explain the adoption of vertical restraints by a manufacturer for procompetitive or price-discrimination reasons. A supplier may guarantee territorial protection to each downstream distributor so that the distributor can capture a higher percentage of the returns from investment in establishing a local market for the product. A car dealership that built up a local market through years of investment, only to see half of its investment captured by the entry of a second dealership in the same local area, would be a victim of the "hold-up" problem. Anticipation of hold-up reduces the incentive to invest in the first place.

Exclusivity restrictions are observed in contracts throughout the economy, often for efficiency reasons. Suppose that you and I enter a contract that is incomplete in the sense that future prices will be negotiated as time passes rather than specified entirely at the outset of the contract. For example, you may own a crude oil field and I may be a nearby refinery. You will have the incentive to develop a pipeline to other refineries not for the purpose of shipping oil but for the "threat" of shipping oil—and the private benefit that this threat carries in future negotiations with me. This investment is privately beneficial but collectively wasteful. An exclusivity clause at the outset can be efficient in preventing this kind of wasteful investment. Exclusivity restrictions in contracts render private investment more efficient.

Exclusivity restrictions and even simple long-term contracts can also have anticompetitive effects, notably the effect of excluding an upstream rival from a market. The simplest example is of a monopoly manufacturer sourcing an essential input from (say) ten upstream suppliers but facing a new threat of entry from a producer of an identical product. Entry would reduce profits to zero. The incumbent monopolist can bribe each of the input suppliers with a share of monopoly rents in return for exclusive rights to the inputs. This preserves the monopoly rents, which are shared among the incumbent monopolist and the input suppliers. The exclusivity contracts are efficient for the parties signing the contracts but reduce social surplus; the contracts impose an externality on downstream buyers, who are not parties to the contract.[22]

The literature, starting with Aghion and Bolton (1987), examines a set of incentives for exclusionary contracts that may involve exclusivity restrictions or simply long terms. Like the example above, these contracts are inefficient when they impose externalities on parties outside the contracts. Contracts between an incumbent firm and buyers can extract surplus from an entrant by inducing the entrant to set a lower price in those states of the world in which entry is successful (Aghion and Bolton 1987). A set of exclusivity contracts between an incumbent and buyers can inefficiently preserve the incumbent's monopoly when each contract imposes externalities on other buyers; that is, each buyer ignores the harmful consequences that accepting the contract has on other buyers (Rasmusen et al. 1990; Segal and Whinston 2000). An incumbent, threatened by entry, may enter into downstream contracts in order to extract better terms from an existing monopolistic upstream supplier.

Vertical restraints may, in short, be adopted for efficient reasons or for anticompetitive reasons. The perspective that we adopted for vertical price restraints, that the restraints should be legal when they have purely vertical effects rather than suppressing interbrand competition, remains valid for vertical restraints in general. An upstream firm, like any firm with market power, aims to both increase the total surplus achieved in its supply chain and capture as large a share of this surplus as it can. Not every element in a vertical contract is efficient, or surplus-increasing, because contracts designed to increase the monopolist's "share" of surplus may decrease total surplus. But it is, as a practical measure, impossible to identify inefficient purely vertical contracts. The optimal policy remains as discussed in our section on vertical price restraints: contracts that have purely vertical effects, without horizontal anticompetitive effects, should be allowed.

The perspective, or rule is, however, less clear-cut for exclusivity restrictions than for vertical price restraints. This is because exclusivity restrictions may appear, by definition, to have horizontal exclusionary effects. Two case examples show that even exclusivity contracts that have the effect of excluding suppliers from providing a given set of buyers may nonetheless be efficient.

The first of these cases highlights the following efficiency effect of exclusionary contracts. Consider a dominant firm, signing exclusive contracts that transfer some demand from a competitive fringe of suppliers. One effect of the contracts is to "increase the output" of the dominant firm, through the transfer of output from the fringe. This has the effect of reducing the deadweight loss from monopoly, the inefficiency of monopoly being that monopoly quantity is too small. The transfer of output to a larger, dominant firm can be expected to increase efficiency.

The facts of the case example are these.[23] An upstream supplier of a building material supplies producers of machine parts. In addition to the upstream supplier, there is a competitive fringe of material suppliers. The dominance of the upstream supplier is due to the high quality of its product. The demand facing the supplier from downstream purchasers is stochastic.

In this setting, the dominant supplier of material engaged in "Disneyland pricing," two-part pricing in which the variable price exceeds marginal cost of production. This is a standard pricing strategy, adopted so as to extract greater net revenues from downstream demanders in states of the world in which demand is high. The strategy extracts a higher share of total surplus for the upstream supplier but comes at a cost: the excess of variable price over marginal cost means that each downstream demander purchases less of the building material than it would in a first-best efficient contract (one that maximized the combined profits of the parties to the contract). In a simple two-part pricing contract, downstream purchasers would be induced by the distortionary gap between variable price and marginal cost to substitute inefficiently towards purchases from the competitive fringe. An exclusivity clause in the contract played the role of preventing this inefficient substitution. An important set of suppliers was excluded, but the contracts were nonetheless efficient.

The second case is *Standard Fashions*.[24] In this case, a dominant firm used an exclusivity contract to "monopolize" a market, but in order to make the contract acceptable to buyers it had to substantially lower the price of the product. Standard Fashions, a dress pattern manufacturer, offered exclusive dealing contracts to department stores, but, to attract stores to these exclusive contracts, it reduced its prices by about 50 percent. Given the alternatives available to department stores and to consumers, Standard Fashions had to reduce its price to make its contract offers acceptable. In many US towns at the time, there was a single department store. The US Supreme Court decision against Standard Fashions was based on a concern that the contracts would create monopolies in "hundreds if not thousands of communities" where there was a single retailer. The sale of dress patterns in each town with a single department store may well have been a separate geographic market, and the contracts thus may well have changed the structure in each of these small markets to an apparent monopoly. But the power of potential competition—competition "for the market"—under exclusive dealing was even stronger than the previous competition "within the market" in terms of keeping prices low. The key is that other dress manufacturers could enter any local market without substantial market-specific investment and therefore remained a constant source of discipline while the exclusive dealing contracts were signed. These two case examples go beyond the classic efficiency explanations of exclusivity as protecting the returns on specific investment (Joskow 1987) and preventing free-riding on manufacturer investment in dealer services (Marvel 1982).

The two case examples discussed above suggest a condition under which exclusivity restrictions should, as a matter of policy, be allowed. If the firms excluded from the set of buyers remains in the market (for other buyers), the exclusivity contract should be allowed. In the first example (building materials), the constant presence of the competitive fringe means that the purpose of the restrictions was not to eliminate a competitive alternative. And in the second example, *Standard Fashions*, the competitive discipline provided on the dominant firm's pricing was even stronger under the exclusionary contract that it was prior to the contract. In both examples, efficiency was served even when firms were excluded.

CONCLUSION

This chapter has reviewed the economic foundations of competition policy towards vertical restraints with an emphasis on RPM. The economics can be summarized in two propositions.

First, vertical restraints can, in theory, be anticompetitive in two senses. Vertical restraints can support collusive pricing across manufacturers. Vertical restraints can serve to exclude competitors at either the upstream or downstream retail level. Competition policy should focus specifically on these two theories in formulating rules against vertical restraints.

Second, consistent with the enormous range of markets in which vertical restraints are observed—far beyond the range that can possibly be explained by the anticompetitive hypotheses—these restraints are profitably adopted by manufacturers for other reasons. A manufacturer, other things being equal, benefits from competition downstream and would therefore restrict it only if the result is an increase in some private benefit such as sales effort. The manufacturer's willingness to trade-off competition for sales effort may or may not signal the social efficiency of the same trade-off. But the mere possibility that the manufacturer gets the trade-off wrong is not a justification for intervention. As the Standing Committee on Industry, Science and Technology (SCIST) of the Canadian Parliament stated,

> The classical example of [resale] price maintenance is where a supplier requires someone to whom it sells . . . to maintain prices at a particular level as a way of encouraging that retailer or wholesaler to engage in competition on something other than price. A higher retail margin thus encouraged the retailer to engage in providing a high level of service to clients or to ensure that the brand image associated with the product is maintained and not sullied in any way. (Standing Committee on Industry, Science and Technology 2002, chapter 5)

From the consumer's perspective, RPM results in an increase in services, which is likely to be welfare-improving, but also higher prices, which are likely to be welfare-decreasing. Prohibiting RPM under the *per se* rule is effectively regulating the manufacturer's decisions on how best to maximize the sale of his products. By way of an analogy, we do not prohibit by law high levels of advertising even when such advertising raises prices; for the same reason, we should not prohibit vertical price maintenance under a *per se* rule.

I criticized the state of competition policy towards vertical price restraints by describing six fallacies contained in law and often in policy discussions. The first is that the best policy rule for RPM is to allow the restraint when it is efficient or in consumers' interest. This rule would be unworkable, just as unworkable as a rule to allow price discrimination only when it is efficient. Second, in many competition regimes, the burden of proof lies on the side of the firm engaged in the practice. Third, the market power of a firm is often the key indicator of whether the resale practice is allowed. The practice is less likely the more the market power. Fourth is the fallacy that policy should require the demonstration of benefits to be balanced against the cost of suppression of intrabrand competition. The fifth fallacy is that evidence that RPM increases prices is evidence that the restraint is anticompetitive. The final is a fallacy on the laissez-faire side of the debate: since we already have laws against cartels, there is no need for a rule-of-reason approach to research price maintenance. The practice should be *per se* legal.

In extending the policy discussion to vertical restraints, I suggested that the basic message remains the same. Competition policy should focus on the two kinds of anticompetitive effects: collusive price or exclusion. But exclusion is not by itself a sufficient reason for prohibiting exclusivity restraints. Even restraints that exclude competitors from selling to a particular set of buyers may be efficient. These restraints may correct a monopoly pricing distortion. Or they may enhance competition "for the market" instead of competition within a market. In either case, exclusion is not at odds with efficiency.

ACKNOWLEDGMENTS

This paper draws on joint work with both Edward Iacobucci and Frank Mathewson. I am grateful to these coauthors for their intellectual input.

NOTES

1. Even among United States (US) policymakers, there is a divergence in views. In September 2008, the US Department of Justice released a 200-page report on single-firm conduct, largely dealing with vertical restraints. Three of the four sitting commissioners at the Federal Trade Commission (FTC) objected to the report on the grounds that it offered insufficient protection to consumers against abuse of market dominance. President Obama's new antitrust appointee then withdrew the report.
2. *Continental T.V., Inc., v. GTE Sylvania Inc.*, 433 U.S. 36 (1977).
3. *State Oil Co. v. Khan*, 522 U.S. 3, 22 (1997).
4. *Leegin Creative Leather Products, Inc., v. PSKS, Inc.*, 127 S. Ct. 2705 (2007).
5. *Albrecht v. Herald Co.*, 390 U.S.S.C 145 (1968).
6. Korean Supreme Court decision no. 2009Du9543 of 25 November 2010. There may be a justifiable reason if the minimum RPM:
   - promotes interbrand competition
   - promotes competition on customer service among distributors

- diversifies consumer choices in products
- enables new firms to smoothly secure distribution channels to make easier entry into markets for the relevant product.

The enterprise has the burden of proof to establish a justification. See discussion in "Enforcement of competition law in the South Korean pharmaceutical industry," Chul Ho Kim and Jiyul Yoo, Yoon & Yang LLC, 1 May 2013, available at http://uk.practicallaw.com/1-525-5401?q=*&qp=&qo=&qe=# (accessed 23 June 2013).

7.   Korea's Fair Trade Commission fined cookware manufacturer Fissler Korea 175 million won ($156,000) for RPM.

8.   *Dr. Miles Medical Co. v. John D. Park and Sons*, 220 U.S. 373 (1911).

9.   The discussion in this section is based on Mathewson and Winter (1984) and Winter (1993).

10. In stating that a wholesale contract will maximize combined profits of the parties to the contract, we are assuming that the manufacturer has the ability to set a fixed fee in contracts with retailers. More generally, even if a simple fixed fee is impossible (for example, because of limited wealth on the part of retail agents), manufacturers benefit from profits at the retail level in a number of ways. Higher retail profits encourage more outlets to carry a product, to the manufacturer's benefit, and also provide incentives to encourage higher retail quality if this quality is being monitored by the manufacturer (Klein and Murphy 1988). The assumption that a wholesale contract maximizes the combined profit of the contract parties is surely a reasonable approximation.

11. In a simple model of a symmetric retailer duopoly downstream, one can show that the individual firm elasticity of demand is equal to the sum of the market elasticity of demand and the cross-elasticity of demand. One can therefore pose the question as the following: why would the ratio of cross-elasticities between retailers differ from the ratio of own-elasticities?

12. Both the direct and the indirect mechanism work in the same direction: increasing sales effort at the expense of higher prices. If we extend the setting to one in which effort takes on multiple important dimensions, the single instrument of a price floor will not achieve first-best profits (unless the key elasticity-ratio condition holds for all effort dimensions simultaneously). If one effort dimension is perfectly substitutable for price, in buyer preferences, then the price floor may be limited in its usefulness altogether. For example, when American Airlines tried to constrain travel agents from undercutting their price schedule, agents simply offered exceptionally low prices on hotel and car rental packages with the tickets (see discussion by Judge Frank Easterbrook in *Illinois Corporate Travel v. American Airlines. Inc.*, 889 F. 2d 751). Both the direct and indirect mechanisms break down when an increase in a non-contractable dimension of effort is a perfect substitute for a lower price. There is also the question of whether price floors, as opposed to some other reward, are necessary to protect downstream incentives to provide effort.

13. As an example, in *Applewood Stoves v. Vermont Castings, Inc.*, USC.A 7th CC No. 86-2818, Judge Richard Posner 1981 writes: "As a new company, selling a somewhat complex product [wood-burning stoves], Vermont Castings ... needs dealers who understand the product, can explain it to consumers and can persuade them to buy it in preference to substitute products . . .. These selling efforts, which benefit consumers as well as the supplier, cost money—money that a dealer can't recoup if another dealer 'free-rides' on the first dealer's efforts by offering a discount to consumers who have shopped at the first dealer . . .. As one of Vermont Casting's dealers explained in a letter to it, 'The worst disappointment is spending a great deal of time with a customer only to lose him to Applewood because of price . . .. This letter was precipitated by the loss of 3 sales of V.C. stoves today [to] people whom we educated and spent long hours with.'"

14. The retailer cartel theory requires that prices be maintained *across products*. The retailer cartel theory of vertical price floors is sometimes explained in terms of a set of retailers coercing a single manufacturer into implementing the retail monopoly price via RPM, to the benefit of retailers with the result an increase in the retail price. In a model where only price affects demand and where retailers compete imperfectly, a price ceiling would

maximize total profits. A cartelized retail sector might gain from a higher share of rents through a lowering of the wholesale price as it exercised monopsony bargaining power. But a price floor would not increase profits.

15. Rey and Vergé (2010) show that the impact of RPM in dampening interbrand competition is particularly strong when manufacturers and retailers have interlocking relationships. In their model, rival manufacturers distribute products through the same competing retailers, in a competing-common-agency framework. Industry monopoly pricing is a non-cooperative equilibrium in the model. But in a richer model of a market with many retailers and many manufacturers, a retailer–manufacturer pair would profitably undercut monopoly pricing. This would rule out an equilibrium of monopoly pricing.

16. See also Paldor (2008).

17. In 1952, the McGuire Act authorized states to allow the enforcement by manufacturers of non-signer clauses, under which a manufacturer could enforce RPM even with retailers that had not signed RPM agreements.

18. McKay and Smith used the Nielsen Consumer Panel Data Set, consisting of 1.4 million unique products, which are organized into 10 departments and 1,083 modules. Private-label or store-branded products are omitted.

19. McKay and Smith find statistical significance in examining the proportion of product categories for which prices and quantities changed with statistical significance. ("Significance" is measured with careful attention to a multiple hypothesis correction.)

20. The guidelines also recognize limited roles for RPM for new products and for short-term price promotions.

21. From more sophisticated observers, the question is posed as, "How do you know that retailers are not better representatives of the *average* buyer, in terms of the trade-off between lower price and greater service, than consumers on the manufacturer's margin, or product margin?" In a classic article, Michael Spence (1975) showed that a distortion in a firm's choice of quality (here, service) depends on preferences of marginal consumers, whereas the socially optimal quality depends on preferences of average consumers.

22. This example is the simplest to show that contracts among vertically related (and therefore complementary) suppliers are not always efficient.

23. These facts are drawn from an actual (but confidential) case and simplified.

24. *Standard Fashion Co. v. Magrane-Houston Co.*, 258 U.S. 346 (1922).

REFERENCES

Aghion, Philippe and Patrick Bolton (1987), "Contracts as a barrier to entry," *American Economic Review* 77, 388–401.

Andrews, P.W.S. and Frank A. Friday (1960), *Fair Trade: Resale Price Maintenance Re-examined*, London: Macmillan.

Asker, John and Heski Bar-Isaac (2014), "Raising retailers' profits: on vertical practices and the exclusion of rivals," *American Economic Review* 104(2), 672–86.

Cooper, J., L. Froeb, D. O'Brien and M. Vita (2005), "Vertical restraints as a problem of inference," *International Journal of Industrial Organization* 23, 639–64.

Deneckere, R., H. Marvel and J. Peck (1996), "Demand uncertainty, inventories, and resale price maintenance," *Quarterly Journal of Economics* 109, 885–913.

Dorfman, R. and P.O. Steiner (1954), "Optimal advertising and optimal quality," *American Economic Review* 44, 826–36.

Hourihan, Anthony P. and Jesse W. Markham (1974), *The Effects of Fair Trade Repeal: The Case of Rhode Island*. Cambridge, MA: Marketing Science Institute and Center for Economic Studies.

Ippolito, P. (1988), *Resale Price Maintenance: Economic Evidence from Litigation*, Washington, DC: Federal Trade Commission.

Ippolito, P. (1991), "Resale price maintenance: empirical evidence from litigation," *Journal of Law and Economics* 34, 263–94.

Ippolito, P. and T. Overstreet (1996), "Resale price maintenance: an economic assessment of the Federal Trade Commission's case against the Corning Glass Works," *Journal of Law and Economics* 39, 285–328.

Joskow, Paul (1987), "Contract duration and relationship-specific investments: empirical evidence from coal markets," *American Economic Review* 77, 168–85.

Jullien, Bruno and Patrick Rey (2007), "Resale price maintenance and collusion," *RAND Journal of Economics* 38, 983–1001.

Klein, Benjamin (2009), "Competitive resale price maintenance in the absence of free-riding," *Antitrust Law Journal* 76(2), 431–81.

Klein, B. and K. Murphy (1988), "Vertical restraints as contract enforcement mechanisms," *Journal of Law and Economics* 31, 265–98.

Krishnan, Harish and Ralph A. Winter (2007), "Vertical control of price and inventory," *American Economic Review* 97(5), 1840–57.

Lafontaine, F. and M. Slade (2005), "Empirical assessment of exclusive contracts," in *Handbook of Antitrust Economics*, Cambridge, MA: The MIT Press, pp. 391–414.

Lambert, Thomas and M. Sykuta (2013), "Why the new evidence on minimum resale price does not justify a *per se* or 'quick look' approach," *CPI Antitrust Chronicle* November 2013 (1) and University of Missouri School of Law Legal Studies Research Paper 2013-20, available electronically at https://ssrn.com/abstract=2363139 (accessed 3 December 2019).

Marvel, H. and S. McCafferty (1984), "Resale price maintenance and quality certification," *Rand Journal of Economics* 15, 340–59.

Marvel, Howard P. (1982), "Exclusive dealing," *Journal of Law and Economics* 25, 1–25.

Mathewson, G.F. and R.A. Winter (1984), "An economic theory of vertical restraints," *Rand Journal of Economics* 15, 27–38.

McKay, A. and D.A. Smith (2016), "The empirical effects of minimum resale price maintenance," *Chicago Booth-Nielsen Dataset Paper Series 2-006*.

Overstreet, T. (1983), *Resale Price Maintenance: Economic Theories and Empirical Evidence*, Washington, DC: Federal Trade Commission.

Paldor, Ittai (2008), "RPM as an Exclusionary Device," unpublished paper.

Posner, Richard A. (1981), "The next step in the antitrust treatment of restricted distribution: per se legality," *The University of Chicago Law Review* 48, 6–26.

Rasmusen, Eric B., J. Mark Ramseyer and John Shepard Wiley, Jr. (1991), "Naked exclusion," *American Economic Review* 81, 1137–45.

Rey, Patrick and Thibaud Vergé (2010), "Resale price maintenance and interlocking relationships," *Journal of Industrial Economics* 58(4), 928–61.

Scherer, F.M. and D. Ross (1990), *Industrial Market Structure and Economic Performance*, 3rd edn, Chicago, IL: Rand McNally.

Segal, Ilya and Michael Whinston (2000), "Naked exclusion: comment," *American Economic Review* 90, 296–309.

Shepard, L.G. (1978), "The economic effects of repealing the fair trade laws," *Journal of Consumer Affairs* 12, 220.

Spence, M. (1975), "Monopoly, quality and regulation," *Bell Journal of Economics* 6(2) 417–29.

Spengler, J. (1950), "Vertical integration and antitrust policy," *Journal of Political Economy* 53, 347–52.

Standing Committee on Industry, Science and Technology (2002), "A Plan to Modernize Canada's Competition Regime" (adopted by the committee on 9 April 2002; presented to the House on 23 April 2002).

Telser, L. (1960), "Why should manufacturers want fair trade?" *Journal of Law and Economics* 3, 86–105.

Williamson, Oliver (1983), *Markets versus Hierarchies. Analysis and Antitrust Implications: A Study of the Economics of Internal Organization*, New York: Free Press.

Winter, R.A. (1993), "Vertical restraints and price versus nonprice competition," *Quarterly Journal of Economics* 108, 61–76.

Zerbe, Richard (1969), "The American Sugar Refinery Company, 1887–1914: the story of a monopoly," *Journal of Law and Economics* 12(2), 339–75.

9. Resale price maintenance in a multi-producer and multi-distributor setting

Se Hoon Bang and Yangsoo Jin

INTRODUCTION

Recently the attitude of competition law toward minimum resale price maintenance or resale price fixing (hereinafter "resale price maintenance," RPM) has changed considerably.[1] In the United States (US), the Supreme Court has adopted the "rule of reason" approach to RPM instead of the "*per se* illegality*" that had been maintained for almost a hundred years since *Dr. Miles Medical Co.* (1911).[2] In other words, in the famous *Leegin* case (2007), the US Supreme Court declared that RPM should be evaluated according to the "rule of reason."[3]

Being influenced by the *Leegin* case, the European Union (EU) has also reviewed its regulation framework of RPM and revised the "Guidelines on Vertical Restraints" (2010/C 130/01). Specifically, the new guidelines added detailed explanations about the market conditions under which RPM is likely to have either procompetitive or anticompetitive effects. Similarly the ruling of the *Leegin* case contained comprehensive explanations regarding the market conditions under which either procompetitive or anticompetitive effects are likely to emerge. It also explained the mechanisms through which these effects work.[4]

Both the *Leegin* case and the revision of the EU guidelines, which are influenced by knowledge development in economic theories, have recently affected Korea. For example, in *Hanmi Pharmaceutical Co.* (2009)[5] the Supreme Court of Korea ruled that "RPM can be allowed exceptionally, provided that it can be justifiable by the effect that it enhances consumer welfare by promoting interbrand competition although it appears to restrict intrabrand competition." Regarding the justifiability, the Supreme Court suggested the following criteria: whether interbrand competition is active in the relevant market; whether the RPM concerned promotes non-price competition among distributors; whether the RPM concerned provides consumers with more choices; and whether the RPM concerned helps new firms secure distribution channels and hence enter the relevant market easily.

This ruling is important in Korea since it begins requesting effective assessments for RPM—which had, for a long time earlier, been treated as "*per se* illegal." The criteria outlined above, however, are no more than a summary of the market outcomes that RPM may produce.

In contrast, the ruling of the *Leegin* case and the EU guidelines explain not only the outcomes but also the market conditions in which respective outcomes are likely to emerge. Additionally, they illustrate in detail the mechanisms through which outcomes are produced in particular market conditions. Therefore the ruling of the *Leegin* case and the EU guidelines provide guidance, referred to in assessing individual RPM cases, for both the competition authority and lawyers in Korea.

The focus of this chapter is the fact that the ruling of the *Leegin* case and the EU guidelines explain respective market conditions separately and independently. For example, the EU guidelines state that RPM is likely to be procompetitive when the possibility of free-ridings among distributors is extant, while anticompetitive when multiple producers are involved in RPM. To put it the other way around, the EU guidelines do not consider the possibility that various market conditions may interact and determine the competition effect of RPM. Thus, the EU guidelines fail to provide adequate direction for RPM cases in which, for example, both the free-riding possibility and the problem of multiple producers are involved at the same time. This is also the case for the ruling of *Leegin*.

Such a case, where various market conditions may interact and determine the competition effect of RPM, is not merely plausible but actually came into question recently in Korea. In *Callaway* (2010),[6] eight golf club manufacturers practiced RPM at the same time for several years. A golf club is a good such that a consumer needs substantial information in order to choose a product that fits her physical characteristics. Such information can be provided by golf club distributors in the form of presale services.[7] A distributor, however, has incentive to free-ride on the presale services provided by its competing distributors. In the RPM cases like this, the market conditions of multiple producers and the free-riding problem may interact to determine the impact of RPM on competition. Therefore, assessments that do not adequately consider this point but depend heavily on the EU guidelines may fail to reach correct conclusions.

Recognizing this problem, we analyse the effect of RPM under a market environment in which various market conditions are simultaneously involved. In addition to the two conditions above, we also consider the degree of brand-specificity of presale services and the cost of service provision.

For our purpose, it is useful to understand the RPM-related part of the EU guidelines since it explains, using "non-economist language," the economic theories related to the market conditions of our interest. Hence, in the next section, we summarize the RPM-related part of the EU guidelines along with the overall framework of RPM regulation. In subsequent sections, we develop a theoretical model and analyse how the market conditions in which we are interested work to determine the effect of RPM. The final section summarizes the implications of our analysis.

RETAIL PRICE MAINTENANCE REGULATION IN THE EU

Overall Framework

In the EU, Article 101(1) of the Treaty on the Functioning of the European Union (TFEU) prohibits agreements between firms, horizontal or vertical, that restrict competition. Anticompetitive vertical agreements (or restraints) are, therefore, prohibited by this provision. At the same time, Article 101(3) of the TFEU allows an efficiency defense. Accordingly, possible illegalities of Article 101(1) TFEU are exempted for vertical restraints having the efficiency effects defined in Article 101(3) that prove to be procompetitive.

Meanwhile, the Block Exemption Regulation (hereinafter "the regulation"),[8] pursuant to Article 101(3) TFEU, stipulates conditions needed for the exemption. Briefly, the regulation establishes a "safe harbor" based on the market shares of the parties to vertical agreement. More specifically, the exemption applies on the condition that the market shares of both manufacturers and distributors do not exceed 30 percent in their respective relevant markets. Thus, when the market-share threshold is not met in a vertical restraint, the EU Commission assesses whether it infringes Article 101(1) TFEU. The parties to the restraint are then able to defend with a claim of improved efficiency in accordance with Article 101(3) TFEU.

However, RPM is treated differently although it is a form of vertical restraint. The regulation defines a category of vertical restraint as the "hardcore restrictions" that are presumed to restrict competition and hence fall within Article 101(1) TFEU. The hardcore restrictions are also presumed to be unlikely to fulfill the conditions in Article 101(3) that are to be met to claim efficiency. RPM belongs to the hardcore restrictions.[9] It is therefore presumed to be unlawful even when the market shares of the parties do not exceed 30 percent. However, this does not mean that RPM is treated as *per se* illegal.[10] Even in such a case, the parties in an individual

RPM case may demonstrate, with the burden of proof on the defendants, its efficiency or procompetitive effect.

Analytical Framework

The overall framework for RPM regulation outlined above employs an effect-based (rather than form-based) approach in that it admits the possibility of both procompetitive and anticompetitive effects of RPM.[11] To put it differently, it adopts a version of the "rule of reason" approach.[12] That is, the illegality of an individual RPM case depends on whether or not its procompetitive effect outweighs its anticompetitive effect.

In this regard, Article 101(3) TFEU provides general conditions for efficiency claims for vertical restraints (including RPM) to satisfy. That is, for a vertical restraint to be exempted from illegality, it should contribute to improving the production or distribution of goods or promote technical or economic progress; allow consumers a fair share of the resulting benefit; not be indispensable to the attainment of these objectives; and not afford (the parties) the possibility of eliminating competition in respect to a substantial part of the products in question.

An individual RPM therefore should meet the above four conditions in principle in order to receive exemption. In the meantime, the "Guidelines on Vertical Restraints" (2010/C 130/01; hereinafter "the guidelines") provide detailed directions that can be used to assess individual RPM cases. Specifically, the guidelines explain in what market conditions or with what mechanisms RPM is likely to be either procompetitive or anticompetitive based on economic theories.[13]

First of all, the guidelines mention a few market conditions in which RPM is likely to produce anticompetitive effects. It explains the following, for example: RPM may facilitate collusion between manufacturers by enhancing price transparency. This effect becomes more plausible when the manufacturers form a tight oligopoly and a significant part of the market is covered by RPM.[14] In this case, RPM reduces interbrand competition. (As previously mentioned, this market condition—RPM by oligopoly producers—is a focus of this chapter.[15]) RPM may facilitate collusion by distributors leading to the elimination of intrabrand competition.[16]

The guidelines then explain some mechanisms through which RPM may result in efficient or procompetitive outcomes. It explains that procompetitiveness will be more likely to emerge when RPM is driven by manufacturers. For example, RPM may help a manufacturer successfully launch a new product by inducing its distributors to increase sales efforts that, in turn, benefit consumers.[17] More notably, the guidelines state that a manufacturer's RPM may induce presale services, which are not likely to be provided absent the RPM, by distributors. In the latter case, the possibility of free-riding among distributors precludes provision of presale services that the manufacturer wants to be provided by distributors. RPM by a manufacturer may, in this case, eliminate incentives for free-riding by its distributors and, hence, enable presale services to be provided.[18]

Burden of Proof

As mentioned earlier, RPM is not treated as *per se* illegal.[19] The parties in an individual RPM case have the possibility to plead an efficiency defense. In this regard, the guidelines outline the assessment procedure. According to the guidelines, parties in an RPM bear the burden of proof to substantiate the likely procompetitive effect and to demonstrate that all the conditions in Article 101(3) TFEU are fulfilled. Then it falls on the European Commission to effectively assess the likely negative effects on competition and consumers before deciding whether the conditions of Article 101(3) TFEU are fulfilled.

MODEL SETUP

In the previous section, we discussed some of the RPM-related contents of the EU guidelines. In the discussion, we tacitly focused on two market conditions—simultaneous RPMs by oligopoly manufacturers and the possibility of free-ridings by distributors. In this section, we develop a theoretical model that addresses these conditions at the same time. In addition, we add to our model two more components: the brand-specificity of presale services and the cost of service provision incurred by distributors.[20]

Manufacturers and Distributors

There are two manufacturers $M \in \{A,B\}$ in the upstream of the market and each of them produces a single product M. The single product, though, is offered in a variety of types. Each manufacturer's product M consists of n types, $M_\tau \in \{M_1, M_2, M_3, \ldots, M_n\}$, and n is sufficiently large. Therefore, once the information about the product is perfectly provided, every consumer can find a type M_τ which exactly matches his own preference or idiosyncratic taste. Manufacturer M offers its product to distributors at the price of w^M regardless of the type of its product. It cannot price discriminate against distributors. If a manufacturer decides to implement RPM, we denote this RPM price with $\bar{p}^M$. The manufacturers compete in price. We assume that there is no production cost for analytical simplicity.

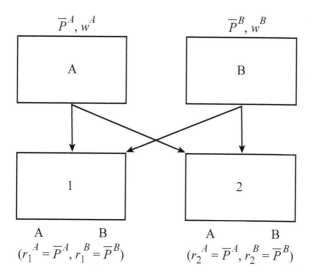

Figure 9.1   Retail prices when resale price maintenance is used

Furthermore, there are two distributors $i \in \{1,2\}$ in the downstream market. Each distributor purchases the products from both or either of the manufacturers at the wholesale price of w^M. They then resell the products to final consumers at the retail price of r_i^M. Two distributors compete in price. Again, we abstract away any costs that the distributors might incur in selling the product, except for the costs of providing product information or presale service to their potential customers. We further assume that the distributors incur the cost of s $(0 < s < 1)$ when providing presale services to each consumer. Figure 9.1 above summarizes the market structure and prices chosen by each manufacturer or distributor.

Consumers

There exists a continuum of t types of infinitesimal consumers. The total mass of these consumers is normalized to 1 and t is uniformly distributed between 0 and 1. Each consumer views products A and B as perfect substitutes and has unit demand for the product. Before gathering information about the product, in other words, prior to or in the absence of presale services by distributors, type-t consumer's willingness to pay for the product A or B is $1 - t$. 1 is the utility that a consumer can obtain when she finds the product that exactly matches her preference. However, she obtains no utilities from other "undesirable" types of product. We can interpret t as the level of prior information about a product, more specifically the information about the characteristics of all its types. If a consumer has perfect information ($t = 0$) about the product M, he knows exactly which type M_τ of the product M matches his preferences. Hence his expected utility when purchasing the product M would be 1. Alternatively, a consumer who has no prior information ($t = 1$) will not be able to find the type of product that matches his preferences. So his expected utility from the product M is zero since the probability that he happens to pick the "desirable" type of the product is almost zero. Lastly, if a consumer has some information about the product ($0 < t < 1$), he can sort out surely-unmatched types of the product and randomly choose one among the types that possibly match his taste. Therefore, his expected utility for the product is in-between, $0 < 1 - t < 1$.[21]

Presale Services (Information Provision)

Once a consumer receives presale services or information about, for example, product A, his willingness to pay for A goes up from $1 - t$ to $1 - \beta t$, where $\beta \in (0,1)$. Furthermore, since the information about product A can render some information about B to some extent, his willingness to pay for product B also increases to $1 - \beta' t$. We incorporate informational loss or imperfect information transferability by assuming $0 < \beta < \beta' < 1$. Thus, the information about product A is more valuable and useful when buying product A than product B. In this model, we assume that consumers are under no obligation to buy the product after receiving presale services on it. In other words, consumers can freely switch to distributor 2 after being offered presale services by distributor 1. They can even purchase the product B from the distributor either 1 or 2 after collecting information about A from distributor 1. In reality, we frequently observe such consumer behaviors and this is one of the main issues when discussing the free-riding problem and the procompetitive effects of RPM.

EQUILIBRIUM ANALYSIS

This section analyses the equilibrium outcomes of our model. First, we study the case where RPM is not allowed as a benchmark. Then we continue investigating the case where both manufacturers use RPM and compare the equilibrium outcomes with those from the benchmark.

No RPM Case

We begin with the case where manufacturers do not practice RPM. In this case, each manufacturer $M \in \{A,B\}$ quotes his own wholesale price w^M, and then distributor $i \in \{1,2\}$ decides its retail price r_i^M of each product M and whether to provide presale services.[22] If one of the distributors, say distributor 1, provides presale services to her potential customers at the expense of $s > 0$, the other distributor has incentive to undercut the price without offering presale services. This is because consumers will visit distributor 1 only to obtain product information and then switch to distributor 2 to actually purchase the product at a lower price. Due to this free-riding problem, no distributor would provide presale services in the end. Therefore, the distributors compete only on price against each other, hence the retail prices are reduced to the wholesale prices, which allow the distributors no profit.

Effectively, the downstream market competition then becomes the wholesale price-competition between the manufacturers in the upstream market. Since the unit production cost was assumed zero, the wholesale prices are determined also at zero in the equilibrium. Accordingly, we obtain the equilibrium prices, profits and consumer surplus as follows:

$$w^{A*} = w^{B*} = 0; r_i^{A*} = r_i^{B*} = 0 \text{ for } \forall i.$$

$$\pi^{A*} = \pi^{B*} = 0; \pi_1^* = \pi_2^* = 0,$$

$$CS^* = \int_0^1 1 - t \, dt = \frac{1}{2}.$$

Notice that consumers enjoy the entire surplus when no RPM is used. This is because consumers view products A and B as homogeneous absent product information. This intensifies the price competition in the supply side, hence lowering the prices to their marginal costs.

RPM Case

Perfectly generic presale services

Now we consider the case where the manufacturers use RPM. We first analyse the case in which the presale services are perfectly generic across brands. That is, the information obtained for the product of manufacturer A can be perfectly transferable to that of manufacturer B. Perfectly generic presale service corresponds to $0 < \beta = \beta' < 1$ in our model.

In this case, in conclusion, the distributors do not provide presale services even if the manufacturers use RPM. And every consumer ends up buying a product, that is, the market is fully served by the manufacturers. In addition, all surpluses from transaction go to the consumers.

This equilibrium outcome occurs because the manufacturers are able to free-ride. Let us consider a situation in which both manufacturers A and B use RPM. When the distributors provide presale services, each manufacturer should set its resale price at least at the level at which the profit margin (difference between resale price and wholesale price) of its distributors can cover the service costs (s). In other words, the manufacturers should compensate the cost of service provision through RPM.

In this situation, however, manufacturer A ends up having the incentive to cut its own RPM price, instead of inducing its distributors to provide services by compensating the service cost with RPM. This is because A can attract the consumers who are offered the presale service for product B by simply undercutting B's RPM price. Manufacturer B, of course, has exactly the same incentive. Therefore, both manufacturers do not compensate the distributors for the service costs, hence the distributors end up not providing presale services.

In the end, the market competition collapses to a Bertrand competition in RPM prices between manufacturers. The equilibrium prices, therefore, are determined at the marginal production cost. That is,

$$\bar{p}^{A*} = \bar{p}^{B*} = 0.$$

At the equilibrium, therefore, the manufacturers earn zero profit and the market is fully served with consumers enjoying the entire surplus. The consumer surplus in this case is computed as $1/2$.

This outcome is equivalent to the outcome that emerges when the manufacturers do not practice RPM. In sum, whether RPM is involved or not, the equilibrium outcomes regarding service provision and consumer surplus do not change when the presale services are perfectly generic across manufacturer brands.

Brand-specific presale services

Now we consider RPM and brand-specific presale services. Each manufacturer $M \in \{A,B\}$ not only charges his own wholesale price w^M but also determines the retail price of its product M. The RPM price set by each manufacturer M is denoted by $\bar{p}^M$, which is its retail price in effect. Thus, $r_i^A = \bar{p}^A$ and $r_i^B = \bar{p}^B$ for $i \in \{1,2\}$. Among consumers who received presale services on product A, the consumers of type-t satisfying

$$1 - \beta t - \bar{p}^A \geq 1 - \beta' t - \bar{p}^B$$

or

$$t \geq \frac{\bar{p}^A - \bar{p}^B}{\Delta\beta}, \Delta\beta = \beta' - \beta > 0$$

will purchase product A. Otherwise, they switch to product B. $\Delta\beta$ represents the amount of information loss when the information obtained for the product of a brand is applied to the product of the other brand. In other words, $\Delta\beta$ means the degree of brand-specificity of presale services. Of course, the larger is $\Delta\beta$, the more brand-specific is the presale services concerned.

We consider the case where the cost of service provision satisfies $s < 1 - \beta - \Delta\beta$. Let us assume that a consumer visits a distributor and receives the presale services for a randomly chosen brand, A or B, but not both.[23] Therefore, a random half of the consumers receive product information for the brand A product and the other random half for the brand B product.

Without loss of generality, let us suppose $\bar{p}^A \geq \bar{p}^B$. Among the consumers who received product information for product A, the consumers with type t such that $t \geq (\bar{p}^A - \bar{p}^B)/\Delta\beta$ purchase product A. Given this, the demand for product A is written as

$$D^A = \frac{1}{2}\left\{ 1 - \frac{\bar{p}^A - \bar{p}^B}{\Delta\beta} \right\}.$$

Thus, the profit maximization problem of manufacturer A is

$$\max_{(\bar{p}^A, w^A)} \pi^A = \frac{1}{2}\left\{ 1 - \frac{\bar{p}^A - \bar{p}^B}{\Delta\beta} \right\} \cdot w^A$$

$$s.t. w^A \leq \bar{p}^A - s,$$

where $w^A \leq \bar{p}^A - s$ is the condition to be satisfied to induce service provision by distributors. This condition, by the way, binds because the manufacturer can achieve larger profit when it is set higher w^A and the distributors would provide services as long as their retail margin $(\bar{p}^A - w^A)$ is greater than s. Solving the maximization problem, we obtain the best response function of manufacturer A as follows,

$$\bar{p}^A(\bar{p}^B) = \frac{\Delta\beta + \bar{p}^B + s}{2}.$$

Meanwhile, all the consumers who are offered the presale services for product B will stick with product B under the assumption of $\bar{p}^A \geq \bar{p}^B$. Therefore, the demand for the brand B product consists of the consumers who were offered services for the brand B product and the consumers who were offered services for the brand A product but switched to the brand B product. The latter are those with type t such that $t < (\bar{p}^A - \bar{p}^B)/\Delta\beta$. Thus, the demand for the brand B is

$$D^B = \frac{1}{2} + \frac{1}{2}\left\{\frac{\bar{p}^A - \bar{p}^B}{\beta' - \beta}\right\}.$$

The profit maximization problem of manufacturer B is then given by

$$\max_{(p^B, w^B)} \pi^B = \frac{1}{2}\left\{1 + \frac{\bar{p}^A - \bar{p}^B}{\beta' - \beta}\right\} \cdot w^B \, \text{s.t.} \, w^B \le \bar{p}^B - s,$$

where the constraint binds again. The first order condition gives the best response function of manufacturer B as

$$\bar{p}^B(\bar{p}^A) = \frac{\Delta\beta + \bar{p}^A + s}{2}.$$

Solving the two best response functions above, we can characterize the equilibrium as follows:

$$\bar{p}^{A*} = \bar{p}^{B*} = s + \Delta\beta; w^{A*} = w^{B*} = \Delta\beta.$$

$$\pi^{A*} = \pi^{B*} = \frac{1}{2}\Delta\beta; \pi_1^* = \pi_2^* = 0.$$

In the equilibrium, the market is fully served and every consumer purchases the brand for which they are initially offered presale services. That is, RPM effectively precludes free-riding across manufacturer brands (as well as across distributors). Finally, the consumer surplus is computed as

$$CS^* = \int_0^1 1 - \beta t - (s + \Delta\beta)\,dt$$

$$= 1 - s - \Delta\beta - \frac{\beta}{2}.$$

Now, let us compare this consumer surplus to that computed in the benchmark. For the RPM in our model to be procompetitive, in other words, to be beneficial to consumers, $1 - s - \Delta\beta - \beta/2 > 1/2$ should hold. Equivalently,

$$s < \frac{1}{2}(1 - \beta) - \Delta\beta$$

is the condition for the RPM to enhance consumer surplus. This implies that the RPM in our model can be procompetitive only when the cost of service provision is sufficiently small. Otherwise, although it effectively cures free-riding problems and induces presale services, the RPM harms consumers. The above condition tells us that RPM can be procompetitive if (i) presale service is sufficiently useful and informative that it can improve the chances for consumers to choose the "right" product (that is, β is fairly small), (ii) the costs in providing presale service are so negligible that the prices will not increase too much (that is, s is small enough) or (iii) the information on one product that consumers obtain from presale service can be readily applicable and transferable to other products (that is, $\Delta\beta$ is considered small).

To put it differently, even if RPM enables presale service provision, it may harm consumers since the price competition between manufacturers can be mitigated. The reason is straightforward. Once a consumer receives the information about a product, her expected utilities for the product increase because now the probabilities that she can choose the right product for her tastes are higher. Unless the information about a product is perfectly applicable to all other products, she will be biased or inclined toward the product for which the presale service is provided since her expected utilities for the two products differ. In other words, she happens to view the two products (vertically) differentiated after receiving information about one product. Knowing this, the manufacturers will have stronger incentives to raise prices, leading to higher equilibrium prices and lower consumer surplus. The equilibrium outcome is described by Figure 9.2.[24]

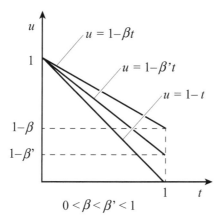

Figure 9.2   Comparison of consumer surplus

CONCLUSION: IMPLICATIONS FOR RPM ASSESSMENT

In the previous section, we analysed the procompetitiveness or the anticompetitiveness of RPM in a market environment where multiple producers (and multiple distributors) exist and free-riding concerns are involved. Our analysis shows that these market conditions closely interact with the degree of the brand-specificity of presale services and the cost of service provision determining the effect of RPM on competition.

This result provides important implications with respect to the competition assessment of individual RPM cases. As noted in the introduction of this chapter, on the one hand, the EU guidelines emphasize the effect of reducing interbrand competition via tacit collusion among producers when the market is composed of oligopoly producers and the RPM concerned is driven by the producers. On the other hand, when free-riding concerns are extant, the guidelines stress the effect of promoting interbrand competition since RPM eliminates the free-riding incentives for distributors. In other words, contrasting these two market environments, the EU guidelines state that the competition effects are likely to be realized in opposite directions. The explanations in the ruling of the *Leegin* case are not very different.

Our analysis, however, shows that one should be cautious when applying this guidance to the RPMs in reality.

First, if multiple producers are involved in RPM simultaneously, one needs to examine additionally whether the presale services concerned are generic across brands even though the free-ridings by distributors appear to be plausible within a brand. In such a case, RPM cannot prevent interbrand free-ridings by producers, although it can prevent intrabrand free-ridings by distributors. The result is that presale services will not be provided. Therefore, if RPM is nevertheless observed in this circumstance, one should find the incentive of RPM somewhere else other than service provision.

Second, one may observe that presale services are widely provided by distributors within a multiple producers' RPM environment. This does not, however, necessarily mean that the RPM in question is procompetitive. In this case, one needs to investigate also the value of presale services to consumers. Valuable presale services benefit consumers, of course. At the same time, however, one should also consider the degree of the brand-specificity of the services provided. Even when highly valuable services are provided to consumers, they should be generic across brands to some degree in order for the RPM to enhance competition. If the valuable services are too brand-specific, they increase only the degree of product differentiation and, hence, in the end, soften interbrand competition.

Finally, the costs of service provision should be considered as well. If the costs to distributors for providing presale services are too high, producers have to compensate for these costs with excessively high resale prices. This, in turn, makes it likely that the RPM reduces consumer surplus.

ACKNOWLEDGMENTS

We are grateful to Jay Pil Choi, Ralph A. Winter and all of the other contributors to the EWC–KDI research project for their helpful comments and suggestions. Any errors are our own.

NOTES

1. Unless otherwise noted, RPM in this chapter means minimum RPM and/or resale price fixing only. In other words, we do not consider maximum RPM. Accordingly, this chapter does not discuss any economic theory and competition laws regarding maximum RPM.
2. *Dr. Miles Medical Company v. John D. Park and Co.*, 220 U.S. 371 (1911).
3. *Leegin Creative Leather Products, Inc. v. PSKS, Inc.*, 551 U.S. (2007). "*Per se* illegality" of maximum RPM was abandoned earlier, that is, in the *Kahn* case (1997; *State Oil Co. v. Khan*, 522 U.S. 3). Shin (2009) provides a detailed survey of the changes in the legal attitudes toward RPM in the US.
4. The US Department of Justice generated "Vertical Restraints Guidelines" in 1985, which were applied only to non-price vertical restraints. They were abolished in 1993.
5. The Supreme Court of Korea, 2009Du9543.
6. The Supreme Court of Korea, 2010Du9976.
7. The presale services related to golf clubs are, for example, measuring a customer's height, arm length and swing mechanism. Golf club distributors are sometimes equipped with machines that analyse a customer's swing speed or trajectory and so on. These presale services may help customers choose the golf clubs that best fit their physical characteristics.
8. Commission Regulation (EU) No. 330/2010 of 20 April 2010 on the application of Article 101(3) of the TFEU to categories of vertical agreements and concerted practice.
9. Besides RPM, four more types of vertical restraint belong to the hardcore restrictions. For example, the restriction of sales territory and the restriction of customers belong to the hardcore restrictions. See Article 4(a)–(e) of the regulation.
10. See OECD (2008).
11. For the details of RPM regulation in the EU and its meaning, see Reindl (2011), for example.
12. One needs to notice that this is not a "rule of reason" approach in an exact sense. Under "rule of reason," a competition authority investigates whether a case is either procompetitive or anticompetitive with the burden of proof. However, in the EU, the burden of proof to claim procompetitiveness of an RPM falls on the firms concerned.
13. The previous "Guidelines on Vertical Restraints" (Commission Notice 2000/C 291/01) did not contain explanations for minimum RPM or resale price fixing. It explained only recommended or maximum RPM.

14. This is one component of the market environments we formally analyse in the next section.
15. "Guidelines on Vertical Restraints" VI.2.10.(224): "RPM may facilitate collusion between suppliers by enhancing price transparency on the market, thereby making it easier to detect whether a supplier deviates from the collusive equilibrium by cutting its price. RPM also undermines the incentive for the supplier to cut its price to its distributors, as the fixed resale price will prevent it from benefiting from expanded sales. Such a negative effect is particularly plausible where the market is prone to collusive outcomes, for instance if the manufacturers form a tight oligopoly, and a significant part of the market is covered by RPM agreements." This explanation is based on Mathewson and Winter (1998) and Jullien and Rey (2007), for example.
16. "Guidelines on Vertical Restraints" VI.2.10.(224): "[B]y eliminating intra-brand price competition, RPM may also facilitate collusion between the buyers, that is, at the distribution level. Strong or well organised distributors may be able to force or convince one or more suppliers to fix their resale price above the competitive level and thereby help them to reach or stabilise a collusive equilibrium. The resulting loss of price competition seems especially problematic when the RPM is inspired by the buyers, whose collective horizontal interests can be expected to work out negatively for consumers."
17. "Guidelines on Vertical Restraints" VI.2.10.(225): "[W]here a manufacturer introduces a new product, RPM may be helpful during the introductory period of expanding demand to induce distributors to better take into account the manufacturer's interest to promote the product. RPM may provide the distributors with the means to increase sales efforts and if the distributors on this market are under competitive pressure this may induce them to expand overall demand for the product and make the launch of the product a success, also for the benefit of consumers."
18. Guidelines on Vertical Restraints VI.2.10.(225): "If enough customers take advantage from such pre-sale services to make their choice but then purchase at a lower price with retailers that do not provide such services (and hence do not incur these costs), high-service retailers may reduce or eliminate these services that enhance the demand for the supplier's product. RPM may help to prevent such free-riding at the distribution level." This explanation is mainly based on Bowman (1955) and Telser (1960).
19. In fact, unlike in the US, the competition framework in the EU does not use the terminology of "*per se* illegality." Instead, the terminology of "restriction by object" closely corresponds to "*per se* illegality."
20. The model introduced here is based on the analysis in Bang and Jin (2015).
21. We implicitly assume that consumers have to incur considerable costs when returning the product. This assumption is often made in order to focus on the effects of incomplete information on product quality upon consumers' choices and firms' decisions. See Loginova (2009); Bang et al. (2014) and Bang and Kim (2013), for instance.
22. The retailer can always decide not to deal in products of a certain manufacturer, for the sake of her own profits.
23. This assumption can be easily relaxed without changing the main arguments. Suppose, for instance, a simpler model setting where each consumer is initially uninformed about which brand is a better match for her. Then it would not matter from which distributor a consumer receives presale services.
24. Notice that we analysed only the case where the service cost satisfies $s < 1 - \beta - \Delta\beta$. When $s > 1 - \beta - \Delta\beta$, distributors also provide presale services—and free-ridings across manufacturer are prevented. Meanwhile the market is served either fully or partially depending on the size of s. However, it can be easily shown that RPM always harms consumers and, hence, is anticompetitive. See Bang and Jin (2015) for a more detailed and full-fledged analysis in this setting.

REFERENCES

Bang, Se Hoon and Yangsoo Jin (2015), "Brand-specificity of pre-sale services and inter-brand competition with resale price maintenance," *International Review of Law and Economics* **43**, 1–9.

Bang, Se Hoon and Jaesoo Kim (2013), "Price discrimination via information provision," *Information Economics and Policy* **25**(4), 215–24.

Bang, Se Hoon, Jaesoo Kim and Young-ro Yoon (2014), "Reverse price discrimination with Bayesian buyers," *Journal of Industrial Economics* **62**(2), 286–308.

Bowman, Ward S., Jr. (1955), "The prerequisites and effects of resale price maintenance," *University of Chicago Law Review* **22**(4), 825–73.

Jullien, Bruno and Patrick Rey (2007), "Resale price maintenance and collusion," *Rand Journal of Economics* **38**(4), 983–1001.

Loginova, Oksana (2009), "Real and virtual competition," *Journal of Industrial Economics* **57**(2), 319–42.

Mathewson, Frank and Ralph A. Winter (1998), "The law and economics of resale price maintenance," *Review of Industrial Organization* **13**, 57–84.

OECD (2008), *Roundtable on resale price maintenance*, DAF/COMP/WD (2008) 62, Paris: Organisation for Economic Co-operation and Development.

Reindl, A.P. (2011), "Resale price maintenance and article 101: developing a more sensible analytical approach," *Fordham International Law Journal* **33**(4), 1300–32.

Shin, K. (2009), "Law and economics of resale price maintenance: the golf club case," *Korean Journal of Law and Economics* **6**(1), 45–90.

Telser, L.G. (1960), "Why should manufacturers want fair trade?" *Journal of Law and Economics* **3**, 86–105.

10. Retail price coordination in Korean department stores: the specific purchase contract

Woohyun Chang

INTRODUCTION

It is widely recognized that, in Korea, retail prices in department stores for the same products are uniform nationwide. This coordination of prices is primarily generated by legal agreements between producers and retailers that allow the producers to set the retail price for each product. This chapter reviews this practice, using a simple model to discover how the practice can become anticompetitive and thereby harmful to social welfare. The chapter draws on policy research carried out by the Korea Development Institute (KDI).

Direct control of retail prices by producers can lead to anticompetitive behavior such as collusion between an upstream producer and downstream retailers. One example is resale price maintenance (RPM), in which the producer sets the minimum and maximum prices that can be charged to the consumer for a product and thus forces the retailers to honor the price restrictions imposed vertically. Even though RPM is no longer *per se* illegal in the United States (US), it is still regarded as a potentially crucial anticompetitive practice on a rule-of-reason basis. In other countries, such as Korea, it is still *per se* illegal for a producer to impose a minimum-price RPM. RPM is an old issue and there is a rich body of literature and legal cases, which will be considered in a section below, related to its anticompetitive nature.

The main focus of this chapter is another type of price control or "coordination" by producers that has thus far received relatively less attention. It is similar to the RPM in the sense that producers—sometimes producers and retailers together—systematically coordinate the retail price, but it is unique in making use of a special form of contract that is legal in Korea. Under the specific purchase contract (SPC), the producer does not sell directly to the retailer (who would then acquire the property rights to the product). Instead, the producer rents the retail space itself and retains the property rights to the product until it is sold.

As, under this contract, the property rights to the product still belong to the producer, the producer can set the retail consumer price. Perhaps even more interesting, under this system the retailer sets a "purchase fee rate," to allow the producer to use the space in the retailer's store, and that fee applies also to the sales of the product. Under this system the producer sets the retail price, whereas the retailer sets a part of the producer's costs—resulting in a swap of the usual pricing roles.

When SPCs are used, it is often observed that retail prices are equal everywhere for the same product. Like other cases of vertical price coordination, such as RPM, attention should be paid to SPC-based price coordination because it naturally shares the problems originating in price equalization, even though SPC is a legal practice. In addition, as the SPC has its own special characteristics, the effects of the contracts should be analysed in depth as SPCs can also have unique anticompetitive issues of their own.

The next section reviews the literature concerning RPM and the problems of vertical price constraints, while the third section reviews SPCs and how these contracts prevail in the department store sector in Korea. It also illustrates the level of price coordination through a sample price survey on cosmetic goods and apparel goods. In the fourth section a simple model, as an example of price equalization, is developed to investigate how, even though (unlike RPM) no collusive actions are involved in the price restrictions, such contracts can end up with an anticompetitive equilibrium that reduces social welfare.

LITERATURE ON RPM

RPM, in its economic nature, is similar to retail price coordination. Before examining the anticompetitive effects of retail price coordination, it will be helpful to first review some of the anticompetitive effects of RPM. RPM has long been a target of competition policy and is discussed extensively in scholarly and policy circles. This section reviews the existing views on RPM and draws implications for the anticompetitive effects of retail price coordination.

The Debate on Prohibiting RPM

The literature on prohibiting RPM examines both generally agreed and individual issues. The most widely accepted general agreement among scholars is that RPM creates a problem more from its anticompetitive effects than from its direct effects (such as the price increase it may create).[1] Starting with this agreement, those who advocate treating RPM as illegal *per se* proceed according to the following logic. If upstream firms or downstream firms have no anticompetitive intentions, a manufacturer has, under the reasonableness assumption, no reason to choose RPM. Therefore, RPM should be *per se* illegal. In other words, it is not unreasonable to restrict RPM, without even considering the merits of individual cases, because RPM cannot be viewed as a rational strategy for individual firms. RPM is, moreover, clearly anticompetitive.[2]

Opponents of treating RPM as *per se* illegal question the assumption that RPM is irrational for individual firms. If individual firms engage in RPM while not pursuing anticompetitive goals and conducting normal business activities, they argue that it is unreasonable to treat RPM as *per se* illegal and that individual cases should be reviewed on their own merits in accordance with the "rule of reason" principle.

A key issue in this debate is presale services that may accompany the sale of a product. These may lead to a free-riding issue that may confront individual retailers. If the nature of the product makes presale services necessary (for example, testing and product information), a customer may use the presale services at one reseller and end up shopping at another where prices are lower because presale services are not offered. In such a case, the customer can free-ride on retailers that do offer presale services and this undermines competition between brands, leading to a harmful effect on social welfare. This argument has a long history (see, for example, Tesler 1960 and Bork 1966) and appears frequently in documents advocating RPM today. In 2007, for example, the US Supreme Court decided in the *Leegin* case that each individual case should be decided on the basis of reasonableness, imposing the rule of reason (*Leegin Creative Leather Products, Inc. v PSKS. Inc.*, 551 U.S. 877 2007). This decision overturned the longstanding doctrine that RPM is *per se* illegal, which was established in the *Dr. Miles* case in 1911 (*Dr. Miles Medical Co. v John D. Park and Sons*, 220 U.S. 373 1911).

Literature on the Anticompetitive Effects of RPM

Hart and Tirole (1990) show that monopolistic manufacturers can use RPM to maximize their monopolistic rents by using a price floor as a commitment to retailers that they will not offer lower prices to new retailers. Likewise, retailers can effectively deter the entry of new competitors to the retail market thanks to the RPM introduced by manufacturers. This is because RPM effectively makes it impossible for entrants to secure a market share using the strategy of offering low retail prices (see, for an example, Marvel and McCafferty 1985).

In another view, RPM may facilitate collusion among downstream firms—in this case, retailers. If retailers intend to collude, it is much easier to do so when the price is fixed by the upstream firm engaging in RPM. In such a situation, retailers with superior bargaining power over manufacturers may have effective control over the manufacturers. In the extreme case, resale prices set by manufactures may well be the prices set by colluding retailers. Overstreet (1983) and Rey and Verge (2009) offer theoretical support for such an argument.

The shortcoming of this logic is that it assumes retailers intend to collude. But even if there is no direct evidence, collusion could be assumed in the absence of reasonableness for the RPM. Neither possibility makes any difference, however, to the conclusion that RPM may facilitate collusion.

A critique by Overvest (2012) focuses on the possibility that colluding downstream firms could, if the upstream firms are monopolistic, reduce the monopolistic profits of upstream firms. Such a measure would lead upstream firms to promote competition and weaken incentives for implicit collusion among downstream firms. They would do so by reducing the upper bounds of punishment for cheating. In other words, the lower bounds of prices would decrease from the collusion price. This result would make upstream firms set lower bounds for the consumer prices through RPM.

This argument, however, poses two problems. First, it assumes (as well as tolerates) anticompetitive behavior (monopolistic price setting and monopolistic profit maximization) on the part of the upstream firms. Second, and more importantly, it would be more direct and intuitive for upstream firms to make use of the maximum price RPM (which is not *per se* illegal), which could be done without much controversy, instead of using the minimum price RPM.

In another line of research, Jullien and Rey (2007) argue that RPM may facilitate collusion among upstream firms. Their work shows that upstream firms in a cartel can use RPM for monitoring any cheating by cartel members. It assumes that downstream firms in each region are perfectly competitive and myopic, whereas upstream firms maximize profits over the long term and produce products that are substitutes for, yet sufficiently differentiated from, each other. And each product has probabilistic variable factors, which are independently given, for ultimate demand. Under such a condition, upstream firms in the cartel find it difficult to judge whether a reduction in the retail price by a cartel member was the result of cheating or was caused by a market-driven change in demand. This leads to a situation where not cheating may be punished as cheating and cheating may go unpunished, resulting in losses. RPM can prevent cheating by cartel members in such situations by fixing the retail prices at the level expected by the members.

Finally, O'Brien and Shaffer (1992) suggest that RPM can be anti-competitive, even when upstream firms do not collude with downstream firms, if each firm engages in a strategic behavior with market influence. They show that, if manufacturers opt for a price-setting strategy other than RPM when retailers are unable to check each other's contracts, the retail price can be set lower that the monopolistic price set under vertical integration of manufacturers and retailers. In such a situation, RPM can be considered anticompetitive because manufacturers have an incentive to pursue anticompetitive behavior using RPM.

KOREAN DEPARTMENT STORES AND THE SPC

Department Stores and Retail Price Equalization

The motivation for this chapter springs from a single surprising observation regarding the department store industry in Korea. In many cases, the price of a specific product is the same in all department stores regardless of the location and the retail chain to which the store belongs.

This phenomenon is economically unnatural, because supply and demand conditions differ depending on the combination of chain and location. Even though the same manufacturing price is applied to the product, there should be differences in the retail prices if the retailers are making optimal decisions. How, then, does this phenomenon occur? There are contracts that facilitate price coordination by vendors in the department store sector in Korea. The SPC is an expanded, nationwide, consignment contract. As described in the introduction, under an SPC the producer rents space from the retailer and withholds property rights to the product until it is sold, rather than selling the product directly to the retailer (who would thereby acquire property rights to the product).

It should be noted that an SPC implies only that the producer will set the retail price, which does not automatically mean that the retail price should be the same at all locations. Nonetheless, a survey by KDI researchers established that, when a producer decides to sell a product in department stores under an SPC arrangement, the producer, by convention, charges the same price in every store regardless of where the stores are located. The producer's justification is that, under SPC arrangements, the producer should not discriminate among retailers by setting different retail prices. Price samples collected by KDI researchers, who also conducted interviews with producers, showed conclusively that, in actual practice, the SPC includes a guarantee of a consistent retail price in Korea nationwide.

To establish that SPC arrangements in Korea really lead to nationwide price uniformity, KDI researchers carried out a survey of prices for 258 cosmetics and 655 products for women. Prices were found to be the same everywhere in the country, without a single exception. For each product, the price was consistently the same throughout the country. An unexpected finding was that distributors were quite willing to reveal their prices.

The effects of such price coordination are, in principle, not so different from those of price coordination under RPM arrangements—and RPM arrangements are illegal in Korea. Given that the RPM system creates problems, other forms of price coordination, such as the SPC, would also be expected to be susceptible to similar problems—especially when such price coordination is managed on as large a scale as it is under SPC arrangements in Korea.

Sales revenue for the Korean department store sector in 2011 was approximately $23.44 billion, representing 9.1 percent of the entire Korean retail industry (Table 10.1). The Fair Trade Commission (FTC; Fair Trade Commission 2010) reported that the concentration ratio has been increasing significantly in retail industry. The concentration ratios of the sum of the three biggest firms (CR_3) for sales revenue and number of stores were 56.4 percent and 27 percent, respectively, in 1999 and, by 2008, these figures had become 80 percent and 52 percent, respectively.

In the Korean retail industry, purchasing may be divided into various types. Direct purchase is the typical wholesale model in which the retailer buys directly from the producer and sells the product to the consumer—adding a price margin for profit but also assuming the risk of not selling the product. Indirect purchase types include SPC and variations of the basic SPC. For research purposes, the indirect types have one characteristic

Table 10.1   Retail sales in Korea, 2007–11

	2007	2008	2009	2010	2011
Retail sales (million won)					
Department stores	19,005,188	19,799,920	21,783,591	24,316,754	27,088,391
Total retail sales	226,630,177	241,996,385	251,697,903	275,783,669	299,079,407
Department store sales					
Share of total sales (%)	8.4	8.2	8.7	8.8	9.1
Annual growth rate (%)	3.1	4.2	10.0	11.6	11.4

Note: The 2012 exchange rate was US$1 = 1,154 won.

Sources: Statistics Korea and Ministry of Knowledge Economy data.

Table 10.2   Shares of retail purchasing in Korea by type, 2005–09

	Share of total purchasing (%)				
	2005	2006	2007	2008	2009
Direct	5.9	6.8	6.2	5.2	5.6
Nondirect					
SPC	71.7	70.7	70.8	70.7	69.2
Other variations of the basic SPC	12.4	12.5	13.0	14.1	15.2
Subtotal nondirect	94.1	93.2	93.8	94.8	94.4

Source: Korea Distribution Association data.

in common: the producer, not the retailer, has the right to set the price. For this reason, in the present chapter all indirect-purchase contracts are regarded, in a broad sense, as SPC arrangements. Under this assumption, as shown in Table 10.2, indirect contracts account for about 94 percent of total sales in the department store sector and SPC arrangements make up the great majority (about 70 percent of total sales) of this share.

Agency Model

A well-known court case illustrates the conflict between the wholesale model and the agency model, which resembles the conflict between the direct purchase contract and the SPC in the Korean department store sector.

In the US government's antitrust lawsuit against Apple, Inc., and five major publishers of electronic books (e-books), the agency model became the heart of the debate. The five publishers who produced the e-books were provided by Apple with the virtual retailing space, selling electronic versions of the books at an agreed price over the Internet. Amazon Corporation, however, was already selling the same e-books but using a wholesale model. Apple, instead of buying the e-books at a discount and reselling them at a profit, decided to collect fees in proportion to the sales volume (as is the case with SPC arrangements in Korea).

Under this "agency model," the publishers agreed to higher prices for Apple's sales and could withhold new releases to Amazon. Apple was protected from competition not only because its competitor was obliged to raise prices but also by an agreement with the publishers that Apple could sell at a lower price if a competitor did so. In April 2013 the US District Court issued its verdict. "Understanding that no one publisher could risk acting alone in an attempt to take pricing power away from Amazon, Apple created a mechanism and environment that enabled them to act together in a matter of weeks to eliminate all retail price competition for their e-books" (US District Court, Southern District of New York 2013).

This case is interesting for the speed at which a new agency model was introduced, which was highly dependent on the technical ease of providing nationwide or worldwide retail virtual space through the Internet's virtual world of business. In the physical world of the department store, development of the SPC model in East Asia took such a long time historically because of coordination difficulties. By contrast, the agency model of Apple was developed in mere weeks, according to the judgment in the case. This implies that the SPC model can be made use of more easily and frequently in the rapidly growing virtual world than in the physical world of retail sales.

A MODEL OF PRICE EQUALIZATION UNDER THE SPC

This section provides a model to demonstrate how to determine the harmful effects of price equalization caused by the SPC. The model provided is very simple; more rigorous general models are needed and should be developed for more sophisticated analysis. For the purposes of the present study, this model, with its clear numerical results, suffices as one of the first economic models to analyse and identify the implications of the SPC.

The model assumes that there are two regions. Each region has one retailer (a department store). Each retailer has some level of market power in the region, but it is assumed that consumers have some level of mobility too. So, the demand function of each retailer is described as follows:

$$D_L(p_L, p_H) = d - P_L + \sigma P_H$$

$$D_H(p_L, p_H) = d - P_H + \sigma P_L$$

The subscripts (L and H) to the demand (D) identify retailers (that is, store L and store H) and P is the consumer price. σ has a value between 0 and 1, which means that, for consumers, the two stores are substitutable. Consumers have higher preferences for the nearest store or for a particular department store chain, but consumers also react to the product pricing at each department store.

The next step is to set the production model of the manufacturer. It is assumed that there is only one manufacturer producing a single product and the manufacturer sells the product to both stores.[3] The producer needs to pay the cost c_0 of each unit produced. In addition, the producer would pay a fee (F) proportional to the sales, not to the profit, which is a special feature of this model and this fee is paid to the retailer for renting space in the store.[4]

Therefore, the profit function of the producer is as follows:

$$\pi = D_L \times (P_L - f_L - c_L) + D_H \times (P_H - f_H - c_H) - C.$$

Fee F is defined as $F = f \times D$.[5] Thus the total cost for the producer when selling the product to the two respective stores is defined as $c_L = c_0 + l_L$ and $c_H = c_0 + l_H$, where l is the cost related to the circulation.

The profit function for each retailer is defined as follows. In this model, retailers are maximizing profit by setting the fee and there is only a fixed cost for each retailer: c_L and c_H. Therefore,

$$\pi_L = f_L \times D_L - C_L$$

$$\pi_H = f_H \times D_H - C_H.$$

The sequence of the decision is as follows. First, the retailer sets f and, with a given f, the producer then sets the retail price P.

For simplicity, it will also be assumed that the circulation costs for each firm are identical (that is, $c_L = c_H l$)—and that these costs can be normalized by $c_L = c_H = 0$.

Next, three cases will be reviewed under this setting. First, we will consider the competitive outcome. In this case the retailers are setting f competitively. Therefore, the producer is solving the following profit maximization problem, with f given.

Case I: Competition

In Case I (competition), the producer's maximization problem is as follows:

$$Max_{P_L, P_H}(D_L \times (P_L - f_L - c_L) + D_H \times (P_H - f_H - c_H) - C).$$

First order conditions are

$$\frac{\partial \pi}{\partial P_L} = d - 2P_L + f_L + 2\sigma P_H - \sigma f_H = 0$$

$$\frac{\partial \pi}{\partial P_H} = d - 2P_H + f_H + 2\sigma P_L - \sigma f_L = 0$$

and therefore

$$P_L = \frac{d - \sigma f_H + f_L}{2} + \sigma P_H, \quad P_H = \frac{d - \sigma f_L + f_H}{2} + \sigma P_L$$

are the equilibrium consumer prices for the two stores.

The result shows that the producer is considering the level of the fee for each store when the level of the price is set. If a fee for one store is higher, the price at that store will be higher.

The equilibrium quantities will be as follows:

$$D_L^* = \frac{1}{2}(d - f_L + \sigma f_H), \quad D_H^* = \frac{1}{2}(d - f_H + \sigma f_L).$$

According to this result, the producer will sell more in one store if the fee of that store is lower than the fee of the competing store. Because the producer will be better off by attracting consumers to a store where the fee is lower, the outcome is not surprising.

Next, the retailers will solve the profit maximization problem respectively as follows:

$$Max_{f_L}\left(\pi_L = f_L \times D_L - C_L = \frac{d}{2} \times f_L - \frac{f_L^2}{2} + \frac{\sigma f_L f_H}{2} - C_L\right)$$

$$\frac{\partial \pi_L}{\partial f_L} = \frac{d}{2} - f_L + \frac{\sigma f_H}{2} = 0$$

$$Max_{f_H}\left(\pi_H = f_H \times D_H - C_H = \frac{d}{2} \times f_H - \frac{f_H^2}{2} + \frac{\sigma f_L f_H}{2} - C_H\right)$$

$$\frac{\partial \pi_H}{\partial f_H} = \frac{d}{2} - f_H + \frac{\sigma f_L}{2} = 0.$$

Assuming the Bertrand–Nash equilibrium, the fee will be determined as follows:

$$f_L^* = f_H^* = \frac{d}{2 - \sigma}.$$

And therefore, finally, the retail prices and quantities can be computed as follows:

$$P_L^* = \frac{d}{2(1 - \sigma)} + \frac{f_L^*}{2} = \frac{d}{2} \times \frac{3 - 2\sigma}{(1 - \sigma)(2 - \sigma)}$$

$$P_H^* = \frac{d}{2(1 - \sigma)} + \frac{f_H^*}{2} = \frac{d}{2} \times \frac{3 - 2\sigma}{(1 - \sigma)(2 - \sigma)}$$

$$D_L^* = \frac{1}{2}(d - f_L^* + \sigma f_H^*) = \frac{1}{2} \times \frac{d}{2 - \sigma}$$

$$D_H^* = \frac{1}{2}(d - f_H^* + \sigma f_L^*) = \frac{1}{2} \times \frac{d}{2 - \sigma}.$$

The profits, too, for the retailers and the producer, can be obtained as follows:

$$\pi_L^* = f_L^* \times D_L^* - C_L = \frac{1}{2}\left(\frac{d}{2 - \sigma}\right)^2 - C_L$$

$$\pi_H^* = f_H^* \times D_H^* - C_H = \frac{1}{2}\left(\frac{d}{2 - \sigma}\right)^2 - C_H$$

$$\pi^* = D_L \times (P_L - f_L - c_L) + D_H \times (P_H - f_H - c_H) - C$$

$$= \frac{d^2}{2} \frac{3 - 2\sigma}{(1 - \sigma)(2 - \sigma)^2} - \left(\frac{d}{2 - \sigma}\right)^2 - C$$

$$= \frac{1}{2} \frac{d^2}{(1 - \sigma)(2 - \sigma)} - C.$$

Case II: Collusion (Retailers)

In Case II, retailers set the purchase fee collusively. That is, they act together as though they were a single retailer, which maximizes the total profit for all.

The retailers' profit maximization problem is as follows:

$$Max_{f_L, f_H}(\pi_L + \pi_H = f_L \times D_L - C_L + f_H \times D_H - C_H$$

$$= \frac{d}{2} \times f_L - \frac{f_L^2}{2} + \frac{\sigma f_L f_H}{2} - C_L + \frac{d}{2} \times f_H - \frac{f_H^2}{2} + \frac{\sigma f_L f_H}{2} - C_H)$$

$$\frac{\partial \pi_L}{\partial f_L} = \frac{d}{2} - f_L + \sigma f_H = 0$$

$$\frac{\partial \pi_H}{\partial f_H} = \frac{d}{2} - f_H + \sigma f_L = 0.$$

The solution of the equations is as follows:

$$f_L^{**} = f_H^{**} = \frac{d}{2(1 - \sigma)}.$$

As expected, the f value is higher than that of Case I, the competitive case. In other words,

$$f^* = \frac{d}{2-\sigma} < \frac{d}{2-2\sigma} = f^{**}, 0 < \sigma < 1.$$

The consumer prices in Case II are

$$P_L^{**} = P_H^{**} = \frac{d}{2(1-\sigma)} + \frac{f^{**}}{2} = \frac{3}{4} \frac{d}{(1-\sigma)}$$

and they, too, are higher than those of Case I. In other words,

$$P^* = \frac{d}{(1-\sigma)} \times \frac{3-2\sigma}{4-2\sigma} < \frac{3}{4} \times \frac{d}{(1-\sigma)} = P^{**}, 0 < \sigma < 1.$$

The quantities are given by the following equation:

$$D_L^{**} = D_H^{**} = \frac{1}{4} d.$$

The producer's profit also can be computed as follows:

$$\pi^{**} = 2\left(D^{**} \times (P^{**} - f^{**}) \right) - C = \frac{1}{8} \frac{d^2}{(1-\sigma)} - C.$$

Not surprisingly, this is less than the profit of Case I, which can be shown as follows:

$$\frac{1}{8} < \frac{1}{4} < \frac{1}{2(2-\sigma)} < \frac{1}{2}, 0 < \sigma < 1.$$

Each retailer in Case II will therefore enjoy the following profits:

$$\pi_L^{**} = f^{**} \times D^{**} - C_L = \frac{1}{2}\left(\frac{d}{1-\sigma}\right) \times \frac{d}{4} - C_L = \frac{1}{8} \frac{d^2}{(1-\sigma)} - C_L$$

$$\pi_H^{**} = f^{**} \times D^{**} - C_H = \frac{1}{2}\left(\frac{d}{1-\sigma}\right) \times \frac{d}{4} - C_H = \frac{1}{8} \frac{d^2}{(1-\sigma)} - C_H.$$

These profit levels are higher than those of Case I, which can be shown as follows:

$$2(2-\sigma)^2 > 8(1-\sigma), 0 < \sigma < 1.$$

Comparisons between cases, showing the relative magnitudes of these and other results, are provided in summary tables at the end of this section.

Case III: Price Coordination through SPC

In Case III (price coordination by means of an SPC), the producer sets a single price for the two retail stores and this fact is known to the retailers. The profit maximization problem of the producer is therefore as follows:

$$Max_P(D \times (P - f_L - c_L) + D \times (P - f_H - c_H) - C),$$

$$D = D_L = D_P = d - P + \sigma P.$$

Therefore, by the first order condition,

$$\pi = 2dP - 2P^2 + 2\sigma P^2 - (f_L + f_H)(d - P + \sigma P) - C$$

$$\frac{\partial \pi}{\partial P} = 2d - 4P + 4\sigma P + (1 - \sigma)(f_L + f_H) = 0$$

$$P = \frac{d}{2(1 - \sigma)} + \frac{f_L + f_H}{4}$$

$$D = \frac{d}{2} - \frac{(1 - \sigma)(f_L + f_H)}{4}.$$

The retailer of the L store will now set the fee to maximize profits as follows:

$$Max_{f_L}(\pi_L = f_L \times D - C_L$$

$$\pi_L = \frac{d}{2}f_L - \frac{(1 - \sigma)}{4}(f_L + f_H)f_L$$

$$\frac{\partial \pi_L}{\partial f_L} = \frac{d}{2} - \frac{(1 - \sigma)}{2}f_L - \frac{(1 - \sigma)}{4}f_H = 0$$

$$f_L = \frac{d}{(1 - \sigma)} - \frac{1}{2}f_H.$$

Similarly solving for the H store,

$$f_H = \frac{d}{(1 - \sigma)} - \frac{1}{2}f_L.$$

To solve the equations, the equilibrium fee levels can be computed as follows:

$$f^{***} = f_L = f_H = \frac{2}{3}\frac{d}{1 - \sigma}.$$

This f can now be used to compute the consumer price and quantities sold:

$$P^{***} = \frac{\sigma}{6}\left(\frac{d}{1-\sigma}\right), D^{***} = \frac{1}{6}d.$$

Note that the fee level is higher in Case III than in Case II. The price also is higher than in Case II and quantities are less. According to the result, if there is a convention of equalizing the retail price through SPC, the consumer price will be set at a level even higher than the level involving collusion.

Intuitively, the result can be explained as follows. If the producer can set different prices for different retailers, the producer can raise (or lower) any individual price as a reaction to an increase in the fee by the individual retailer. However, if there is a constraint causing the producer to set only one price, the producer cannot set an optimal price according to individual fee levels. If the producer does so, an externality would occur between retailers, in the sense that neither store recognizes the loss of the other store by raising the fee to raise the common price. As a result, the fee and price are set even higher than they would be in a collusive case.

If the profits for the producer and the retailers are computed, the producer's profit becomes the following:

$$\pi^{***} = 2\left(D^{***} \times (P^{***} - f^{***})\right) - C = \frac{1}{18}\frac{d^2}{(1-\sigma)} - C.$$

And this profit level is less than that of both cases I and II, which can be shown as follows:

$$\frac{1}{18} < \frac{1}{8} < \frac{1}{4} < \frac{1}{2(2-\sigma)} < \frac{1}{2}, 0 < \sigma < 1.$$

Retailers L and H will achieve the following respective profits:

$$\pi_L^{***} = f^{***} \times D^{***} - C_L = \frac{2}{3}\left(\frac{d}{1-\sigma}\right) \times \frac{d}{6} - C_L = \frac{1}{9}\frac{d^2}{(1-\sigma)} - C_L$$

$$\pi_h^{***} = f^{***} \times D^{***} - C_H = \frac{2}{3}\left(\frac{d}{1-\sigma}\right) \times \frac{d}{6} - C_H = \frac{1}{9}\frac{d^2}{(1-\sigma)} - C_H.$$

These results highlight two interesting points. First, the profits in Case III are always less than those in Case II. Second, the profit in Case III can be more or less than the profit in Case I, depending on the substitution parameter. If $0 < \sigma < 0.5$, the profits in Case I are higher (see Table 10.3). However, if $0.5 < \sigma < 1$, the profits in Case III are higher than the profits in Case I, which can be shown as follows:

Table 10.3   Comparisons of variables between cases I and III

Variable	Case I		Case III
Retail price	$P^*_L = P^*_H = \dfrac{d}{2} \times \dfrac{3 - 2\sigma}{(1 - \sigma)(2 - \sigma)}$	$<$	$P^{***} = \dfrac{5}{6}\left(\dfrac{d}{1 - \sigma}\right)$
Retail quantity	$D^*_L = D^*_H = \dfrac{1}{2} \times \dfrac{d}{2 - \sigma}$	$>$	$D^{***} = \dfrac{1}{6}d$
Fee per unit	$f^*_L = f^*_H = \dfrac{d}{2 - \sigma}$	$<$	$f^{***}_L = f^{***}_H = \dfrac{2}{3}\dfrac{d}{1 - \sigma}$
Producer's profit	$\pi^* = \dfrac{1}{2}\dfrac{d^2}{(1 - \sigma)(2 - \sigma)} - C$	$>$	$\pi^{***} = \dfrac{1}{18}\dfrac{d^2}{(1 - \sigma)} - C$
Retailer's profit (1) $(0<\sigma<0.5, \text{i}=\text{L},\text{H})$	$\pi^*_i = f^*_i \times D^*_i - C_i = \dfrac{1}{2}\left(\dfrac{d}{2 - \sigma}\right)^2 - C_i$	$>$	$\pi^{***}_i = \dfrac{1}{9}\dfrac{d^2}{(1 - \sigma)} - C_i$
Retailer's profit (2) $(0.5<\sigma<1, \text{i}=\text{L},\text{H})$	$\pi^*_i = f^*_i \times D^*_i - C_i = \dfrac{1}{2}\left(\dfrac{d}{2 - \sigma}\right)^2 - C_i$	$<$	$\pi^{***}_i = \dfrac{1}{9}\dfrac{d^2}{(1 - \sigma)} - C_i$

$$2(2 - \sigma)^2 < 9(1 - \sigma), 0 < \sigma < \frac{1}{2}, 2(2 - \sigma)^2 > 9(1 - \sigma), \frac{1}{2} < \sigma < 1.$$

The fact that the Case II (collusion) equilibrium is definitely illegal in Korea may provide a retailer with an incentive to prefer Case III together with Case I, at the expense of both the consumers and the producer, when the consumers are sensitive to a price set by another retailer.

Table 10.4 provides a summary of the results of this section, showing comparisons between cases I and II and cases II and III.

Although the model presented above is merely a simple example, it also has general implications. As long as the optimal consumer price (which is set by the producer for each retail store) is affected by the level of fee set by the retailer, the result could be a loss of social welfare, if the price coordination (or equalization) is conventionally applied *ex ante*, as it is in the case of the department store sector in Korea.

CONCLUSION

This chapter has reviewed the popular SPC-based price coordination in Korea's retail industry, demonstrating how it can be anticompetitive, just as illegal coordination cases, such as RPM, can be. The mathematical analysis also demonstrates, with a simple model, that the harm to social welfare can be even greater under specific settings.

Given the debate about whether RPM is illegal *per se*, it may likewise be difficult to call SPC-based price coordination illegal *per se*. Even so, as

Table 10.4   Comparisons of variables in cases I and II and cases II and III

Variable		Case I		Case II		Case III
P^T	Retail price	$P_L^* = P_H^* = \dfrac{d}{2} \times \dfrac{3-2\sigma}{(1-\sigma)(2-\sigma)}$	$<$	$P_L^{**} = P_H^{**} = \dfrac{3}{4}\dfrac{d}{(1-\sigma)}$	$<$	$P^{***} = \dfrac{5}{6}\left(\dfrac{d}{1-\sigma}\right)$
D^T	Retail quantity	$D_L^* = D_H^* = \dfrac{1}{2} \times \dfrac{d}{2-\sigma}$	$>$	$D_L^{**} = D_H^{**} = \dfrac{1}{4}d$	$>$	$D^{***} = \dfrac{1}{6}d$
f^T	Fee per unit	$f_L^* = f_H^* = \dfrac{d}{2-\sigma}$	$<$	$f_L^{**} = f_H^{**} = \dfrac{d}{2(1-\sigma)}$	$<$	$f_L^{***} = f_H^{***} = \dfrac{2}{3}\dfrac{d}{1-\sigma}$
$\dfrac{f^T}{P^T}$	Fee rate	$0 < \dfrac{2-2\sigma}{3-2\sigma} < \dfrac{2}{3}, 0 < \sigma < 1$	$<$	$\dfrac{2}{3}$	$<$	$\dfrac{4}{5}$
π^T	Producer's profit	$\pi^* = \dfrac{1}{2}\dfrac{d^2}{(1-\sigma)(2-\sigma)} - C$	$>$	$\pi^{**} = \dfrac{1}{8}\dfrac{d^2}{(1-\sigma)} - C$	$>$	$\pi^{***} = \dfrac{1}{18}\dfrac{d^2}{(1-\sigma)} - C$
π_i^T	Retailer's profit (i=L,H)	$\pi_i^T = f_i^* \times D_i^* - C_i = \dfrac{1}{2}\left(\dfrac{d}{2(2-\sigma)}\right)^2 - C_i$	$<$	$\pi_i^{**} = \dfrac{1}{8}\dfrac{d^2}{(1-\sigma)} - C_i$	$<$	$\pi_i^{***} = \dfrac{1}{9}\dfrac{d^2}{(1-\sigma)} - C_i$

Note: See Table 10.3 for alternate comparisons of the retailer's profit between cases I and III.

long as concerns about the anticompetitiveness of RPM do exist, competition authorities should pay as much or greater attention to SPC-based price coordination.

Future model development should include a more generalized model that can add more producers and products and can introduce a variety of costs and dynamics. Such a model should also allow the consumer the choice of not buying as well as allowing producers the choice of entry to or exit from the market.

For further analysis of SPCs, a model could be developed in which it is in the interest of the manufacturer to use SPCs and to commit to a common retail price for all retailers. The results might provide a better understanding of the incentives and motivations for the use of such pricing policies. Another possibility is to consider procompetitive explanations, such as those proposed for RPM, including sharing risk, enhancing retail services, reducing transactions costs and eliminating double markups.

The department store industry in Korea is merely a single example. But, because this business model is shared by department stores in Japan, China and other countries, there is a great, potential welfare benefit in studying and reviewing the anticompetitiveness of SPC-based price coordination in depth. More importantly, there is particular concern about the rapid growth of sales through the virtual world of the Internet as an alternative to the real world of the traditional retail store. Given the ease with which the Internet can provide nationwide or worldwide retail space almost instantaneously, vertical price coordination may become ever easier in the new business models of the virtual world. For this reason, it is strongly recommended that competition authorities pay more attention to this topic. The virtual sales world is growing fast and it will be the place where new businesses will flourish and new value-added markets will be created from now on.

NOTES

1. RPM has been a subject of intensive research because of the potential for negative effects on consumer and social welfare by creating an environment conducive to collusion. This literature is highly relevant to competition restriction created by retail price coordination.
2. It can be argued that innocent, although irrational, decisions by individual firms should be punished. Yet, according to this view, such irrational decisions can be prevented by this provision, if RPM is clearly an irrational practice.
3. If we want to consider the entry decision of the producer for each retailer, we need to compute the demand function under a condition starting from the indirect utility functions of the consumers. For simplicity, this chapter considers only the case where the producer has contracts for both of the stores.
4. It would appear natural to pay the fee in proportion to the profit, but, conventionally, the

fee is charged according to the sales. One possible reason is that the sales level is easier to observe than the profit level. Note that, in the Apple e-book case, Apple charged the publishers a fee according to the sales of the e-books.

5. For reference, f here is not the "fee rate," but the fee rate can be computed directly from f by the equation $\frac{F}{P \times Q} = \frac{f \times Q}{P \times Q} = \frac{f}{P}$.

REFERENCES

Bork, R. (1966), "The rule of reason and the *per se* concept: price fixing and market division," *Yale Law Journal* **75**, 373–475.

Fair Trade Commission (2010), *Enhancement Plan for the Department Store Home-Shopping Sales Fee*, Seoul: Fair Trade Commission.

Hart, Oliver and Jean Tirole (1990), "Vertical integration and market foreclosure," *Brookings Papers on Economic Activity: Microeconomics 1990* (June), 205–76.

Jullien, B. and P. Rey (2007), "Resale price maintenance and collusion," *Rand Journal of Economics* **38**(4), 983–1001.

Marvel, H.P. and S. McCafferty (1985), "The welfare effects of resale price maintenance," *Journal of Law and Economics* **28**(2), 363–70.

O'Brien, D. and G. Shaffer (1992), "Vertical control with bilateral contracts," *Rand Journal of Economics* **23**, 299–308.

Overstreet, T. (1983), *Resale Price Maintenance: Economic Theories and Empirical Evidence*, Bureau of Economics Staff Report, Washington, DC: Federal Trade Commission.

Overvest, Bastian (2012), "A note on collusion and resale price maintenance," *European Journal of Law and Economics* **34**(1), 235–39.

Rey, P. and T. Verge (2009), "Resale price maintenance and interlocking relationships," *Journal of Industrial Economics* **58**(4), 928–61.

Tesler, L. (1960), "Why should manufacturers want fair trade?" *Journal of Law and Economics* **3**, 86–105.

US District Court, Southern District of New York (2013), *United States of America v Apple, Inc., et al.* 12 Civ. 2826 (DLC), New York, 10 July 2013.

Index